CLEVELAND ON FOOT

"A superb introduction to our neighborhoods and natural areas"—*Northern Ohio Live*

"Useful for beginners and people who are new to this area. For experienced hikers . . . the book is a fun way to add variety when planning outings."
—*Explorer*, Cleveland Museum of Natural History

"A straightforward, no-nonsense guide that should be in every hiker's glove compartment."
—*Ohioana Quarterly*

"In their efforts to inform, the Camerons leave no stone unturned."—*Akron Beacon Journal*

"User-friendly . . . Informative"—*Currents*

"It's tough to get lost with a book like this"
—**WEWS TV 5 News**

CLEVELAND ON FOOT

SECOND EDITION

A Guide to Walking and Hiking
in Cleveland and Vicinity

Patience and Harry Cameron

GRAY & COMPANY, PUBLISHERS
CLEVELAND

Gray & Company, Publishers
11000 Cedar Avenue
Cleveland, Ohio 44106

Library of Congress Cataloging in Publication Data
Cameron, Patience
Cleveland on foot: a guide to walking and hiking in Cleveland and vicinity / Patience and Harry Cameron. —2nd ed.
Includes bibliographical references
1. Hiking—Ohio—Cleveland Metropolitan Area—Guidebooks. 2. Walking—Ohio—Cleveland Metropolitan Area—Guidebooks. 3. Cleveland Metropolitan Area (Ohio)—Guidebooks. I. Cameron, Harry. II Title.
GV199.42.032C543 1995   95-1337

ISBN 0-9631738-9-8
Printed in the United States of America.
10 9 8 7 6 5 4 3 2 1

Permissions
The quotation on p. 4 is from *Walden* by Henry David Thoreau, copyright 1910, Grosset & Dunlap.
The poems by Emily Dickinson, numbers 888 on p. 6 and 328 on p. 15, are reprinted by permission of the publishers and the Trustees of Amherst College from *The Poems of Emily Dickinson*, Thomas H. Johnson, Ed., Cambridge, MA: The Belknap Press of Harvard University Press, Copyright 1951, 1955, 1979, 1983 by the President and Fellows of Harvard College.
The quotation on p. 8 is from *The Writings of Ralph Waldo Emerson*, copyright 1940 by Random House, Inc.
Permission was granted by Random House, Inc., to quote Colin Fletcher in *The Complete Walker*, copyright 1968 by Alfred A. Knopf on p. 15.

We dedicate this book to all the people who had the foresight to create Cleveland Metroparks, Cuyahoga Valley National Recreation Area, and all other natural areas, and to the dedicated staff and host of volunteers who help maintain the parks, trails, historic buildings, and other interesting places that make Cleveland a prime area for outdoor recreation.

I am monarch of all I survey,
My right there is none to dispute.

—Henry David Thoreau, *Walden*

When I have seen the Sun emerge
From His amazing House—
And leave a Day at every Door
A Deed, in every place—

Without the incident of Fame
Or accident of Noise—
The Earth has seemed to me a Drum,
Pursued of little Boys

—Emily Dickinson, c. 1864

CONTENTS

CONTENTS (*continued*)

The civilized man has built a coach, but has lost the
use of his feet.

    —Ralph Waldo Emerson, *Self Reliance*

PREFACE TO THE SECOND EDITION

In the two years since it was first published, *Cleveland On Foot* has brought new outdoor adventures to many Clevelanders and other northeast Ohio residents.

After two repeat printings, we felt it was time to expand *Cleveland On Foot* to include other areas worth visiting on foot and to make a few revisions to our descriptions because some trails have changed. In this edition we have also expanded the book from 33 to 45 walks and hikes, including 19 new walks and hikes.

Because our urban and suburban walks have been particularly popular, we have added new Cleveland city walks in Tremont and Brooklyn Centre (areas now experiencing a renaissance), a downtown Cleveland geology walk with a hunt for fossils embedded in building stones, a historic tour of the town of Chagrin Falls, and a new walking tour of some quiet streets and lanes in Cleveland Heights. A new walk in historic Riverside Cemetery, together with the walk in Lake View Cemetery, expands the view of well-known Clevelanders—many of whom attained national prominence. We have increased walks in Cleveland Metroparks and added a series of new walks in Mentor Marsh State Nature Preserve and a new hike in Punderson State Park.

Among the new hikes in Cleveland Metroparks, we have included five easy hikes in South Chagrin, Big Creek, Bradley Woods, Garfield Park, and Hinckley Reservations, three moderate hikes in Bedford, Rocky River, and North Chagrin Reservations, a moderately strenuous hike in South Chagrin Reservation, and one strenuous hike in Brecksville Reservation.

As in the first edition of Cleveland on Foot, we carefully walked and re-walked all the walks and hikes and reviewed our descriptions thoroughly to avoid conveying any misleading information. We hope no one has yet gotten lost using our directions, and anticipate that this second edition will be equally reliable.

ACKNOWLEDGMENTS

We are indebted to the following people, all of whom helped us in one way or another to put together the first edition of *Cleveland On Foot*:

Jane Christyson, Chris Brabander, and the staff of Cleveland Metroparks; John Debo, Diane Chalfant, and the staff of Cuyahoga Valley National Recreation Area; Katherine Kohl of Lake View Cemetery; Ivan Bezugloff, David and Gail Broughton, Kerry J. Kelly, Sol Weiss, and our editor, Florence J. Cunningham.

In this second, expanded and revised, edition of *Cleveland On Foot* we wish especially to thank the following persons who substantially assisted us in the preparation of special chapters:

Nancy M. Csider, for the chapter on Mentor Marsh State Nature Preserve; William R. Halley, for the chapter on Riverside Cemetery; Dr. Joseph T. Hannibal, for the chapter on Downtown Geology; Emily A.P. Lipovan and Laura McShane, for the chapter on Tremont; Steven McQuillin, for the chapter on Brooklyn Centre; Pat and Scrap Zalba, for the chapter on Chagrin Falls

Other persons who have assisted us in one way or another with the second edition and whom we wish to thank are:

Helen and Bernie Doherty, Annie Gumprecht, Sandy Paliga, and Elinor Polster.

We also wish to acknowledge our fellow hikers in the Buckeye Trail Association, Cleveland Hiking Club, and others with whom we have spent many pleasant hours enjoying our great outdoors.

Photo Contributors:

Steven B. Stregevsky, Bill Baughman. All photos are by the authors unless otherwise credited.

Maps illustrated by Drawbridge Studio.

CLEVELAND ON FOOT

DISCLAIMER

This guide was prepared on the basis of the best knowledge available to the authors at the time of publication. However, because of constantly changing trail conditions due to natural or other causes, the authors disclaim any liability whatsoever for the condition of the trails described herein, for occurrences happening on them, or for the accuracy of descriptions. Users of this guide are cautioned not to place undue reliance upon the continuing validity of the information contained herein and to use this guide at their own risk.

INTRODUCTION

This book has been developed primarily for newcomers to Cleveland who have both the time and interest to spare for its exploration on foot. There are undoubtedly many in the Cleveland area for whom these excursions will prove to be both innovative and enjoyable. As the title implies, all the activities described here are walking tours or hikes.

This book is also for people who have lived in Cleveland for many years, possibly all their lives, but who perhaps have never learned about the wonderful hiking opportunities that abound in our area. The activities described can be enjoyed in as little as an hour or two, or as long as a full day.

Please check our descriptions carefully. We hope there are no errors or omissions, but if some have crept in please send us a note and let us know how we can improve this guide to make it better for you the next time. Even if the descriptions are satisfactory, we'd like to know that, too.

We encourage you to partake of the special joy that comes from walking and hiking, and the sharpening of senses that makes one feel more alive. We hope you have as much pleasure taking these walks and hikes as we have had in describing them to you, and that this guide will be only a start for you on a lifelong adventure of hiking.

What is in this guide?

The walks and hikes described here are categorized by degree of difficulty for the average walker and hiker.

Easy Urban and Suburban Walks are located in and around the city of Cleveland and its suburbs. They are short walks of one to five miles, often with features of historic, scenic, architectural, or other unusual interest to enjoy. They usually follow sidewalks and involve no exertion beyond the pace and distance you set for yourself. They are also generally suitable for children.

Easy and Moderate Trail Hikes are located in the parks surrounding Cleveland, some in Cleveland Metroparks, many including stretches of the blue-blazed Buckeye Trail (BT). They are usually three to five miles or more and may ascend or descend some hills. They may have uneven footing or obstacles such as stream crossings, but they are suitable for average and more experienced hikers in good health.

Moderately Strenuous and Strenuous Trail Hikes are also located in the Cleveland Metroparks, Cuyahoga Valley National Recreation Area (CVNRA), or state parks. They are usually about 10 miles or more over hilly or rough terrain, on the BT or other marked trails. Some of these hikes are in remote areas and require sturdy boots and a day pack with food and liquid. On these hikes there may be steep ascents and descents, and stream crossings without the aid of bridges.

Why walk?

Years ago everyone walked out of necessity—to work, to school, to the store. Taking a stroll was a common pastime. Nowadays, having grown up with all sorts of transportation available, we seem to have far less need to walk. But there is value in taking to the woodland trails or even to the neighborhood sidewalks to get away from a frenetic modern lifestyle. We have learned to love the peacefulness and rhythm of walking and hiking. We appreciate the benefits of physical exercise and the mental relaxation that ensues from participating in this sport. This guide will introduce you to some of the treasures and pleasures of northeast Ohio that you can easily observe on foot.

When out walking, slow down and observe. Look for wild animals and their footprints, many kinds of birds in all their splendor, a wide variety of ferns, mushrooms, trees, wildflowers, cloud formations, and stunning views.

How do you get started? Most important is mental attitude. The hardest part is making a determined effort to get out, perhaps alone, or with a friend or an organized group. Once you get past all the excuses you can invent for not walking, you will soon find yourself anxious to go outdoors and begin exploring. We have beautiful days for outdoor exploring in northeast Ohio in every season.

. . . .my mind, set free by space and solitude and oiled by the body's easy rhythm, swings open and releases thoughts it has already formulated. Sometimes, when I have been straining too hard to impose order on an urgent press of ideas, it seems only as if my mind has slowly relaxed; and then, all at once, there is room for the ideas to fall into place in a meaningful pattern.

—Colin Fletcher, *The Complete Walker*

A Bird came down the Walk—
He did not know I saw—
He bit an Angleworm in halves
And ate the fellow, raw,

And then he drank a Dew
From a convenient Grass—
And then hopped sidewise to the Wall
To let a Beetle pass—

He glanced with rapid eyes
That hurried all around—
They looked like frightened Beads, I thought—
He stirred his Velvet Head

Like one in danger, Cautious,
I offered him a Crumb
And he unrolled his feathers
And rowed him softer home—

Than Oars divide the Ocean,
Too silver for a seam—
Or Butterflies, off Banks of Noon
Leap, plashless as they swim.

—Emily Dickinson, c. 1862

Section I
Hiking Preparation

The most basic item to take with you on a hike or walk is a map of the area. This guide contains a map for each hike it describes. Cleveland Metroparks provides free trail maps and information about hiking at all four of its nature centers—in Rocky River, Brecksville, Garfield Park, and North Chagrin Reservations—and at Ranger Headquarters in Mill Stream Run Reservation and Look About Lodge in South Chagrin Reservation. More information about Cleveland Metroparks can be found in Section II, *Hiking Resources*.

Maps of trails in the Cuyahoga Valley National Recreation Area (CVNRA) are available at Park Headquarters in Jaite and at the two visitor centers: Canal Road and Happy Days. More information about the CVNRA is also found in Section II, *Hiking Resources*.

For city walks, we suggest the maps published by the American Automobile Association (361-6000) and the street atlases published by Commercial Survey Company (771-3995). Other Cleveland maps and atlases are also available—look for them at most area bookstores.

Mentioned throughout this introduction and listed in Section II, *Hiking Resources* are organizations from whom more hiking maps can be obtained. These sources will enable you to expand your hiking information beyond that contained in this guide.

The key to successful and enjoyable hiking is advance planning. Before starting out, read through the hike descriptions and familiarize yourself with the features, landscape, and terrain you will encounter on the walk or hike.

It is a good practice to take a compass with you as a guide should you become lost. Even if you are unsure how to read maps, a compass is invaluable in the woods. It always points close to north in this part of the country and thus helps you travel in a chosen direction. If, despite your best efforts, you become lost while hiking, try to retrace your footsteps. This often gets you back to a missed turn in the trail. When following blazes, glance up frequently to be sure you are still on the route. (A blaze is a mark, usually on a tree, to indicate a trail.) Look down also to see the trodden footpath and footprints of others having gone this way before you. Or just stop completely, look around, and go back to the last blaze. Position yourself alongside the tree or post with the last mark painted on it and look in all directions. Often you'll spot the trail going in an entirely different direction. If you are with others, shout or blow on your whistle to attract attention to your location. If all else fails, follow a stream downhill to its entry into a larger body of water. This is a useful method to get you out of the woods and often back to an identifiable landmark. Distances on our listed hikes are generally so short that you will not find it difficult to reach one of the access roads shown on these maps.

Group hiking

Hiking alone poses dangers such as getting lost or becoming injured without available assistance. To lessen these hazards, hike with a partner or in a group. Group hiking, for most people, is also simply more fun and companionable.

When in a group, stay together. A rule of thumb is that the last person in line always keeps the person ahead in sight. If you find yourself last and unable to keep up, the group is going too fast and you need to notify the person ahead to get word of your predicament to the designated leader. The leader is responsible for all the hikers in the group and should adjust the pace or wait at intersections for everyone to regroup, or decide how a slower hiker may return to the starting point.

Trail courtesy on a group hike includes: 1) allowing faster hikers to proceed ahead of you; 2) holding back branches for the closely following hiker; 3) warning the person behind you of danger ahead, such as a tree root or deep hole; 4) assisting hikers, if they wish, in crossing streams or making their way over rough terrain; and 5) warning of an approaching car, bicycle, or horse when on a roadway, All-Purpose Trail, or Bridle Trail.

Clothing and footwear

When hiking and walking, comfort is of utmost importance. Most people have found greatest ease in wearing layers of clothing that can be removed or added as temperatures change. You will need to experiment with kinds and combinations of clothing to find those that are most comfortable for you in different weather conditions. On a cool day while waiting for a group hike to start, resist the temptation to don heavy clothing that will soon need to come off after the hike starts and you start perspiring.

Wearing cotton in hot weather keeps the body cooler than synthetic fabrics. Wool in cool weather has proven again and again to provide the greatest warmth even when it gets wet. Veteran hikers wear cotton next to the skin, with the next layer a cotton or wool shirt that can be buttoned up or down, and sleeves that can be rolled up or down as needed.

Long pants help you avoid leg scratches, insect bites, and poison ivy. An umbrella or waterproof jacket will protect you against the inevitable rain that falls when walking or hiking. Wear a hat to protect your head from sun, low branches, and rain. The head is the best regulator of body temperature, so applying or removing a hat will often provide instant relief from cold or heat.

Proper socks provide insulation, padding, and skin comfort. Most hikers prefer to wear two pairs—an outer thick wool sock and an inner thin cotton or propylene sock. The exact combination of weight and thickness depends upon what kind of hiking or walking you are doing and upon the boot or shoe being worn. Some people wear one pair of socks with cushioned insoles that fill out the shoe space and provide extra comfort.

Sometimes you will find you need to carry an extra pair of socks to change into after getting wet feet, a precursor of the dreaded foot blisters. Some dedicated hikers apply rubbing alcohol to their feet before a difficult hike, followed by talcum powder or a medicated foot powder to help keep the feet dry. Applying moleskin or similar protection to a reddened pressure area often prevents a blister from forming. If an area of the foot starts to get painful, apply moleskin right away. But remember that nothing is more pleasurable on a hot day than bathing tired feet in a cool stream for a few moments. Try it sometime.

Boots are the single most important piece of equipment you will acquire and the most difficult to choose. Waterproofed hiking boots that are sturdy and comfortable and have non-slip soles will serve you well on most woodland trails. Sturdy running or walking shoes are most comfortable on sidewalks and paved paths.

Talk to experienced hikers about the advantages and disadvantages of different types of boots. Stick with a tried and true brand. Try on new boots using both pairs of socks you expect to wear while hiking. Be sure the boots fit your feet comfortably, provide adequate support for your ankles, and allow a little space beyond the toes for downhill hiking. When selecting a walking shoe, as with boots, search until you find the best-fitting shoes for your feet. If you expect to do winter hiking, apply a snow sealer to footwear when new and periodically thereafter to protect them from water and keep the leather supple.

Food and liquid

No stream, pond, lake, river, or other body of water in our area of northeast Ohio is safe to drink from without water treatment. Always carry a canteen of water or fruit juice with you when you hike or walk, especially on a warm day. Apples or oranges to quench thirst and replace lost body liquids are handy also. You will lose body fluids quickly when hiking, not only through perspiration but through expiration. This is true even on winter hikes; you can become dehydrated quickly and not even suspect it until unusual fatigue sets in. When perspiring heavily, take small sips of liquid often for optimal body metabolism rather than gulping a large amount at once.

During a walk or hike over a period of several hours you will wish to carry food—a sandwich, fruit, raw vegetable snacks, a trail mix of raisins, nuts, and dried fruit, hard candy, or a high-energy bar to provide the nourishment needed for this energetic sport. Eating small amounts frequently rather than a large amount at once provides a steady flow of fuel to your body without overloading your digestive system.

First aid

Anyone entering the woods needs to be prepared for emergencies. A turned ankle, an eyeball scratch, a bruised elbow, a heel blister, or a deep briar scratch all can be experienced when walking or hiking in the woods. On a group hike the leader is usually responsible for carrying first aid equipment.

The amount of first aid you take depends upon the type and length of the hike and the number of people on the outing. Adhesive bandages will take care of small scratches, blisters, and cuts. As mentioned, moleskin is best applied to foot blisters or hot spots. A roll of two- or three-inch elastic bandage will handle a sprained wrist, ankle, or knee. Small sterile gauze squares and tape can stem a bleeding cut or patch an eye. Aspirin, alcohol pads, personal items, insect repellent, and sun lotion can also be included as needed.

What to carry

The hike length, difficulty, and location will help you determine what to carry and how. Pockets will hold a map, compass, and some food; a belt will carry a canteen and a pedometer to measure your hike; a belt pack will carry first aid, snack food, a small flashlight, a knife, and tissues; and a day pack will hold all of these items plus clothing, a hat or bandanna, rain gear, and a camera. Eventually, each hiker will determine how much is necessary and comfortable to carry.

It is a good idea to carry a flashlight with you on the short days of winter to aid you in finding the trail if darkness descends. A whistle is useful for calling attention to yourself in case of emergency. Always carry personal identification and notify someone before you leave as to where you are hiking and when you expect to return.

Bird-watching is a fast-growing hobby. To take part, you may wish to carry binoculars and a bird identification book such as The National Geographic Society's *Field Guide to the Birds of North America*.

Identifying wildflowers is also a pastime for many hikers, but please leave them there. It may be tempting to carry out wildflowers, but they will wilt before you get them home. It is more fun to take along a wildflower book and study the flower right where it grows. It is enriching to look at the leaves, petals, and all the intricate and fascinating parts, as well as the environment in which it lives. A very helpful flower identification book is Lawrence Newcomb's *Wildflower Guide*.

Safety

Safety is one of the prime considerations of hiking. Consider it whenever you are out alone or with a group. If a situation seems unsafe to you, avoid it. Note any caution reminders on the trail and in the trail descriptions in this guide. They are suggestions for your protection.

When on a paved trail, keep to your left to allow bicyclists, joggers, runners, and faster hikers to pass on your right, and allowing you to face oncoming traffic. On road hikes, make a habit of facing traffic as you walk, and walk in single file if traffic is heavy. On bridle trails when a horse and rider approach, trail safety requires that you stop immediately, step off to the side of the bridle path, and remain quiet and still until they are well beyond you. This behavior prevents the fearful horse from rearing up and injuring you or the rider.

When going out in wet, icy, or snowy weather you might find that once-benign trails, sidewalks, and black-topped paths have become treacherous. Many hikers find it helps to have a walking stick and never go out without their "third leg." This support helps maintain an easy rhythm and provides substantial help in going up and down slopes. It can also be useful in beating a path through overgrown terrain and in crossing streams. A disadvantage of a walking stick is the extra weight. Often you can pick up a suitable stick on the trail when you need one and leave it at the trailhead for the next hiker to use.

How long to walk

Try to take one of the easy, shorter hikes in this guide if you are a novice, to see how your body reacts. Are you sore and aching the next day? You will find you may need to work gradually into the longer and more strenuous hikes. You are the judge of the type and length of your outing. Most persons find they can gradually increase their distance by mentally challenging themselves: "I did three-and-a-half miles today … I'm going to do four miles next time." Listen to your body.

Pace

Most walkers and hikers who start out slowly soon build up their endurance and speed to about two to two-and-a-half miles per hour. The approximate times listed in this guide are calculated for the "average" hiker. But there may be times when you would like to go slower to enjoy the birds, flowers, trees, waterfalls, colorful foliage, or magnificent views. Your legs, lungs, and heart will tell you the proper pace for you to walk. It is usually better to go at a slow, steady pace for several hours than to speed-hike for one or two. You'll see more, of course, by slowing your pace. If the group you are hiking with consistently goes faster than you, then consider hiking with another group or select slower hikes. An important aspect of pacing is maintaining an easy rhythm, one that can take you along for hours without your awareness of the passage of time.

Resting

There is no formula for frequency of rests while on a walk or hike. As with taking in food, it is usually much more effective to take frequent and short rest stops, especially when ascending a steep hill, rather than an occasional long rest. Lunch and snack stops provide a natural opportunity to rest, as does contemplating a view. When public facilities are not available, a call of nature away from the trail is a chance to stop. Remember always to bury excrement and tissues.

Walking uphill and downhill

Hiking uphill requires meeting steepness with a slower pace. It takes some practice to take small, steady steps upward with very brief rests until the top is reached. If you find your heart is pounding rapidly or you are gasping for breath, you need to stop right then until it resumes a slower beat, then slowly continue your ascent and stop for a longer rest at the top. Try placing your boot flat on the slope when going up, avoiding rocks as much as possible. This maneuver stretches and strengthens the calf muscles so they will help you more the next time you ascend a slope.

Downhill walking is easier on your heart but harder on your knees because you are using different muscles in descending. Go downhill slowly, making sure your footing is secure. Again, as you descend, avoid coming down on rocks, slippery mud, leaves, or tree roots. Take advantage of firmly rooted trees to assist you, checking their reliability first before trusting them to help you descend. Some hikers find their walking stick very useful in walking downhill.

Carrying in and carrying out

Why do some people discard trash on the trail? Are they immune to the unsightly view of cans, bottles, paper, foil, and plastic that spoil our pleasure in nature's beauties? The volume of trash left behind by increasing numbers of trail users is of genuine concern. Part of your responsibility in hiking and walking and enjoying our great outdoors is to carry *out* whatever you carry *in*. Many dedicated hikers take along a small trash bag and routinely pick up litter and recyclable cans as they walk. Some hiking clubs and other out-door organizations regularly schedule trail clean-up hikes. Present-ly the carry in/carry out philosophy includes carrying out *more* than you carry in. If everyone did this, consider how much we would enhance the walking experience for all.

Staying on the trail

It is important to stay on the trail no matter how easy it may be to take a shortcut. If one leaves the designated trail, new pathways are started that others will follow, creating new areas for unwanted soil erosion.

The need to respect private property is also essential. Stay on des-ignated trails, paved paths, and sidewalks. As mentioned above, when walking on a paved All-Purpose Trail, it is best to walk to the left facing oncoming bicycle traffic. All of the walks and hikes in this guide are in areas specified for public use and do require one to remain on the described pathway or trail.

Trail sense

Part of trail sense is plain common sense, but some of it has to be developed. It means the sense not to get lost, and if temporarily dis-oriented, to find one's way back. Even a well-marked trail will occa-sionally have a lapse. As discussed earlier, the only thing to do is to walk a short distance in the most likely direction, then return to the last marker until the continuation is found.

Observation is the key. It bears repeating that the worst thing is to yield to panic. Sit down until you have calmed down, and decide on a course to follow. Observe the terrain and the features through which you are walking. Much of the woodland has similar features so that it is often difficult to remember where you have walked. After a while one fallen tree may look like another you have passed previ-ously. Is it? Is the ground well trodden? This seems to be the trail . . . but is it the one you came on? Trails along streams and ravines are easy to retrace. Brook crossings help orient you, and certain features observed can be unique and memorable.

Even if you are not particularly friendly with a compass, it helps to keep you walking in the proper direction. It is all too easy to walk in circles without being aware of it. Use the sun for direction and your watch to tell you how long you have walked.

You will find that your trail sense will develop very naturally as you enjoy discovering the beautiful parks and woodlands in northeast Ohio.

Buckeye Trail Tree Blazes

Typical trail blazes: a single blaze indicates the hiking trail is straight ahead. The tree on the right shows two blazes, the upper blaze indicating the direction of turn.

 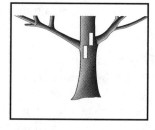

Section II
Hiking Resources

We selected a variety of the walks and hikes included in this guide from the many resources below. There are, however, many more walks available in the facilities described than we could possibly include here. We hope you will try some of these hiking opportunities on your own and obtain information from the organizations listed here.

City of Cleveland

Located on the shores of Lake Erie and divided by the Cuyahoga River, Cleveland—a city of half a million people—has much to offer visitors and residents alike. It is a thriving metropolitan area with many older and restored ethnic neighborhoods and lovely tree-shaded suburbs. The University Circle area contains an unusual concentration of cultural facilities. And the vast Cleveland Metroparks system, often called "The Emerald Necklace," circles the city with green spaces.

The walks and hikes listed in this guide will lead you to these and other outstanding areas of scenic natural beauty or historical distinction.

Information about the city of Cleveland can be obtained from the Convention and Visitors Bureau of Greater Cleveland, Inc., Terminal Tower, Cleveland, OH 44114, or by calling 621-4110, or from the Greater Cleveland Growth Association, Tower City Center, Cleveland, OH 44114, 621-3300.

Cleveland Metroparks

Cleveland Metroparks, established in 1917, celebrated its 75th anniversary in 1992. The Park District consists of 19,069 acres of land in five counties and is governed by a three-person Board of Park Commissioners that oversees the 13 reservations and connecting parkways, as well as Cleveland Metroparks Zoo and RainForest. The tax district for Cleveland Metroparks includes all of Cuyahoga County and Hinckley Township in Medina County. Lake, Lorain, and Summit counties own 3,428 acres of this land.

Hiking trails are an integral part of Cleveland Metroparks. Many trails were built or improved during the Depression era by crews in the Works Progress Administration (WPA) and Civilian Conservation Corps (CCC) crews. Their fine craftsmanship is still evident in shelters, stone walls, bridges, steps, and benches of most of the parks.

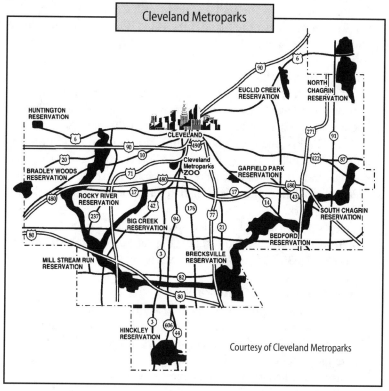

Courtesy of Cleveland Metroparks

The 13 Cleveland Metroparks reservations are: Bradley Woods, Huntington, Rocky River, Big Creek, Mill Stream Run, Brecksville, Bedford, Garfield Park, South Chagrin, North Chagrin, Euclid Creek, Hinckley, and Brookside. This guide describes a selection of hikes in several of the reservations. Naturalists in the four nature centers (Brecksville, Garfield Park, Sanctuary Marsh in North Chagrin, and Rocky River) can provide information and maps of Cleveland Metroparks. The reservations are generally open from 6 a.m. to 11 p.m. every day of the year. A few buildings and special facilities, such as the Cleveland Metroparks Zoo and RainForest, may have varying hours and charge admission fees. An overview map of Cleveland Metroparks is shown on page 27.

The Emerald Necklace, a monthly listing of Cleveland Metroparks activities, including hikes, is a free publication for residents of Cuyahoga County and Hinckley Township. For this publication and for information about the parks write or call: Cleveland Metroparks, 4101 Fulton Pkwy., Cleveland, OH 44144-1923, 351-6300 (phone line available 24 hours).

Lake Metroparks

Lake Metroparks consists of 25 parks including about 4,000 acres throughout Lake County. The parks with hiking trails are: Chagrin River Park, Chapin Forest Reservation, Children's Schoolhouse Nature Park, Concord Woods Nature Park, Girdled Road Reservation, Hell Hollow Wilderness Area, Hidden Valley Park, Hogback Ridge, Indian Point Park, Lake Farmpark, Lakeshore Reservation, Paine Falls Park, Penitentiary Glen Reservation, Riverview Park, and Veterans Park.

Information about Lake Metroparks can be obtained from: Lake Metroparks, Concord Woods, 11211 Spear Rd., Concord Township, OH 44077, 639-9226 or 1-800-699-9226.

Headlands Beach State Park

Headlands Beach State Park and Headlands Dunes State Nature Preserve are located in Painesville Township in Lake County, just west of Fairport Harbor. These parks are directly on Lake Erie and offer pleasant beach walking. Walking on the dunes is permitted, but visitors are asked not to walk on any growing plants.

Ohio's statewide Buckeye Trail begins (or ends) in Headlands Beach State Park and is marked with two-inch by six-inch blue rectangles painted on trees or posts. Information about the park can be obtained from: Headlands Beach State Park, 9601 Headlands Rd., Mentor, OH 44060; 257-1330.

Mentor Marsh State Nature Preserve

Mentor Marsh State Nature Preserve consists of 644 acres of land and is jointly owned by the Ohio Department of Natural Resources and the Cleveland Museum of Natural History. It is located 3.5 miles west of Painesville on State Route 283 and 0.5 mile north on Corduroy Rd. The blue-blazed Buckeye Trail is identified here as the Zimmerman Trail. There are other short hiking trails in the preserve accessible from local roads; these are described in Chapters 24 and 25. Information can be obtained from: Mentor Marsh State Nature Preserve, 5185 Corduroy Rd., Mentor, OH 44060; 257-0777.

Hach-Otis State Nature Preserve

Hach-Otis State Nature Preserve is in Willoughby Township, 1.0 mile east of Willoughby Hills. Also managed by the Ohio Department of Natural Resources (ODNR), Hach-Otis can be reached by going east on State Route 6, then 200 yards north on State Route 174, and east on Skyline Dr. to a dead end where parking is available. Short boardwalks and trails provide spectacular views of the Chagrin River 150 feet below (see Chapter 14). More information can be obtained from: Ohio Department of Natural Resources (ODNR), Division of Natural Areas and Preserves, Bldg. F, Fountain Square, Columbus, OH 43224.

Punderson State Park

Punderson State Park is located about 30 miles east of Cleveland in Geauga County, near the junctions of State Routes 87 and 44. The main entrance to the park is on State Route 87, 1.0 mile west of this junction. A stately Tudor Manor House provides guest rooms, dining rooms, and meeting rooms. The 996-acre park also has housekeeping cabins, a camping area, an outdoor swimming pool, and Punderson Lake for boating, swimming, and fishing. Hiking trails surround the golf course and the glacially formed lakes and go through the wooded hills and open fields. Two such hikes are presented in Chapters 39 and 40. Information can be obtained from: Punderson State Park, Box 338, 11755 Kinsman Rd., Newbury, OH 44065; 564-2279 or 564-2201.

Nelson-Kennedy Ledges State Park

Nelson-Kennedy Ledges State Park is located north of the town of Nelson on State Route 282 in the northeast corner of Portage County. This small 167-acre park has interesting hiking trails that wind through caves and ancient ledges formed 350 million years ago. Information is available from Punderson State Park at the above address and phone number.

West Branch State Park

West Branch State Park is near the town of Campbellsport on State Route 14, east of Ravenna. It offers 5,352 land acres and 2,650 water acres for recreational enjoyment. The Buckeye Trail follows the perimeter of Kirwan Lake over rolling terrain with ever -changing views for a challenging 8+ mile hike. Information about facilities in the park can be obtained from: West Branch State Park, 5708 Esworthy Rd., Route 5, Ravenna, OH 44266-9659; 296-3239.

Cuyahoga Valley National Recreation Area

The Cuyahoga Valley National Recreation Area (CVNRA), created in 1974, is a 33,000-acre natural valley administered by the National Park Service of the U.S. Department of the Interior. It preserves a beautiful 22-mile corridor of pastoral green space between Cleveland and Akron. It is easily accessible to residents of both cities for active recreation, for education, for study of nature and history, and for that refreshment of body and spirit so needed by those of us who are city-dwellers. The Cuyahoga River, remnants of the Ohio and Erie Canal and its towpath, and the historic Cuyahoga Valley Scenic Railroad extend down the center of the CVNRA. Miles of trails are found throughout the CVNRA, including those in Cleveland's Bedford and Brecksville Reservations, and Akron's Furnace Run, Deep Lock Quarry, O'Neil Woods, and Hampton Hills MetroParks. The 19.5-mile Ohio & Erie Canal Towpath Trail is open to hikers, bicyclists, and joggers between Rockside and Ira roads. Many hikes in the CVNRA are of varying degrees of difficulty, and some are described in this guide. An overview map of Cuyahoga Valley National Recreation Area is shown on page 31.

The National Park Service (NPS) maintains headquarters in the small historic town of Jaite on Vaughn Rd. at Riverview Rd. The restored, yellow-painted buildings in Jaite are those that the Park Service has rehabilitated from old homes that once belonged to Jaite Paper Mill workers. They are now used for official activities of the NPS. Their address and phone are: National Park Service, 15610 Vaughn Rd., Brecksville, OH 44141-3018; 526-5256.

Park rangers at two visitor centers provide scheduled programs, visitor assistance, trail maps, and information about the CVNRA. Canal Visitor Center is located in an old restored house near Hillside Rd., at 7104 Canal Rd., Valley View, OH 44147; 524-1497. Happy

Days Visitor Center is in Virginia Kendall Park on State Route 303, east of the town of Peninsula and west of Rte. 8; 650-4636. Both centers are open from 9 a.m. to 5 p.m. daily.

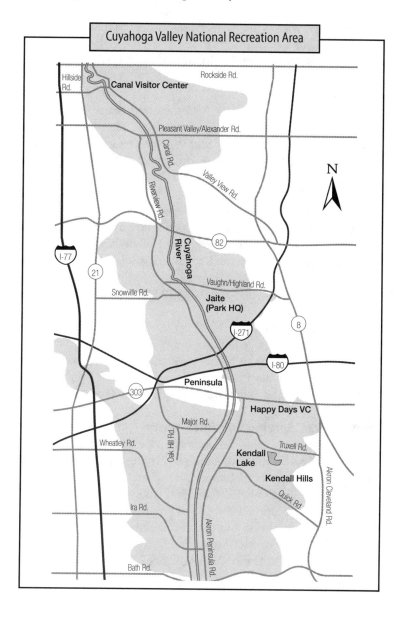

Holden Arboretum

The Holden Arboretum is a unique 2,800-acre private preserve of natural woodlands, horticultural collections, display gardens, ponds, fields, and ravines. A daily admission fee is charged to non-members who wish to use the many resources and trails available at Holden. Membership information is available from: Holden Arboretum, 9500 Sperry Rd., Kirtland, OH 44094-5172; 946-4400.

Geauga Park District

The Geauga Park District publishes trail maps of Whitlam Woods, Eldon Russell Park, Big Creek Park, Metzenbaum Park, Swine Creek Reservation, and Best Wildlife Preserve. Information can be obtained from: Geauga Park District, 9160 Robinson Rd., Chardon, Ohio 44024; 286-9504 or 285-2222.

Lorain County Metro Parks

Lorain County Metro Parks offers hiking trails in the reservations of Black River, French Creek, Mill Hollow, Wellington Creek, and Carlisle. Information and maps are available from: Lorain County Metro Parks, 12882 Diagonal Rd., LaGrange, Ohio 44050; 458-5121 or 246-2010, or 1-800-LCM-PARK.

Findley State Park

Findley State Park is in Lorain County near Wellington, Ohio, on State Route 58. It contains hiking trails and recreational swimming and boating on Findley Lake. Information is available from: Findley State Park, 25381 State Route 58, Wellington, OH 44090; 647-4490.

Metro Parks, Serving Summit County

Created in 1921, Metro Parks consists of over 6,600 acres of land in a series of parks with hiking trails of varying lengths and degrees of difficulty. The parks in Summit County are: Cascade Valley, Deep Lock Quarry, Firestone, Furnace Run, Goodyear Heights, Gorge, Hampton Hills, Munroe Falls, O'Neil Woods, Sand Run, Seiberling Naturealm, Silver Creek, and the 23-mile Bike and Hike Trail. For more information contact Metro Parks, Serving Summit County, 975 Treaty Line Rd., Akron, Ohio 44313; 867-5511.

Portage Lakes State Park

Portage Lakes State Park is near State Routes 93 and 619, close to Akron. It consists of 1,000 land acres with hiking trails and 2,520 water acres. Information is available from: Portage Lakes State Park, 5031 Manchester Rd., Akron, OH 44319-3999; 644-2220.

Tinker's Creek State Nature Preserve

Tinker's Creek State Nature Preserve is located in both Portage and Summit counties and has several short hiking trails surrounding seven ponds. From Twinsburg the preserve is 2.0 miles south on Rte. 91 then east on Old Mill/ Davis Rd. Adjacent to it is Tinker's Creek State Park containing a 10-acre man-made lake for water recreation and one short hiking trail. Information about both parks is available from: Tinker's Creek State Park, 5708 Esworthy Rd., Route 5, Ravenna, OH 44266-9659; 562-5515.

Eagle Creek State Nature Preserve

Eagle Creek State Nature Preserve in Nelson Township is a 441-acre park in Portage County with a bird observation blind, boardwalk, and a system of trails. It can be reached from Garretsville by going 2.0 miles northeast on Center Rd., then 1.0 mile south on Hopkins Rd. Information is available from Ohio Department of Natural Resources (see address under Hach-Otis State Nature Preserve).

Sierra Club

The Sierra Club's northeast Ohio Chapter can be reached by calling 843-7272. This group holds regular meetings and offers hiking, canoeing, and other outings for its members. Environmental education and conservation are major interests of the Sierra Club.

Buckeye Trail Association

The Buckeye Trail (BT) is a blue-blazed 1,200-mile-long trail extending around the perimeter of the state of Ohio, from Lake Erie in the north, to Cincinnati in the south, to Toledo in the west. Much of the BT is on country roads but a large portion of it goes through city and state parks, canal towpaths, forests, woods, and public and private lands.

Along the BT the light blue 2-inch by 6-inch blaze is painted at frequent intervals on trees, fence posts, telephone poles, or other permanent objects. If the trail makes a turn, either a blue arrow is used or a special double blaze is designated, with the upper blaze offset in the direction toward which the trail turns.

This Ohio footpath was put together by volunteers of the Buckeye Trail Association (BTA) who conceived the idea, planned, laid out, and blazed the routes, and today take care of maintaining the trail. The BTA sells maps and guides for many portions of the trail, holds annual and chapter meetings, and publishes a quarterly newsletter called *The Trailblazer*. To obtain information or to join, write to: Buckeye Trail Association, Inc., Box 254, Worthington, Ohio 43085.

Cleveland Hiking Club

The Cleveland Hiking Club (CHC), founded in 1919, just celebrated its 75th Anniversary and is one of the largest and oldest continually operating hiking clubs in the country. The CHC offers many opportunities for large group hiking. Selected club hikes are listed in *The Emerald Necklace*, published by Cleveland Metroparks. Additionally, the club publishes its own schedule and requires that six club hikes be completed before membership is obtained. For information call 749-4762 or 398-5852.

Other local and national resources

After getting started with walking and hiking in northeast Ohio by means of this guide or others, you may wish to consider joining a hiking organization as you get more involved in the sport. The foregoing sections have listed many local organizations to write to for information and maps. In addition, the organizations listed below may offer you an opportunity to do more walking, enlarge your knowledge and enjoyment of nature, participate in volunteer trail maintenance work, and, of course, enjoy the friendship and fellowship of others who love walking and hiking and the out-of-doors.

Akron Metro Parks Hiking Club, 1435 Carey Ave., Akron, OH 44314

American Hiking Society, 1015 31st St. N.W., Washington, D.C. 20007

Appalachian Mountain Club, 5 Joy St., Boston, MA 02108

Appalachian Trail Conference, Box 807, Harpers Ferry, WV 25425

Cleveland Museum of Natural History, Wade Oval, Cleveland, OH 44106; 231-4600

Cuyahoga Valley Trails Council, Inc., 1607 Delia Ave., Akron, OH 44320

Keystone Trails Association, Box 251, Cogan Station, PA 17728

Nature Conservancy Ohio Chapter, 1504 West First Ave., Columbus, OH 43212; (614) 486-4194

North Country Trail Association, Box 311, White Cloud, MI 49349

Ottawa National Wildlife Refuge, 14000 West State Route 2, Oak Harbor, OH 43449; (419) 898-0014

Rails-to-Trails Conservancy Ohio Chapter, Suite 307, 36 West Gay St., Columbus, OH 43215; (614) 224-8707

Wilderness Center, 9877 Alabama Ave. S.W., Box 202, Wilmot, OH 44689-0202; 359-5235

DESCRIPTIONS AND MAP SYMBOLS

In this guide paragraph numbers in the trail descriptions correspond to numbers on the maps. Mileage in the trail descriptions is approximate. Measurements were made with a pedometer set to an average gait; the gait changes with the terrain (up or down), hence slight variations are inevitable. Please note that the maps are not drawn precisely to scale. The map symbols are presented in the table below.

All Purpose Trail	‑‑‑‑‑‑‑‑	Pedestrian Underpass	
Boardwalk		Picnic Area	
Body of Water		Railroad Tracks	
Boulders		Ravine	
Bridges: (Foot)	] [	Restroom	
Bridges: (Road)		Road	
Buckeye Trail	Ⓑ	Stairs	
Building	■	Stream or River	
Camping		Tower	
Cliff, Ledge		Trail	
Marsh		View	
Monument		Waterfall	

Section III
Easy Urban and Suburban Walks

1 DOWNTOWN CLEVELAND

This walk introduces several distinctive historical buildings of downtown Cleveland. Chapter 2, a Downtown Geology Walk, will introduce some of the building stones and fossils to be found downtown. That chapter can be followed alone or in conjunction with this one.

Many building tours are available by individual or group arrangement and are so noted in the descriptions. It is best to take this walk on a weekday when most of the public buildings are open.

For an even more comprehensive walking tour, please see the *Guide to Cleveland Architecture* listed in the bibliography or call the Cleveland Restoration Society (521-1498) for a guided architecture walk.

Distance: 1 mile

Walking time: 2 ½ hours

Description: Although this walk does not cover much geographic area, it requires crossing many busy streets and calls for extra care at rush hour times.

Directions: Take any major artery to Public Square in downtown Cleveland and follow signs to the Tower City Center Parking Garage, beneath Tower City Center. Access to the parking area is off Huron Rd. near Ontario Ave.

Parking & restrooms: Tower City Center

1. Start the tour by viewing the three levels of shops in Tower City Center. This building complex was created from a former railroad station, completed in 1930 along with the Terminal Tower. The Terminal Tower was then the second tallest building in the world, and

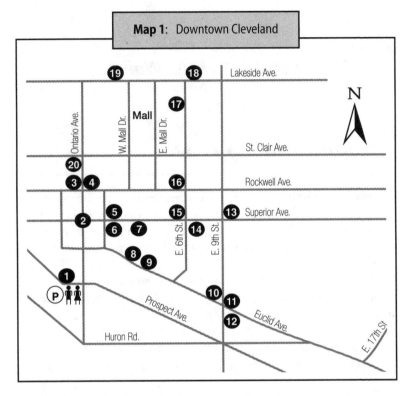

Map 1: Downtown Cleveland

has been Cleveland's landmark ever since. (On weekends, its enclosed 42nd-floor observation deck is open to the public for a unique view of the city.) The 1990 renovation and expansion added a new concourse space and shopping mall, offices, and the Ritz-Carlton Hotel.

Leave Tower City Center at the Public Square exit. Note the elaborate portico of this building, with rosettes on the vaulted ceiling, vast windows, and allegorical murals—all recently refurbished. Sloping roofs remain over the ramps that formerly led down to the trains.

2. Public Square was laid out in 1796 when Moses Cleaveland arrived to survey Connecticut's Western Reserve. A statue of Cleaveland (the "a" was left out of his name when it would not fit into a newspaper headline!) stands in the southwest quadrant of the square. In the northwest quadrant is a statue of Tom L. Johnson, an influential mayor of Cleveland (1901–09), sculpted by Herman

Matzen. Most prominent, in the southeast quadrant, is the 1894 Soldiers and Sailors Monument dedicated to 10,000 Cleveland-area soldiers who served in the Civil War. This 125-foot-high memorial is open to the public.

3. From Public Square, walk north to Old Stone Church, an 1853 Presbyterian Church reconstructed in 1857 and again in 1884 after being destroyed by fires. The entrance to the sanctuary is at the Old Stone Center around the corner on Ontario St. Tours are offered to see the Tiffany and LaFarge stained-glass windows and the beautiful oak interior designed by the architect Charles Schweinfurth.

4. Opposite is the old (1890) red sandstone Society National Bank Building, incorporated into the new (1992) Society Center. This old building was Cleveland's first skyscraper, a heavy, fortresslike building with granite pillars, arched windows, and an ornate lamp fixture at one corner. Inside are a beautiful stained-glass ceiling, marble columns, and murals by English painter Walter Crane. The new Society Center combines the old bank, a Marriott Hotel, and a 57-story office tower, now Cleveland's (and Ohio's) tallest building at 888 feet.

5. Turn south to Superior Ave. The red polished-granite BP America building, built in 1985, faces the square. Its eight-story pedestrian atrium with indoor waterfall, plantings, and granite stairs was planned to conform to the sloping grade of the site and offers fine views of Public Square through its high glass windows. Across the Square is the eye-catching facade of the former May Company building with its prominent terra-cotta clock and ornamental detail.

6. Also on Public Square and Superior Ave. is the Old Federal Building identified as "United States Post Office." This was Cleveland's first post office and from here home delivery of mail originated in 1863—the first ever in America. No longer a post office, it now houses most of Cleveland's federal courts. The exterior figures, *Jurisprudence* on the left and *Commerce* on the right, were created in 1912 by sculptor Daniel Chester French, the designer of Washington D.C.'s Lincoln Memorial. Each corner eagle was carved from a single block of granite and has a 20-foot wingspan.

In 1903, Chicago architect Daniel Burnham planned an elaborate mall and civic center for Cleveland. Similar in design, these massive stone buildings with impressive interiors and ornate details were to surround a central mall. Of the buildings in this Group Plan, the Old Federal Building was the first completed (1911). Only six more were finished: Cuyahoga County Courthouse (1912), Cleveland City Hall (1916), the Cleveland Convention Center Public Auditorium (1922) and Music Hall and North Lobby (1927), Cleveland Public Library (1925), and Cleveland Board of Education (1930). The ornate lamps and statues on the exterior of the Old Federal Building are characteristic of the Group Plan buildings. The Mall consists of Mall A, with its War Memorial Fountain commemorating those who served in World War II and the Korean War (adjacent to Society Center), and Malls B and C from Rockwell north to Lakeside, between East and West Mall drives.

7. Continue east on Superior to the Arcade, the only enclosed structure of its kind in the United States when it opened in 1890. It joins Euclid Ave. on the south with Superior Ave. on the north, one level below. Its 400-foot-long and 100-foot-high glass-roofed five-story atrium was designed by Cleveland architect George H. Smith and built by Detroit bridge builders. This forerunner of the suburban shopping mall is sandwiched between two solid nine-story office buildings. The grand marble stairways and elegant interior details are impressive on first view. The central bridge was added in 1900 and the staircase at the Superior end in 1930. Note the mosaic floor and, overhead, the gargoyles.

Walk through the Arcade to the Euclid Ave. entrance.

8. Two smaller arcades were built in Cleveland to protect shoppers from the city's cold and windy winter weather. The Euclid Arcade, at 510 Euclid Ave., was built in 1911 and is a 440-foot-long, one-story terra-cotta passageway to Prospect Ave., formerly connected to the demolished Colonial Hotel.

9. At 530 Euclid Ave. is the slightly smaller Colonial Arcade (1898), also 440 feet long but with a second-story balcony and glass roof in a Classical style. This arcade also led to the old Colonial Hotel and has recently been refurbished.

10. Continue on Euclid Ave. to East 9th St., where there are three outstanding banking institutions: National City Center, Huntington Bank, and Society Bank. At the northwest corner is National City

Center, constructed in 1980 with an open pedestrian plaza and gyroscopic sculpture that can be fascinating to watch when it twirls in the wind. Connected to National City Center and around the corner on East 6th St. and Euclid is the old National City Bank (1895) with its magnificent colonnaded lobby of pink marble and its beautiful ceiling.

11. On the northeast corner of East 9th and Euclid is the Huntington Bank, with one of the largest and most impressive bank lobbies in the United States. Built in 1924 to resemble a Roman basilica, this 30-acre room is L-shaped with entrances on Euclid, East 9th, and Chester. The three-story-high ceiling with skylights, the marble columns, the standing brass light fixtures, and the murals are all exceptional.

12. The Society Bank building, opposite on the southeast corner of East 9th and Euclid, is identified as Cleveland Trust Company. This 1908 building of white granite is highly decorative with a beautiful portico of columns and pediment sculptures representing Industrial Labor, Agriculture, Mining, Commerce, Navigation, and Fishery. The bank lobby is a magnificent rotunda with a Tiffany-like dome of blue, green, and yellow stained glass. There are 13 columned bays with murals depicting life in the Midwest, bronze railings, marble floors and walls, and original banking desks, grilles, and doorways.

13. Walk north on East 9th St. to Superior. On the northeast corner is St. John's Cathedral, the headquarters of the Catholic Diocese of Cleveland. Originally built in 1852, this French Gothic–style center was substantially rebuilt and refurbished, with a new tower added in 1948.

14. Go west on Superior one block. Bank One Center, completed in 1991, is on the left. The massive Federal Reserve Bank of Cleveland is on the right. The sculpture at its Superior Ave. entrance represents Energy, and those flanking the entrance on East 6th St. are figures of Security on the right and Integrity on the left. This grand building of pink granite and marble was designed in 1923 to resemble an Italian palace. The interior has beautiful marble floors, walls, and pillars, and decorative iron screens representing each Federal Reserve district. This bank has one of the world's largest vault doors, which can be seen only on a Friday afternoon tour. For information call 579-2125.

15. Cross East 6th St. to the block-long Cleveland Public Library. Adjacent to it is a new library annex undergoing construction, which is expected to open in 1995. These two buildings will be separated by the Eastman Reading Garden. Third largest in the country, after the Library of Congress and the New York Public Library, the Cleveland Public Library was the first to create the system of placing books on an open shelf for public browsing. Enter the main building at 325 Superior to see the marvelous marble staircases, painted ceiling, light fixtures, and clock globe at the entrance. Straight ahead is the three-story Reading Room (Brett Hall) with four unusual murals in the portals: straight ahead (north) is *The City in 1833*; to the right is *Sommer's Sun*; on the rear (south) wall is *Public Square* and to the west *Night Sky: Cleveland 1978*. A free pamphlet from the Reference Desk describes these murals. Tours of the library are scheduled by calling 623-2800.

16. From the library walk north on East 6th St. past the Board of Education Building, the last Group Plan building to be built (1930). Although the main facade faces the Mall, the entrance on East 6th St. can be used to see the beautiful marble lobby.

17. The long Cleveland Convention Center complex lies along East 6th St. between St. Clair and Lakeside avenues and consists of Public Auditorium (1922) and the Music Hall and North Lobby (1927). An addition with much-enlarged display space and new mall entrance was added in 1964. Complete renovation of the complex took place in 1988, and the Convention Center is now used frequently for gatherings of all kinds. The huge Public Auditorium contains 11,500 seats, all with an unobstructed view of the stage; the smaller Music Hall seats 2,800.

18. Directly ahead on Lakeside Ave. and East 6th St. is the grand Cleveland City Hall. This majestic building was recognized in 1983 by the American Institute of Architects as one of the outstanding city halls in the nation. From its stately portico to its magnificent rotunda, City Hall is an impressive treasure to view. The two-story barrel-vaulted ceiling with skylights, marble floors, walls, columns, murals, and bronze lamps and gates all are stunning. Here is

Archibald Willard's masterpiece painting *The Spirit of '76*, which was restored in 1987. Much of City Hall was renovated in the 1970s. The beautiful mayor's suite contains fine-grained oak walls and five painted tapestries showing scenes of early Cleveland. The handsome City Council Chambers, one of the largest and most elegant rooms for this purpose in the country, contains a gold-leaf ceiling, chandeliers, hand-carved English oak paneling, and a large Ivor Johns mural depicting life in the city. Tours of City Hall may be arranged by calling 664-2000.

19. Proceed west on Lakeside Ave. to the Cuyahoga County Courthouse, another one of the Group Plan buildings. This one has a gorgeous columned portico with statues of important figures in law along the cornice and statues of Alexander Hamilton and Thomas Jefferson in front. The elegant marble interior hall has a beautiful vaulted ceiling and large murals at either end—*Constitutional Convention of 1787* at the north end and *Signing of the Magna Charta* at the south end. On the east side of the hall is a marvelous curving marble stairway with a Tiffany stained-glass window in the center; called *Justice*, it memorializes famous persons in the law.

20. From the Courthouse, walk south on Ontario, returning to Public Square and Tower City Center. Along the way note the ornate Standard Building at 1370 Ontario with its distinctive terra-cotta starburst design on the exterior panels.

Optional
21. Not on this walking tour but of interest historically in the downtown area is Playhouse Square Center, Cleveland's magnificently restored theater district on Euclid Ave. at East 17th St. The Ohio, State, and Palace theaters were once the homes of vaudeville, movies, and legitimate theater; today they house the Cleveland Ballet, Cleveland Opera, Great Lakes Theater Festival, and many other performing arts groups. Regular weekend tours of the Center are offered; call 589-0066 for information.

2 DOWNTOWN GEOLOGY
Every Stone a Story

Most of the information for the following walk was adapted from *Guide to the Building Stones of Downtown Cleveland: A Walking Tour* (Ohio Division of Geological Survey Guidebook No. 5, 1992) by Joseph T. Hannibal and Mark T. Schmidt. Dr. Hannibal, a geologist and Curator of Invertebrate Paleontology at the Cleveland Museum of Natural History, also provided additional information and carefully reviewed this chapter for accuracy.

Distance: Less than a mile

Walking time: Varies, but allow 2 to 3 hours

Description: This walk does not cover a very large area but requires adequate time to fully examine the buildings, stones, and fossils. It can be shortened, of course, to accommodate whatever time is available to you. There are some busy street crossings on this walk. Because entrance to a few public buildings is necessary, it is best to take this walk on a weekday when the buildings are open.

Directions: Drive on any major artery to Public Square in downtown Cleveland and follow signs to Tower City Center Parking Garage beneath Tower City Center. Access to the parking area is off Huron Rd. near Ontario Ave. Tower City Center is also easily reached via the RTA's Rapid Transit. Debark on the lower level and take the escalator to the upper level. Follow signs to the exit at Public Square. Bring a small magnifying glass, if possible, to allow for closer scrutiny of fossil details.

Parking & restrooms: Tower City Center

Much of the city of Cleveland is spread over a giant prehistoric valley carved over 2 million years ago, and later widened and deepened by glacial erosion from several different advancing glaciers that covered this area during the Ice Age, which lasted from about 2 million years ago to about 10,000 years ago. These glaciers, and several

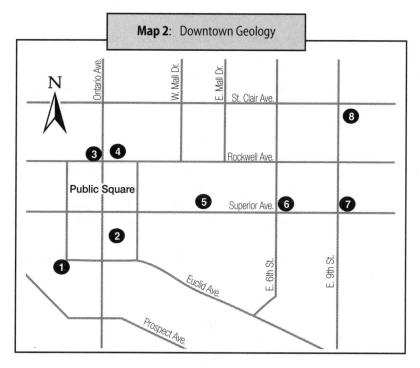

Map 2: Downtown Geology

ancient lakes predating Lake Erie, left layers of material that now fill this valley with silt, clay, and sand. The bedrock supporting Cleveland's tall buildings is more than 200 feet below the surface at Public Square. The area known as The Flats on either side of the Cuyahoga River was formed by cutting action of the present Cuyahoga River.

In constructing Cleveland's larger buildings, architects and builders were (and are) required to excavate many feet below street level to assure a firm foundation. They have used both local rocks and stones imported from various parts of the world for construction. Architects have selected stone for the exteriors and interiors of buildings, and for their ornamentation, by color, texture, pattern, durability, workability, and, of course, cost and availability.

Many of Cleveland's familiar downtown buildings are made of a wide variety of geologically interesting building stones. These rocks, many with fossils embedded in them, provide a fine opportunity for allowing your mind to wander back to prehistoric times and trying to imagine how the earth was when it was in a far different stage of development from where it is now.

1. Begin the walk at Tower City's exit to Public Square. (See Chapter 1, note 1 for description of Tower City.)

The beautiful Tennessee marble flooring in the portico is from the Holston Formation in the Knoxville, Tennessee area. This rock was formed in the Ordovician Period 505 to 438 million years ago when that area was inundated by an inland sea. The small white blobs in the stone are organisms that once lived in the warm sea. In geologic terms, marble is a limestone or dolomite that has been recrystallized below the earth's surface due to heat and pressure. This limestone, however, has not been recrystallized and so is not a true marble in geological terms. In builders' terms, though, marble can be described simply as somewhat soft carbonate rock that can be polished. The irregular black seams in the marble, called stylolites, formed when portions of the limestone dissolved away, leaving dark, concentrated, insoluble materials behind.

The Botticino marble walls in the lobby were also formed as limestone, at the bottom of a warm sea that once covered Italy in the Jurassic period 208 to 144 million years ago. What appear to be round circles in the marble are coated grains, formed by grains of sand or small fossils rolling around in the shallow sea and accumulating surrounding layers of calcium. These spheres now are cut through and appear flat.

The information desk in the inner lobby contains side panels of Botticino marble and a top of Verde Antique, which is a trade name for dark-green serpentine-rich rock containing iron and magnesium, often used as a decorative building stone.

Leave the building and take a close look at its exterior, made of Salem limestone, a frequently used building stone quarried in southern Indiana. It is made mostly of calcium carbonate skeletons of billions of marine animals. These can be seen with or without a magnifying lens. The fossil organisms in the limestone lived in the warm, shallow sea that once covered Indiana about 325 million years ago. The dark gray blocks of stone underfoot are of flame-roughened granite that has been treated to make it less slippery. When wet, it becomes darker and quite beautiful.

2. Cross Public Square to the 125-foot-high Soldiers and Sailors Monument on the southeast quadrant with its 15-foot statue of Liberty at the top. Dedicated in 1894 to commemorate the 10,000 men from Cuyahoga County who served in the Civil War, the monument was designed by the architect, Levi T. Scofield. In front of each of the building's four outer walls are bronze sculptures representing the infantry, artillery, cavalry, and naval branches of the service.

Take a look up at the blackish-gray stone in the column and exterior of the monument. It is polished Quincy (Massachusetts) granite that is probably of Mississippian age formed 360 to 320 million years ago. Each of the 10 blocks composing the column weighs about 14 tons.

The reddish stone of the outer steps and the platform at the top of the stairs is Grimsby Sandstone from Medina, New York, and is 438 to 408 million years old. The curved markings on the platform that you see at the top of the steps represent wave ripples in the sand, frozen by the action of geologic forces.

Much of the light-beige-colored stone of the monument is Berea sandstone quarried in Amherst, Ohio, and is around 360 million years old. This sandstone formed as deposits of beach sand, shallow marine sand, or sand dunes. It is a very hard rock useful in building. What looks like long horizontal grooves along the inner side of the small west pedestal is inclined layering of the sand created during its formation. Geologically speaking, the sand grains in this sandstone are much like those found in beach sand at Edgewater Park.

A United States Geological Survey bench mark is embedded in the stone rail on the northwest side of the monument marking its location 668 feet above sea level.

3. Cross Public Square to Old Stone Church (First Presbyterian Church) at the corner of Ontario St. and Rockwell Ave. Built in 1855 of Berea sandstone, it is the oldest building in downtown Cleveland; its very dark color results from its never having been cleaned. Contrast this sandstone with the normally light-colored Berea sandstone just viewed at the Soldiers and Sailors Monument. Restoration specialists now believe that the process of cleaning may damage and weaken old stone buildings. By looking closely you will see small marks on the facing stones made by stoneworkers' brushhammer work. The exterior sandstone was mined in Carlisle Township, Lorain County. The massive bell mounted on the sidewalk dates from 1865.

It is well worth the time to visit the interior of this church, elaborately redesigned by the architect Charles Schweinfurth in 1884 after a disastrous fire. The entry is through the office of Old Stone Center, 1380 Ontario St. (241-6145). Note the gorgeous mahogany paneling, graceful carvings, barrel-vaulted ceiling with structural tresses, Holtkamp organ, and magnificent stained glass windows. Artist John LaFarge designed the Amasa Stone window on the south wall and Louis Comfort Tiffany designed two of the windows on the west wall—*Beside the Still Waters* and *I Am the Resurrection and the Life*. Tiffany also created two of the windows on the east wall—*The Sower* and *The Recording Angel*. A pamphlet describing Old Stone Church and its art and architecture is available in the office area.

4. Walk across Ontario St. to the Society For Savings building, Cleveland's first skyscraper, which opened in 1890 with five-foot-thick ground-floor walls that help support the 10-story structure. Attached to the southwest corner of the building is an elaborate wrought iron post supporting an ornate street lamp. It is one of Cleveland's original street lights in a city that was among the first to electrify its roads.

The base and columns of the building are Graniteville granite from Iron County, Missouri; it is one of the oldest (about 1.3 billion years) stones used in Cleveland's buildings. The deep reddish stone used in the upper portion is Jacobsville sandstone from Houghton County, Michigan. This rock is composed of tiny grains of quartz and feldspars and its reddish color is derived from hematite.

As you walk east toward the entrance to the new 57-story Society Tower, note the clever glass connector between the old and new structures. At 888 feet, Society tower is now Cleveland's (and Ohio's) tallest building. The facing on the tower's lower floors is Napoleon Red granite from Sweden and on the upper, more than 245-million-year-old pre-Triassic Stony Creek granite from Branford, Connecticut. The sidewalk in front is flame-roughened Stony Creek granite that, on a rainy day, also turns a handsome dark color.

Purplish Rosso Levanto marble from Turkey adorns the interior. This stone was formed in the youngish Tertiary period 66.4 to 1.6 million years ago. The gorgeous Breccia Pernice marble walls in the lobby are from the Mt. Pastello region of Italy and are Jurassic—208 to 144 million years old. These limestone walls contain large and small fragments, with small fossils within, to create unusual rock embedded in rock.

Walk toward the bank of elevators serving floors 24–39 and note the light and dark orange marble walls. The marble is Rosso Verona from the Venice area of Italy and is Jurassic in age. Some of the circular nodules are ammonite fossils. An ammonite is an extinct type of cephalopod with a multichambered shell through which a siphuncle (tube) passes. The chambers of ammonites were separated by complex partitions. (See photo 1). A four-inch-size ammonite can be found on the north side of the bank of elevators serving floors 24-39 between the two west elevators, about seven feet from the floor. Another ammonite, about the same size, lies in the marble on the south bank of elevators 13–23, toward the east side, in the third marble panel from the east opening, about two feet above the floor.

Photo 1

To see the splendid interior of the grandly restored banking hall of the original Society For Savings building, turn toward the doorway, where 12 stone columns support a 26-foot-high ceiling enclosing a spectacular stained glass skylight. Beautiful Walter Crane murals depict the story of the goose that laid the golden eggs. In a small glass-enclosed case are descriptions of the art work.

5. The next stop is generally considered to be one of Cleveland's most beautiful buildings: Cleveland Public Library, built in 1923–25. Walk south on Public Square one block to Superior, and east on Superior to the one-block-long library on the left. (See Chapter 1, note 12 for more information about the library.)

The exterior stone is white Murphy marble (also called Cherokee marble) from Tate, Georgia, which has suffered considerably from general weathering, acid rain deterioration, and rough cleaning methods. Because of this erosion, concrete balusters supporting the upper railing in the building's front have replaced the original marble columns. Murphy marble is Cambrian in age, formed 570 to 505 million years ago. The main entrance steps are made of North Jay (Maine) Gray granite.

Just inside the entrance are Tennessee marble floors with top, side, and bottom views of stylolites, formed where the rock was sutured back together after portions of the limestone dissolved away. Note the beautiful Botticino marble walls, marble staircases, painted ceiling, light fixtures, and clock globe at the entrance. Straight ahead is the entrance to three-story Brett Hall, originally the general reading room and now the general reference room. The travertine flooring has now been covered with carpeting. When the library opened, travertine, a porous freshwater limestone, was ideal for quieting noise created by the many footsteps echoing in this majestic room. The hall is lighted by splendid windows.

Take the impressive marble stairway up to the third floor. On the second floor note the striking building architecture through the windows. These openings were designed strategically to enable librarians and visitors to enjoy pleasant outside views while working inside.

The John Griswold White collection of valuable rare books is located in Room 323. When visiting this room it is necessary to leave identification with the librarian in charge in order to look at the interesting fossils here. Just inside the entry door, take a close look at the round corals in the limestone door trim. This beautiful marble was found in Ozora, Missouri, and is a 380-million-old Devonian rock that was created from remnants of a shallow-water coral reef.

Go to the far east end of the room to the left doorframe of the door marked "Staff Only" and look about four-and-a-half feet up from the floor. Here you will see a fossil of rugose coral, about two inches in diameter, appearing in cross section as a small round formation with spokes. (See Photo 2). It is also called horn coral because it is cone-shaped and sometimes superficially resembles a horn. In the marble windowsills are many more smaller horn corals.

Before leaving this room, be sure to see on exhibit in the glass cases many rare and unusual chess sets.

Leave the White room to go downstairs to the second floor hallway near the History Room. Here in the Botticino marble wainscoting are good examples of coated grains. These five-millimeter-wide

Photo 2

formations appear as flat round fossils with concentric layers of calcium carbonate that enclose tiny grains. In some cases there is even a tiny, comma-shaped snail inside. As mentioned earlier, coated grains were formed by the tumbling action of waves in shallow water that caused accretions to gradually build up over the tiny fossils.

Next, step inside the History Room (Room 210) to see another fossil, foraminiferans. These small 1/2-inch-diameter fossils are embedded in the cream-colored limestone marble windowsills. Foraminiferans are types of one-celled organisms with hard supporting structures consisting of many chambers. They appear fossilized as tightly wound spirals. A good example is found in the third windowsill from the Reference Desk at the east end of the sill.

6. Leave the Cleveland Public Library and continue east on Superior Ave. to East 6th St. to reach the Federal Reserve Bank on the corner. This imposing, fortress-like building was designed in 1923 by the architects Frank Walker and Harry Weeks to resemble a grand Italian palace. It is clad on its lower portion with a reddish-gray Moose-a-Bec granite from Maine, a 408- to 360-million-year-old Devonian rock. The upper portion is a beautiful pink Murphy Marble with dark streaks, called Etowah marble by builders, from the Tate area of Georgia and is Cambrian in age, 570 to 505 million years old. The handsome statues, Security on the right and Integrity on the left, are also of Murphy marble, as are the curbstones that mark the bank's territory.

It is well worthwhile to go inside the Federal Reserve Bank to admire the gorgeous marble floors, the gold Siena, Italy, walls and columns with prominent veins of calcite, and hand-painted cathedral ceiling. (See Chapter 1, note 14 for more information on the Federal Reserve Bank.) Other features of the building can be seen on a Friday afternoon guided tour by calling 579-2125.

7. Continue walking east on Superior Ave. to East 9th St. On the northeast corner is St. John's Cathedral, the headquarters of the Catholic Diocese of Cleveland. Originally built in 1848–52, this French Gothic–style church features an exterior of multi-colored Tennessee Crab Orchard stone (Crossville sandstone) from Cumberland County, Tennessee—320- to 286-million-year-old Pennsylvanian period rock. Its unusual red, brown, and orange patterns have been created by iron oxides. Its sheen, which is visible on a sunny day, is due to small fragments of mica within the rock. The church's exterior trim and statues are Salem limestone containing tiny calcified organisms. On the small north wall next to the square tree planter, and visible at about eye level, are straight and curved tubular burrows or channels up to 2 centimeters wide and 24 centimeters long. These interesting tubes were made by organisms churning through shoal sediments in the sea, leaving behind trace fossils.

8. Continue walking north on East 9th St. to One Cleveland Center at 1375 East 9th St., near St. Clair Ave. This handsome, "silver chisel" building, completed in 1983, contains many easily visible fossils that stand out in the polished Champlain Black marble (Crown Point limestone) in the lobby. The honed grayish base and low walls on the exterior are made of the same stone, but it has markedly deteriorated due to acid rain, and has split off along stylolites, where jagged cracks have developed in the limestone along its seams. This limestone comes from Isle La Motte, Vermont and is Ordovician in age— 505 to 438 million years old.

Step inside the lobby and look on the wall opposite the down escalator near the elevators for a large snail fossil called maclurites. It is about 10 centimeters in diameter. (See Photo 3). Also embedded in this beautiful black stone are smaller nautiloid cephalopods, containing many chambers separated by thin partitions. (See Photo 4).

From here you may return to Tower City Center by retracing your steps, going south on East 9th St. and west on Superior Ave.

There are many other interesting building stones used in downtown Cleveland that invite further exploration. If you wish to continue your investigation, please refer to the Hannibal and Schmidt publication mentioned at the beginning of this chapter; it is available at the Cleveland Museum of Natural History's shop, The Ark in the Park.

Photo 3

Photo 4

This chapter was prepared with the generous assistance of Dr. Joseph T. Hannibal, Curator of Invertebrate Paleontology, Cleveland Museum of Natural History.

3 OHIO CITY

Ohio City, Franklin Circle, and Market Square comprise a Historic District of the City of Cleveland. Located on the west side of the Cuyahoga River along West 25th St., this area was, in the mid-1800s, a bustling little town with many small homes and businesses. Originally a separate city (incorporated as such in 1836), Ohio City was merged with Cleveland in 1854. It is now a culturally rich neighborhood with many early homes and business buildings still surviving. There has been much restoration in Ohio City in the past few years, the results of which can be seen on this walk.

Distance: 4 miles

Walking time: 3 hours

Description: This walk is on sidewalks with one hill to descend and ascend if the portion along the Cuyahoga River in the Flats area below Ohio City is toured.

Directions: From downtown Cleveland, Ohio City can be reached by taking the Detroit-Superior Bridge, the Lorain-Carnegie Bridge, or the Main Ave. Bridge to West 25th St. From I-90, Ohio City can be reached by exiting on W. 25 and following it north. RTA trains (Red Line) and buses stop at the W. 25 St. station.

Parking & restrooms: Park at the West Side Market parking lot near the corner of West 25th and Lorain. Restrooms are located inside the market.

1. Start the walk at 1979 West 25th St., the West Side Market. Built in 1912, this European-style markethall, centerpiece of the Near West Side, is topped with a tall copper-domed clock tower, originally a water tower. It is open on Monday and Wednesday from 7 a.m.–4 p.m. and Friday and Saturday from 7 a.m.–6 p.m. (664-3386). It is interesting to view the food stalls inside and the open-air vegetable stands outside, many of which have been operated by the same fam-

Map 3: Ohio City

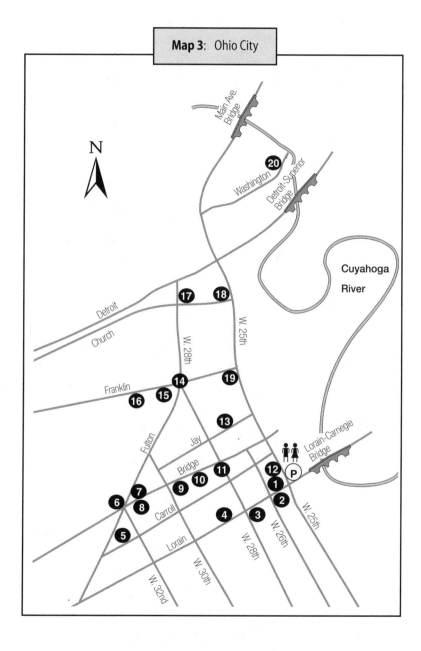

ilies for generations. The market, including its large western window, was restored in 1989 and is now a National Historic Landmark.

2. Go west on Lorain. The Athens Bakery at 2545 Lorain sells Greek foods and imported Greek items both locally and all over the United States.

3. Hansa Imports at 2701 Lorain specializes in German goods and is a travel agency as well.

4. St. Ignatius High School (1888), next on Lorain, was originally St. Ignatius College, which later became John Carroll University and moved to University Heights. The high school remained and in the 1970s added new buildings and a new athletic field.

5. Turn right (north) on West 30th to Carroll. Turn left (west) on Carroll to Fulton. Turn right (north) on Fulton to Bridge Ave. Turn right (east) on Bridge.

6. St. Patrick's Church (1871) at 3602 Bridge was built over a 10-year period by early Irish settlers who quarried the stone in Sandusky for the building and tower. Inside, shamrocks are carved on the support columns, which enclose the masts of the settlers' ships to remind them of their homeland. Information for a visit to the interior of the church can be obtained by calling 631-6872.

7. Carnegie West Branch Library (1910) is across the street. Restored in 1979, it was among the first branch libraries in Cleveland, built with money donated by Andrew Carnegie, who was impressed with Cleveland's progressive library system. This ornate building is triangularly shaped to conform to its three-sided lot.

8. Walk east on Bridge Ave. The oldest house in Ohio City is on Bridge between West 32nd and West 30th. About 150 years old, it is the brick house with green trim, a wrought iron fence, and an antique lamp.

9. Heck's Cafe at 2927 Bridge was at one time a bar and before that a grocery store and confectionary. It was restored and converted to a restaurant in 1974.

10. John Heisman's birthplace (c. 1850) is next on Bridge and is identified with a plaque to commemorate the football innovator for whom the Heisman Trophy was named.

11. The Ohio City Tavern at 2801 Bridge was one of the first buildings renovated in the Ohio City restoration of 1971. It contains a stained–glass ceiling salvaged from St. Mary's of the Assumption Church (1865-1969).

12. Turn right (south) onto West 26th St. The Great Lakes Brewing Co. at 2516 Market St. is off West 26th St. near Lorain. It is the only restaurant in Cleveland with a brewery located right in the building. In the mid-19th century it was a seed and feed supply store.

13. Back on 25th St. go north to Jay Ave. and turn left (west). This is the best-restored street in Ohio City. Note the original paint colors on the homes and the original brick side streets with center gutters.

14. Reach West 30th St. and turn right (north) to Fulton Rd. Turn right (northeast) on Fulton to Franklin Circle. Franklin Circle Christian Church (1875), in Gothic Revival style, is where James Garfield preached after graduating from college and before becoming president of the United States. The church was founded in 1842.

15. Nearby, at 2843 Franklin, is the restored Nelson Sanford House. Built in 1862, it is one of Cleveland's best surviving Italianate style houses.

16. At 2905 Franklin is the Robert Russell Rhodes House, built in 1874 in Italian Villa style. It has recently been restored and is the home of the Cuyahoga County Archives, a property and genealogy research source.

17. Return to Franklin Circle and go north on West 28th to Church St. Turn right (east) on Church St. St. John's Episcopal Church is the oldest church in Cuyahoga County. Built in 1836 in Gothic Revival style with some stones taken from the Cuyahoga River, it served as Station Hope on the Underground Railroad during the Civil War. A secret tunnel extended from it to Lake Erie, through which (it is said) runaway slaves escaped to boats that took them to Canada.

18. The home and office of Dr. George Crile, a founder of the Cleveland Clinic, still remains at the corner of Church St. and West 25th and is so marked.

19. Turn right (south) on W. 25 St. and return to the West Side Market, passing Lutheran Medical Center on the right.

Optional
20. An extension to this walk can be made by walking north from Franklin Ave. past the Detroit-Superior Bridge to Washington Ave. Go downhill on Washington to the Flats area and the recently developed west bank of the Cuyahoga River. Start by exploring The Power House, a shopping mall converted from an old power station. You will recognize it by its tall smokestack. Walk north on the boardwalk, which is located just outside The Power House, along the river, and pass nightclubs, restaurants, and cruise and pleasure boats. Turn around at the end and repeat the always-fascinating boardwalk in the opposite direction. There may be large ore boats slowly navigating up the sharply bending Cuyahoga River to the steel mills. Retrace your steps up Washington Ave. to West 25th St. and the West Side Market.

LAKEWOOD AND LAKE ERIE SHORE

This walk reveals some fine old mansions in Lakewood, sweeping views of Lake Erie, and high-rise apartment buildings in the area along the lakefront's so-called "Gold Coast." Many lovely old homes built between 1900 and 1930 stand on tree-lined Edgewater Dr., Clifton Blvd., Lake Ave., and other wide avenues throughout the city.

Distance: 8 miles

Walking time: 3 ½ hours

Description: This walk is flat and mainly on sidewalks.

Directions: Take I-90 to the West 117th St. exit and drive north to Lake Ave. Turn left (west) on Lake Ave. to Lakewood Park. Enter the park at Belle Ave. off Lake Ave.

Parking & restrooms: At Lakewood Park

Lakewood, which celebrated its 100th anniversary in 1989, was settled by pioneers who were attracted by its abundant water, woods, and game. Later it became a farming community, known as Rockport, and grew into a substantial town and industrial city. Now, Lakewood is an attractive suburb of about 60,000 residents close to Cleveland's downtown.

The Oldest Stone House Museum, located at 14710 Lakewood Ave. in Lakewood Park (where this walk begins) is the home of the Lakewood Historical Society (221-7343). The museum contains period furnishings and memorabilia from the early 19th century and is open for free tours from 1–5 p.m. on Wednesday and 2–5 p.m. on Sunday; the Historical Society office is open every weekday morning. The house itself was built in Lakewood in 1838 by a Scotsman, John Honam, and moved to this site in 1952.

Nearby (but not on this walk) is the oldest surviving structure in Lakewood: Nicholson House, at 13335 Detroit Ave. James Nichol-

Map 4: Lakewood and Lake Erie Shore

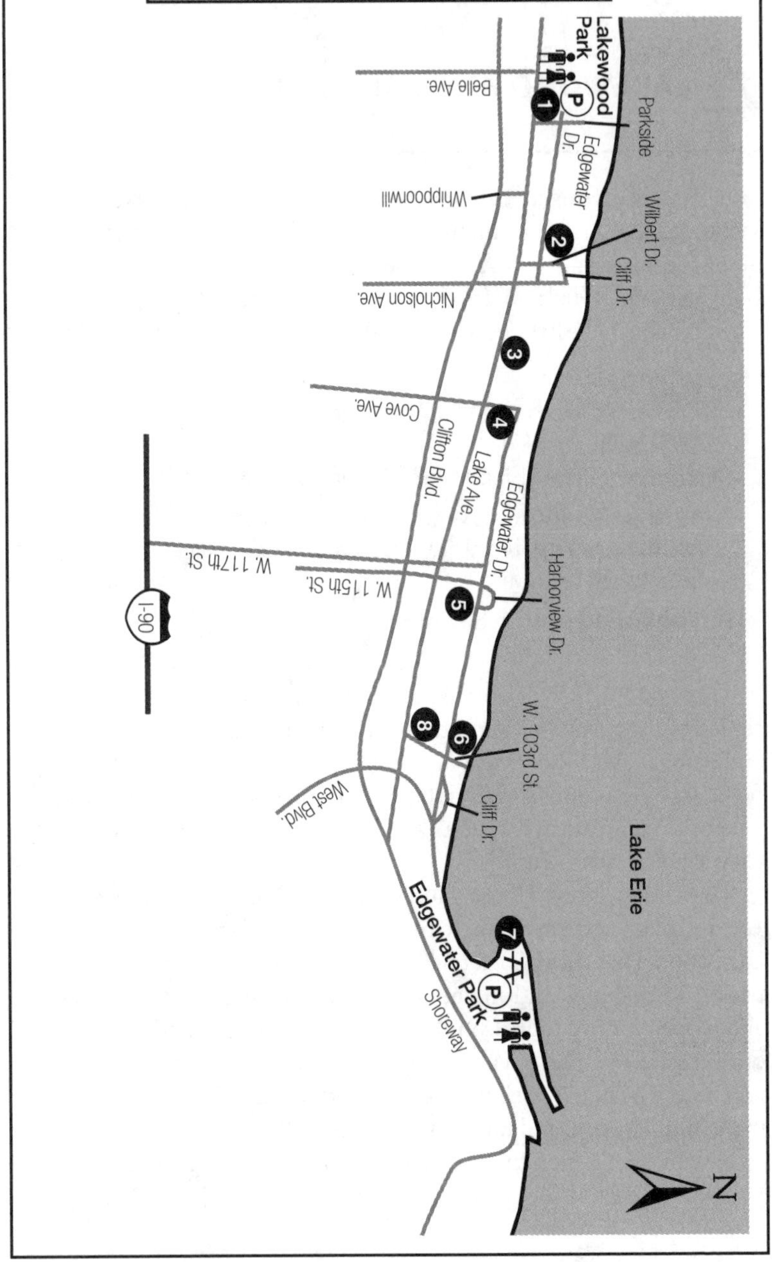

son, the first permanent settler in this area, built his lovely home in 1835; it is now used for special events and is not open to the public.

Both the Oldest Stone House and Nicholson House are listed in the National Register of Historic Places.

1. Start the walk by viewing beautiful Lake Erie from behind the fence at Lakewood Park. Walk out of the park on Edgewater Dr.

2. Follow the drive to Wilbert Rd., then turn left (north) to Cliff Dr. and another sweeping view of the lake.

3. From Cliff Dr. turn right at Nicholson Ave. and left at Lake Ave. Pass the series of tall high-rise apartment buildings called the "Gold Coast"—The Carlyle (1968), Winton Place (1961), The Meridian (1971), The Waterford (1978), and others of newer vintage.

4. At Cove Ave. turn left and walk to Edgewater Dr. Lake Shore Towers, straight ahead, is a remarkable old building (1929), formerly an apartment hotel.

5. Turn right at Edgewater Dr. and continue to West 115th St. and turn left. Take the loop around Harborview Dr. to see a rare all terra-cotta residence at 11320 built in 1913, and other lovely homes along Lake Erie.

6. Back on Edgewater Dr., continue east past West 103rd St. and turn left to Cliff Dr.

7. Turn left (east) onto Edgewater Dr. at West Blvd. and enter Edge-water State Park. A walk through the park to the Edgewater Yacht Club and Marina is especially pleasant in the summer, when several hundred boats are moored here.

8. Return through Edgewater Park to Lake Ave. and walk west on Lake. Finely designed homes are all along this wide street, especially at Nicholson Ave. and at Whippoorwill.

At 13900 Lake Ave. near Chase Lane is a gas station discreetly hidden below street level to avoid disharmony with the residential surroundings.

Continue along Lake Ave. back to Lakewood Park.

5 TREMONT

This interesting walk will take you through 150 years of early settlement, decay, and renaissance.

Distance: 2 miles

Walking time: 1 ½ hours

Description: The walk through Tremont is entirely on sidewalks and provides many stops for enjoyment of the community's historical, architectural, and gastronomic features. A weekday is a good time to visit Tremont when most of the shops are open. To enter some of the churches and other historic buildings it is necessary to telephone ahead.

At the conclusion of the walk are several stops somewhat distant from the central community that are easier to visit by car.

Directions: Drive south on I-71 from Cleveland and exit at Abbey Ave. Turn left (east) and follow Abbey to West 14th St. Turn right (south) at West 14th and continue three blocks to Lincoln Park.

From Akron drive north on I-77 to I-490 west and exit at West 7th St. Follow West 7th St. to Literary Ave. Turn left on Literary and follow it to its end at Lincoln Park, Kenilworth Ave., and West 11th St.

Parking & restrooms: There is free parking on Kenilworth Ave. at Lincoln Park and restrooms are available in any public restaurant or the library.

Tremont is a small community located on an 80-foot-high plateau just south of downtown Cleveland above the Cuyahoga River. The small neighborhood, bounded by Interstate 490, the Innerbelt freeway (I-71), and the ridge above the flats, enjoys an excellent view of the Cuyahoga River and the steel mills below. This somewhat isolated area has a long and interesting history and is home to 25 churches within one square mile—more than in any other part of the city. Its renaissance, celebrated in recent years, is

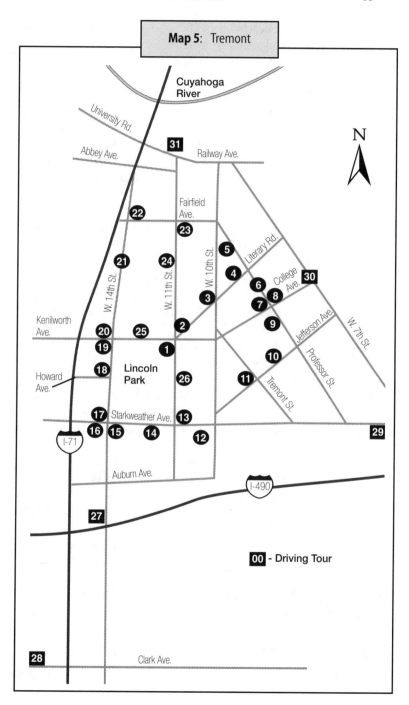

Map 5: Tremont

Cuyahoga River

University Rd.

Abbey Ave.

31

Railway Ave.

N

Fairfield Ave.

22

23

5

Literary Rd.

W. 10th St.

21

24

4

College Ave.

30

W. 14th St.

W. 11th St.

3

6

8

7

Kenilworth Ave.

20

25

2

9

Jefferson Ave.

W. 7th St.

19

1

10

Professor St.

18

Lincoln Park

26

11

Howard Ave.

Tremont St.

17

Starkweather Ave.

13

29

16

15

14

12

I-71

Auburn Ave.

I-490

27

00 - Driving Tour

28

Clark Ave.

due to community development efforts, community cohesion, and its successful art and architecture tours.

The first people to settle in Tremont came from New England in 1818. They were wealthy residents who wished to build their homes outside of Cleveland. Around the middle of that century, Cleveland University was established in Tremont, but it was only in existence from 1850–55. At that time the area was known as University Heights, and today several streets still bear the names given to them at that time: Literary Rd., Professor St., and College Ave. Because of industrial growth, this exclusive section lost many of its illustrious citizens to the eastern suburbs, but some of their attractive old homes still survive and can be seen on this walk.

When immigrants from Central and Eastern Europe flocked into the United States around 1900, numerous families established themselves in Cleveland. Many lived in Tremont to be near the mills where they worked and the churches they built. When these residents died or moved out, others moved in, and changes in the neighborhood caused the community to slide into decline in the 1950s and 1960s.

In the last few years, Tremont has started to come back as a desirable place to live for young families and for people commuting to downtown Cleveland. It is a multicultural and multiracial community with people of Hispanic, Ukrainian, African-American, Russian, Greek, Polish, Slovenian, and other ethnic backgrounds; among these are a number of artists and artisans.

1. Begin the walk at the northeast corner of Lincoln Park, at Kenilworth Ave. and West 11th St. Lincoln Park, formerly Pelton Park, was originally part of a 275-acre parcel purchased by Mrs. Thirza Pelton and Mr. John Jennings for the campus of Cleveland University. When the university closed, the land continued to be used as a park. During the Civil War, President Abraham Lincoln brought troops here for an encampment; after that, residents changed the name to Lincoln Park.

At this intersection are two fine eating establishments: Cravings at 2366 West 11th St. and Patisserie Baroque at 1112 Kenilworth, open at various hours.

2. Wildflower at 2337 W. 11th St. is an eclectic establishment containing a restaurant, secondhand boutique, and flower shop. It is located in a 1911 Romanesque building called Lemko Hall, a former Slavic social hall (Koreny's) that contained a saloon, gambling rooms, and a ballroom. Later the first floor housed a grocery store and, still later, in 1977, was the site of the wedding reception featured in the Hollywood film, *The Deer Hunter.* Note the building's shape conforming to its pointed lot, its arched windows and striking corner tower with pointed dome. Several years ago the upper level of Lemko Hall was converted to residential suites after extensive renovation.

Literary Cafe at 1031 Literary Rd. is a neighborhood bar housed in an 1871 building thought to have originally been a bakery.

3. Continue to the right (northeast) up Literary Rd. to West 10th St. You will pass an unusual, old brick building at 2258 W. 10th St. Note the white decorative stars covering the building's bracings and the former stable doors.

On the right at 2280 Literary is a beautifully renovated home and studio belonging to an artist who practices the ancient art of iconography.

4. On the left at Literary Rd. and Professor St. is the Bohemia Club & Cafe, another fine eating establishment.

5. North of this intersection is Tremont West Development Corporation, at 2190 Professor St. It is an organization whose mission is "to improve and maintain the living, cultural, and business conditions for all of Tremont." This community-based association helps rehabilitate housing for low- and middle-income families, assists businesses in commercial development, and organizes neighbors to work together on common issues to promote the Tremont neighborhood. You may wish to stop in to get some updated information on the area's development.

6. At 2247 Professor is Third Federal Savings and Loan, one of Tremont's early-20th-century commercial buildings.

The owners of Raphael's Draperies at 2253 Professor have completely renovated this building to create a wholly new structure, with attention devoted to keeping its original look. With the exception of the front door and brick walls, everything in this once dilapidated building has been replaced to create a shop, workroom, and three new apartments. Note the stained glass window above the door retained from the original structure.

Matt Talbot Inn, a residential alcohol rehabilitation treatment center, is at 2270 Professor.

7. St. John Cantius Roman Catholic Church and School at the corner of Professor St. and College Ave. is a large complex of many buildings located in the heart of an old Polish neighborhood. Although the parish was organized in 1898, it grew fast, requiring the construction of a new combination church and school in 1913. A convent and parish house were built in the 1920s, followed by the present large and imposing yellow-brick church completed in 1925. With the capacity to seat 1,000 worshippers, St. John's has an inspiring interior. Beautiful marble angel friezes along the barrel-vaulted ceilings, stained glass windows admitting natural light, and a magnificent altar newly installed from the demolished St. Joseph Franciscan Catholic Church, all enhance its beauty. Services are conducted in Polish, English, and Spanish.

8. Note Edison's Pub at 2373 Professor. A favorite neighborhood establishment, Edison's was once a five- and ten-cent store and is now is filled with Thomas Alva Edison memorabilia and other antiques.

9. Continue along Professor St. The building at 2406 Professor was extensively rehabilitated in 1991 by Tremont West Development Corporation into seven apartments for low- and moderate-income Tremont residents.

10. Continue to Jefferson Ave. and turn right (southwest). The Jefferson Branch (1918) of the Cleveland Public Library, at 850 Jefferson Ave., is well worth visiting to see how an old building has been converted for modern library use. This small limestone structure was modernized in 1981 by opening up interior space with small upper level windows, yet it still fits right into its residential neighborhood. The project won an Award of Excellence for Library Architecture in 1983. The library contains a large collection of historical materials on Tremont. Hours vary; call 623-7004 for open times.

11. Continue along Jefferson, past Iglesia De Dios Evangelica (church) serving the Hispanic neighborhood population. On the right at Tremont and Jefferson is Tremont Elementary School.

12. Cross West 10th St. to Starkweather Ave. and walk west on Starkweather past several lovely old renovated homes on the left. These Greek Revival double homes are opposite Merrick House.

13. At the corner of Starkweather and West 11th St. is Merrick House Settlement and Day Nursery, a social service agency offering diverse programs for Tremont residents. Named for Miss Mary Merrick, founder of the National Christ Child Society, the organization developed from an original 1919 program for aiding new residents in Cleveland. The current building was constructed in 1949.

Pulaski Post 30 at 1041 Starkweather is located in an architecturally interesting building with an unusual tower overhang above the entrance.

14. Beyond West 11th on Starkweather are two grand examples of restored Victorian homes at 1103 and 1107 Starkweather. The careful maintenance of these striking residences reflects the pride and respect for heritage in this community.

Dempsey's Oasis Tavern at 1109 Starkweather is another well-known Tremont landmark.

At the south end of Lincoln Park is Lincoln Park Bathhouse. This 1921 bathhouse is a relic of the days when residents of Tremont lacked indoor plumbing and used this facility for bathing. After a planned restoration, it will house four condominiums on two floors and several townhouses at the rear of the property. Public Lincoln Park Pool is opposite on the right.

15. Reach West 14th St. to start walking past a unique cluster of Tremont's churches. Many of these sacred landmarks date from the community's early, more populous days, but today these churches are still active and form a unique place in modern Tremont.

St. George Antiochian Orthodox Church at 2587 West 14th St. was built in 1892 as Lincoln Park Methodist Church. Attached is an addition housing the Tremont Campus of Marotta Montessori School. The massive exterior walls contain few windows and the onion-shaped finials on the bell tower reflect the church's Syrian/Lebanese religious and cultural heritage. In 1933 St. George Church bought and refurbished the building only to have a fire destroy the interior. At the second rebuilding in 1935, a hand-cut crystal chandelier and handmade altar screen were added. The Bishop's Throne is of dark walnut inlaid with ebony, rosewood, and ivory. (781-9020).

16. Cross the street to the 1893 Pilgrim Congregational Church at 2592 West 14th, the largest of the three churches on this corner. The rough ashlar stone exterior features an impressive arched sandstone entrance with metal grillwork and heavy wooden doors on either side of wide stone steps. Ashlar is rough-hewn stone that has been cut, squared, and laid in regular courses on a building's facade.

Organized in 1859 as University Heights Congregational Church, its members first built the church now occupied by St. Augustine's Roman Catholic Church, located a block north of here. Outgrowing that site, the members built the present structure, designed by church architect S. R. Badgley, to accommodate Pilgrim's many social, recreational, and educational programs. Its numerous multi-purpose rooms enabled the church to open the first library on the west side of Cleveland, the first kindergarten, and first cooking school in the city. The building housed a kitchen, library, art museum, and gymnasium. Badgley was known for his design of ceilings with intricate segments and coves unsupported by columns. His unique Akron Plan (originally used in Akron's First Methodist Church) allowed sliding doors and interior windows to open up to accommodate large groups of people. Tiffany glass windows and a Ferran-Votey organ restored in 1992 are among the treasures in this church. Pilgrim continues to be a very active force in the Tremont neighborhood and houses a variety of community programs. To visit the church, call 861-7388.

17. Although it has changed hands several times, services are still held in the handsome church at 2536 West 14th St. Built in 1910 by German immigrants, this structure was originally known as Emmanuel Evangelical United Brethren Church. The building's Gothic and English architectural styles are evident in its large pointed windows with hood moldings (Gothic) and two wide porch entryways and short steeple on the corner tower (English). Until World War I, services were conducted in German, and in the 1930s the church was known for its missionary work in the Far East. In 1968, Cleveland Baptist Temple purchased the building; more recently it has become El Calvario, the church home of a Hispanic congregation.

On the left are more small, old Tremont homes, some of which have been carefully restored.

18. St. Augustine's Roman Catholic Church at West 14th St. and Howard began as a mission church in 1860 to serve Irish parishioners living in Tremont. It soon became large enough to become a parish and, with continued growth, members purchased the present church from Pilgrim Congregational Church in 1896. The Pilgrim congregation had built the simple red Victorian Gothic structure in 1870 with a high first floor to allow light to enter the basement Sunday School rooms, although the windows are covered over now. The attractive interior contains a raised marble altar at the end of a wide nave; the roof is supported by hammer-beam trusses and wrought iron tie rods. No nails were used in the ceiling. The rectory is located in a restored Victorian home at 2486 West 14th St. St. Augustine's is a very active community church, serving as the Deaf Center of Cleveland, and providing free meals to hundreds of needy persons.

19. Holy Ghost Byzantine Catholic Church, just to the west at Kenilworth Ave. and W. 14th St., was built in 1910 by the Ruthenian community, people who had emigrated from their homes in the western part of the Ukraine. An impressive rose window is set above three small entry doors, and the towers are topped by Byzantine domes and crosses. Inside is a striking icon screen made in Budapest in 1924; it is one of the most elaborate in Cleveland and contains 48 icons. Of its three doors, the central, royal door is used only by the priest.

At 2363 West 14th are the Pelton Apartments in a Romanesque-style building named for Mrs. Thirza Pelton, one of the founders of the now-defunct Cleveland University.

20. Just beyond Kenilworth Ave. at 2346 W. 14th St. is St. Joseph-Our Lady of Angels School for the Mentally and Physically Handicapped. The program is run by the Catholic Diocese and its principal is the Rector of St. Augustine's.

21. Continue north on West 14th St., passing St. Andrew Kim Korean Catholic Church and a beautiful "wedding cake" home at 2330. Next is Grace Hospital on the right, and north of it are graceful boarded-up Greek Revival homes that, until recently, housed the Olney Museum with its fine collection of art.

22. At the corner of Fairfield Ave. is the 1918 Greek Orthodox Church of the Annunciation with its familiar blue-topped twin towers and central dome that are seen daily by thousands of freeway drivers. As the mother church for the Greek Orthodox community in greater Cleveland, it reflects that country's culture both inside and outside the building. The impressive interior contains many frescoes and more than 80 icons.

23. Walk east on Fairfield Ave. to West 11th St. On the northeast corner is beautifully restored Sindy's Tavern, a former grocery store located in a Federal Italianate building with attractive windows, decorative stars covering the bracings, and a sidewalk stepping stone used when horse-drawn carriages filled the street.

Turn right (south) on West 11th St. and note the three-story Stacey's Block building and, next to it, a small, white brick, Gothic cottage—one of the oldest in Tremont. All along this street are lovely small homes that have been or are in the process of being rehabilitated. As with many renovations in this neighborhood, owners have tried to preserve as much of the original architecture as possible.

24. The Byzantine-style yellow-brick Spanish Assembly of God Church, (La Nueva Jerusalem) at 2280 West 11th St. was formerly St. Vladimir Ukrainian Orthodox Church established in 1924.

25. Of note at 1202 Kenilworth Ave. (between West 11th and West 14th streets) is the converted home housing the Ukrainian Museum-Archives. Call 781-4329 for open hours. This small museum contains a wealth of historical material of particular interest to those of Ukrainian heritage. The museum has collected hundreds of copies of *Svoboda* (Liberty), a Ukrainian-language newspaper published in Pennsylvania from 1893 to the present, and the *Ukrainian Weekly*, from the same publisher, printed for Ukrainians in English since 1933.

As the repository of the world's largest collection of Ukrainian literature produced in the Displaced Persons Camps of Germany and Austria following World War II, the museum is now cataloging hundreds of books and periodicals published by these refugees between 1945 and 1952. The museum also contains a collection of books, photographs, paintings, art objects, clothing, stamps, medals, currency, letters, leaflets, and historic records.

Continue south on West 11th St. to return to Lincoln Park.

26. On West 11th St. facing the park is the 1948 Our Lady of Mercy Roman Catholic Church, the newest of Tremont's churches. The variegated Tennessee crab-orchard stone exterior is unusual. The interior has beautiful carved wooden statues, several shrines, marble altars, and Slovenian folk painting.

Optional Driving Tour
   To enjoy more of Tremont's treasures, here is a convenient driving tour to several somewhat distant stops. As noted, it is important to telephone ahead for opening times and to make arrangements for tours.

27. Drive south on West 14th St. to 2716 West 14th. The 175-foot-tall octagonal spire of Zion United Church of Christ, soaring above the Gothic-inspired church building, is a Tremont landmark visible for miles around (861-2371). Organized in 1867 as the United German Evangelical Protestant Church to serve German immigrants in Tremont, the congregation soon outgrew its quarters on College Ave. and moved into this new structure in 1884. The front exterior, taking the form of a transept, shows pointed arches over the windows, doors, and above the open belfry. Additions over the years included a parsonage, religious school, kitchen, and auditorium.
   In 1934 Zion was the site of the historical vote to merge the Reformed Church in the United States and the Evangelical Synod of North America to form the Evangelical and Reformed Church. In 1957 another merger created the present Zion U.C.C.

28. Continue driving south on West 14th St. to Clark Ave. and turn right (west) on Clark to St. Michael Roman Catholic Church at 3114 Scranton Rd. and Clark Ave. (861-6297). St. Michael's parish was founded in 1883 to serve German Catholics in the surrounding neighborhood. Today, St. Michael's is also the home of La Iglesia de San Miguel Archangel; services are regularly held here in Spanish.
   When this magnificent Victorian Gothic-style church was built in 1892, it was the largest and most costly church in Cleveland. Its tall, graceful spires, reaching 232 and 180 feet, can be seen for miles around. Above the three arched doorways is a great pointed arch containing a large rose window with elaborate mullions.
   The interior, seating 1,500 parishioners, is filled with a profusion of carved statuary, many of which came from Germany. Behind the

altar are polychrome statues of the 12 apostles, 9 angels, and the patron saint, St. Michael. A marble altar designed by Cleveland's John Winterick, is modeled after the high altar of the Church of St. Francis, Borgo, Italy. The beautiful stained-glass windows permit natural light to enter and feature the Infancy and Childhood of Christ. Tennessee pink marble wainscotting contrasts with white marble flooring containing blue tile insets. Above the wainscotting in the entryway is a frieze of dragon heads. As the frieze continues into the sanctuary, the dragons change to angels, signifying that the power of Satan is broken within the church.

29. Return to Tremont proper by driving east on Clark Ave. and north on West 14th to Starkweather. Turn right (east) on Starkweather until just past Professor St., and on the right is St. Theodosius Russian Orthodox Cathedral at 733 Starkweather Ave. (861-5363). This magnificent Eastern Orthodox church, built in 1911 at the tremendous cost of $70,000, represents one of the best examples of Russian church architecture in this country. Located on a hill as a focal point for the Tremont neighborhood, its striking onion-shaped central dome and 12 smaller surrounding domes represent Christ and the apostles.

The cathedral, named after St. Theodosius, Bishop of Chernigov, is the center of Russian cultural activities in the Cleveland area and was patterned after Moscow's Church of Our Savior Jesus. The inspiring interior, shaped like a Greek cross with four limbs of equal length, contains a huge Czechoslovakian chandelier and a splendid icon screen from Kiev. A $100,000 renovation in 1953 added wall and ceiling murals created by Yugoslavian artist Andre Bicenko. In 1974 the church was placed on the National Register of Historic Places and, in 1977, wedding scenes for the movie *The Deer Hunter* were filmed here. St. Theodosius's parishioners come from all parts of the city for worship. An especially festive service is the Christmas choir concert, a tradition for many Clevelanders.

30. From the cathedral drive north on Starkweather to West 7th St. and turn left (west) to the corner of West 7th St. and College Ave. Sts. Peter and Paul Ukrainian Catholic Church (Byzantine Rite) at 2280 West 7th St. (861-2176) was originally built in 1910. The church was remodeled in 1956 and 1978, and is the mother parish of all the Ukrainian Catholic churches in the greater Cleveland area. The parish has a long history as a social center for Ukrainians arriving in Cleveland. In the past, it provided dramas, concerts, and classes in Ukrainian history, language, and dance. The Greek-style cross atop the tower reflects its Eastern Orthodox heritage. The interior retains the original pews, crystal chandeliers, icon screen with many religious images, and ceiling icon depicting Ukrainians in native dress.

31. Continue on West 7th St. to University Rd. Along the high embankment marking the northern edge of Tremont is a small park with a promenade enabling visitors to view the city of Cleveland from a unique perspective. At 1201 University Rd. is Sokolowski's University Inn, a well-known restaurant owned and operated by the same family since 1923, and now run by the third generation of Sokolowskis. It is open Monday through Friday from 11 a.m.–3 p.m. Its famous homemade food is still priced inexpensively and includes bratwurst, kielbasi, salisbury steak, and other foods.

From Sokolowski's, drive south on West 11th St. one block to Fairfield Ave. and turn right (west) to the freeway entrance off Fairfield Ave. for the return to Cleveland on I-71 north.

To return to Akron from here, take I-71 north as described above to the next exit for I-77 south.

This walk was prepared in consultation with Emily A.P. Lipovan, Director of Tremont West Development Corporation and Laura McShane, TWDC Project Coordinator.

6 BROOKLYN CENTRE
A Community in Renaissance

Brooklyn Centre, a Near West Side neighborhood, is one of Cleveland's oldest settlements. Forming a rough triangle enclosed by I-71 on the north, Riverside Cemetery and Jennings Rd. on the east, and Big Creek and the railroad tracks on the south, Brooklyn Centre is listed on the National Register of Historic Places as a Multiple Resource Area and carries a Landmarks Designation by the city of Cleveland. The community's buildings are a mix of late-19th to early-20th-century styles, including Italianate, Queen Anne, and Colonial Revival.

Distance: 2 miles

Walking time: 1 ½ hours

Description: This urban walk is on sidewalks and requires some street crossings at busy intersections. It includes a walk through tiny Brooklyn Centre Burying Ground (1835). To view the interiors of the churches on this tour it is necessary to call ahead for appointments. Please respect the rights and privacy of the owners by not trespassing onto the lawns of houses.

Directions: From Cleveland take I-71 south and exit at Pearl Rd. (U.S.42) turning right (south) at the top of the exit ramp. Follow Pearl Rd. two blocks to Brooklyn Centre shopping plaza on the right.

Parking & restrooms: At the Brooklyn Centre shopping plaza

The village was first settled in 1812 by early pioneers from Connecticut, including members of the Fish and Brainard families, and developed around the important rural crossroads of what is now Pearl Rd. and Denison Ave. This area was the center of old Brooklyn Township, a farming region west of Cleveland. In 1818 the first churches, now known as Brooklyn Memorial United Methodist Church and Archwood United Church of Christ, were founded. By 1867 the village of Brooklyn was incorporated and gradually devel-

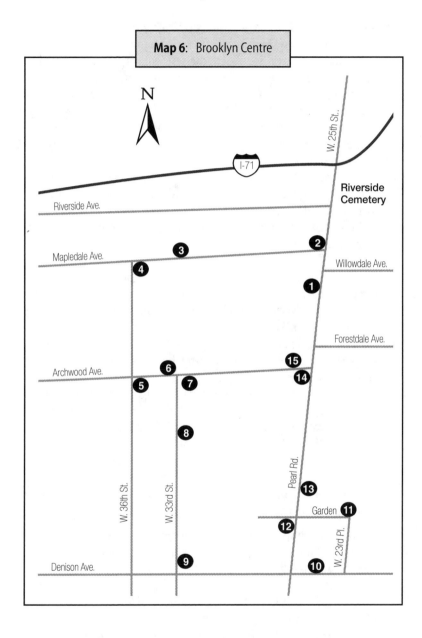

Map 6: Brooklyn Centre

N

I-71

W. 25th St.

Riverside
Cemetery

Riverside Ave.

Mapledale Ave.

Willowdale Ave.

Forestdale Ave.

Archwood Ave.

W. 36th St.

W. 33rd St.

Pearl Rd.

Garden

W. 23rd Pl.

Denison Ave.

oped into a residential community of large homes on spacious lots. Many of the new residents were from Germany.

As the population increased, the residents of Brooklyn voted in 1894 to annex to Cleveland so as to obtain the advantages of a better school system, fire and police protection, paved streets and sidewalks, and other city services. Many of the homes and carriage houses built then are now enjoying a renaissance as current restoration efforts are devoted to preserving the colorful past of this historic community.

To enhance your visit to this interesting Cleveland neighborhood, you might combine this tour with one through adjacent historic Riverside Cemetery (see Chapter 7). Many of Cleveland's earliest West Side families, with names such as Brainard, Lamson, Session, and Rhodes, are buried there.

1. Begin the walk at the Brooklyn Centre shopping plaza. Directly opposite at 3731 Pearl Rd. is the Mallo House (c.1880), an Italianate-style home converted to podiatry offices, one of the oldest houses still standing on Pearl Rd. As seen in this neighborhood, the Italianate style is characterized by tall arched windows, flaring eaves supported by ornate brackets, low-pitched hipped roofs, and ornate entrance porches.

Behind the Mallo House is the former Eighth Reformed Church (1909) at 2409 Willowdale Ave. The building is California Mission style and was designed by architect Paul Motzinger.

North of the Mallo House is the old building of Engine Company #24 (1894) built soon after the Cleveland annexation. Originally hay was stored in the rear of the second floor to feed the fire horses. This fire house served the neighborhood until the new fire station was built in 1985 a few doors away at Pearl and Archwood.

2. Walk north to Mapledale Ave. The Brooklyn Branch Library of Cleveland Public Library stands at 3706 Pearl Rd. Built in 1919, its interior was totally renovated in 1985, but its exterior, with two old stone building signs, was preserved.

At 3648 Pearl Rd. is the stately, symmetrical former Third Church of Christ, Scientist, now Living Word Church (1906). The architect of this Neoclassical-style building was Frederick Striebinger, one of

Cleveland's better-known architects, who also designed the former First Church of Christ, Scientist at Euclid Ave. and East 77th St. Neoclassical style is characterized by robust cornices, columns, entablatures, and other elements derived from the Greco-Roman culture.

Turn left (west) on Mapledale Ave.

At 3000 Mapledale Ave. is the Bomante House (1910), built for a Cleveland restaurant owner. Although reminiscent of a Swiss chalet, its architecture is basically Tudor Revival, and is characterized by half-timbering, flaring eaves, broad porches, and multi-paned windows. Home restoration in the community has placed an emphasis on using historic paint colors, usually three or more colors in warm earth tones such as on the Bomante House.

3. Continue walking west on Mapledale. Many interesting restored homes are here. Note, for example, 3101 Mapledale, the Verona Apartments at 3127-31, and 3221 Mapledale.

At 3400 Mapledale is the three-story orange-brick Karl F. Snow House (1909), originally built with a ballroom on the top floor.

4. At 3503 Mapledale is the former Emmaus Evangelical Lutheran Church, now Holy Gospel Church of God (1910). Note the beautiful Gothic window in the front of this small religious structure.

Turn left on West 36th St. past Virginia to Archwood Ave. and turn left again onto Archwood.

5. Along Archwood are more stunning examples of late-19th-century homes that have been carefully preserved and returned by their owners to their former architectural magnificence.

The Queen Anne–style home at 3515 Archwood is the Weldon Davis House (1895) constructed with an imposing three-story corner tower. Queen Anne–style homes are characterized by gables, broad porches, asymmetrical plans, steep roofs, and an occasional tower or turret. Again, historic paint colors have enhanced this handsome home. A rear apartment addition to the home artfully blends the new with the old. Standing behind the house, on West 36th St., is a newly built carriage house that incorporates design elements matching the home and contains old windows from the demolished 1881 Brooklyn Methodist Church.

Next to the Davis House is a beautiful Italianate home at 3505

Archwood, the Charles Selzer House. Selzer, who was mayor of Brooklyn, a municipal judge, and founder of a weekly newspaper, built this colorful home around 1880.

6. Diagonally across the street at 3340 Archwood is the Doubleday House (c.1880), another noteworthy and finely restored Italianate home built by a family who owned much of the land in this area.

The William R. Coates House (1902) at 3304 Archwood was built by a man who was the mayor of Brooklyn when the village was annexed to Cleveland. The architect who designed this Colonial-Revival-style home was Frederick Striebinger, the architect of Third Church. Colonial Revival homes are characterized by delicate detailing and Classical ornament inspired by early American architecture.

7. At 3101 Archwood is the Adam Poe House (c.1870), one of the finest brick Italianate-style houses in Cleveland. It has elaborate cast-metal hood moldings over the tall windows, porches, and distinctive brackets. Adam Poe was a storekeeper and lay minister at the Brooklyn Methodist Church.

On the corner of Archwood and W. 33rd St. are Archwood Manor and Brooklyn Manor, containing apartments that have recently been renovated by a Cleveland city housing program.

Turn right (south) on W. 33rd St.

8. Next to the elementary school, the F. A. Shepherd House (1914) at 3785 West 33rd St. is a Tudor Revival house that exemplifies the Arts and Crafts style of architecture. It is characterized by finely crafted yet simple oak woodwork, multi-paned windows, and a massive gable roof.

The home at 3800 West 33rd St. is the Italianate Clayton Townes House (c.1865) whose front porch was added later. Townes was president of Cleveland's city council and mayor when William R. Hopkins, founder of the country's first municipal airport, was city manager.

9. On the corner of West 33rd and Denison Ave. is St. Philip the Apostle Episcopal Church (1922), organized in 1894. This Neogothic-style building is also home to St. Agnes Mission to the Deaf. This style is characterized by lancet windows, steep roofs, and Medieval-inspired trim.

10. Turn left (east) on Denison Ave. Continue past Pearl Rd. to 2310 Denison to see the restored Kroehle House (1865). This large, beautiful Italianate structure was the home of the founder of Spang Bakery Co. Note the long 10-car garage at the rear of the property where delivery trucks once were kept. Kroehle claimed to be the first baker in Cleveland to sell wrapped bread.

11. Turn left (north) at W. 23rd Pl. one block to the small Brooklyn Centre Burying Ground (1835). It is also known as Denison Cemetery. The community's first burials took place on this ground. As early as 1823 some of Brooklyn's pioneer settlers were laid to rest here, including members of the Fish, Brainard, Storer, and Booth families. Just inside the cemetery and to the right, about half-way to the end, is the grave of the American Revolutionary War soldier Ebenezer Fish (1757-1827) and his wife Lydia, very early settlers of Brooklyn.

Turn left (west) on Garden St. and return to Pearl Rd.

12. The Neo-classical Brooklyn Masonic Temple building at 3804 Pearl was built in 1932 and remodeled in 1937 for the lodge that had been founded in 1871. Daniel Farnam, the architect of Archwood United Church of Christ, also designed this structure.

13. Turn right (north) on Pearl Rd. The new Aldi's supermarket on the corner of Garden and Pearl is designed to conform to historic district standards, as was the Cleveland Fire Station #20 and EMS Unit No. 4 (1985) at 3765 Pearl Rd. This handsome brick structure designed by Ovington & Glaser, City of Cleveland Division of Architecture, was the first new building in Brooklyn Centre to follow Design Review Committee guidelines. The clock tower used for drying fire hoses is an attractive focal point for the neighborhood.

14. Opposite the new fire station at Archwood and Pearl, note the architecturally striking building on the southwest corner with unusual terra-cotta trim. It is the old Brooklyn Savings & Loan Co. (1904) designed by J. Milton Dyer, who was also the architect of Cleveland's magnificent City Hall.

Just west of this corner at 2607 Archwood is Brooklyn Memorial United Methodist Church (1911) designed by the architect Ray Fulton for the oldest Methodist congregation in greater Cleveland. Founded in 1818, the congregation had three previous buildings before this unusual one was constructed. Of special interest is the wooden eight-sided tower with windows lighting an immense stained glass dome over the sanctuary. The Gothic exterior features two square towers with louvered belfries, lancet windows, pointed arches above the doors, and elaborate stained-glass windows. The interior was built on the Akron Plan with sliding walls to provide flexible room arrangements.

15. Almost directly opposite is Archwood United Church of Christ (1929), home to the oldest Congregational church in Cleveland, founded in 1819, only a few years after the first settlement, by New Englanders. The original church was built in 1879 and extended in 1912. The later wing was retained when the present Georgian Revival structure was built in 1929. Designed by the architect Daniel Farnam to reflect 18th-century New England, its stately exterior includes Georgian details such as the tripartite doorway, front portico with a single round window, 6- and 12-paned windows topped by keystones and fanlights, and the tall copper steeple and weather vane.

Continue north on Pearl Rd. to return to Brooklyn Centre shopping plaza.

This chapter was prepared with the generous assistance of building preservation consultant Steven McQuillin, who is a homeowner and resident of Brooklyn Centre Historic District. A walking tour prepared by the Brooklyn Centre Design Review Committee has been adapted for this chapter, using architectural designations from that source and additional material from Mr. McQuillin.

7 RIVERSIDE CEMETERY
Visiting Cleveland's History

Riverside Cemetery is a 90-acre oasis of serene beauty in the midst of city and freeway traffic and nearby steel mills, and is the burial place of many early developers and wealthy businessmen of Cleveland's West Side. Planned by landscape architect, E.O. Schwagerl and dedicated in 1876, the cemetery was created from Titus N. Brainard farmland high above the Cuyahoga River. The dedication ceremony was attended by many prominent Clevelanders, including Jeptha Wade, president of Lake View Cemetery Association (which had been founded six years earlier), and by Ohio Governor and President-elect Rutherford B. Hayes. Originally the cemetery contained six acres of lakes with seven rustic wooden bridges spanning the waterways. The lakes are now drained and filled in.

Distance: 2 miles

Walking time: 1 ½ to 2 hours

Description: The walk is on cemetery roads that are generally flat, except for one hill. It is permissible to walk on the grassy areas of the cemetery.

Directions: From downtown Cleveland take I-71 to Exit 245 (W. 25th St., Pearl Rd.). Turn right (south) at the exit ramp onto Pearl Rd. Just over the overpass turn sharp left to enter the main gate of Riverside Cemetery at 3607 Pearl Rd.

Parking & restrooms: Park along the road near the Administration Building and office; a restroom is available inside.

Two of the cemetery's buildings are on the National Register of Historic Places: the 1896 Administration Building and the 1876 Stone Chapel, closed since 1953. Preservation plans are currently underway for full restoration of this building as a nondenominational chapel for persons being buried at Riverside.

Map 7: Riverside Cemetery

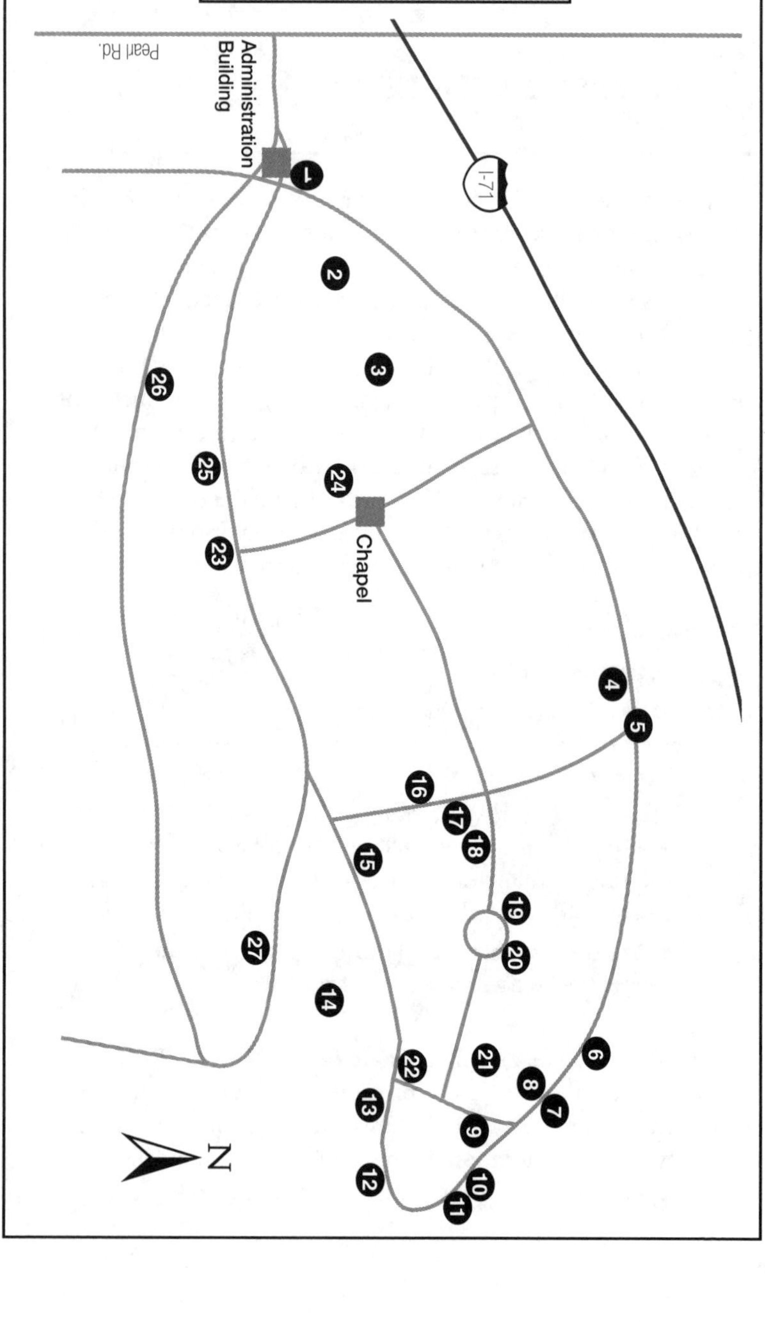

Along the front of the cemetery's property are a row of flowering crabapple trees that bloom magnificently each year in early May. Many lovely shrubs and trees grace Riverside Cemetery, as well as plantings placed by owners who are uniquely permitted to do their own landscaping on grave sites.

The cemetery is open from 7:30 a.m.–5 p.m. daily and the office is open from 8 a.m.–4 p.m. Monday through Saturday. It is best to call ahead for this walk to ensure that a visit to Riverside will not interfere with scheduled services that day (351-4800).

A walk in Riverside Cemetery can easily be combined with the Brooklyn Centre walk described in Chapter 6.

1. Start at the beautiful, red-tile-roofed Administration Building. The turrets, gables, and porch of this Romanesque Revival office building were designed by the building's architect, Charles W. Hopkinson, who also contributed to the design of the James A. Garfield Monument in Lake View Cemetery.

2. From the office go northeast on the road nearest to I-71. (The roads here are not named.) On the right is the tall Francis Branch monument, topped by a weeping woman embracing a cross, near a lovely stand of Austrian pines. Mr. Branch (1812-77) came with his family from Connecticut in 1818. A dairy farmer and one of the first to sell milk in this area, he later served three terms as county commissioner.

3. Farther along, also on the right but in the center of this section, is a tan stone monument with a wreath on the end. This is the memorial for William Jacob Astrup (1845–1915), founder in 1876 of the Astrup Awning Co., now the Astrup Company, which is still in business on West 25th St. as one of the country's largest manufacturers of awning fabric and hardware, tents, and canvas. Mr. Astrup, a Danish sailmaker, first started his company by manufacturing sails for Great Lakes ships.

4. Toward the end of Section 9 on the right near the road and just past the tall buckeye tree, is the unobtrusive grave of Linda Eastman (1867–1963). Miss Eastman was the fourth director of the Cleveland Public Library and the first woman in the world to head so large a library. She served when the present library on Superior and East

6th St. was built in 1925 and was nationally recognized for her achievements in library work, such as developing services for the visually and physically handicapped and establishing travel and business bureaus. Miss Eastman served as president of the Ohio and American Library Associations and lived to be 95 years of age. The Eastman Reading Garden adjacent to the Cleveland Public Library downtown and the Eastman Branch Library at Lorain and West 115th St. were named in her honor.

5. As you continue along this drive, note the beautiful view of MetroHealth Medical Center on the left. On the right note the unusual carving that graces the 1901 Magdalene Fredericks Woehrle monument, especially the hairdo, dress collar, and exquisite folds and fringe of the grieving woman's shawl.

Although no one is buried inside the large casket-shaped, granite Humiston monument also on the right, members of the family are buried all around it.

6. On the left is the Baggett monument, another beautiful stone carving of two grieving women, a common theme of late-19th- and early-20th-century cemetery art.

Next is the 1889 Brainard family mausoleum containing members of an early family of farmers. David S. Brainard owned many acres of farmland where MetroHealth Medical Center now stands. Also on the left is a small burial area for members of the Leisy family. Founded by Isaac Leisy (1838–92) in 1873, the Leisy Brewing Company was the oldest brewery in Cleveland and one of the longest surviving family-operated breweries in the country. A long view of the downtown Cleveland skyline and the Cuyahoga River valley can be seen next to this plot.

7. Farther along on the left is the Byelorussian Orthodox Church burial area maintained by members of this religious community.

8. Opposite on the right is a large boulder under a spreading evergreen tree. This is the burial place of Carlos Jones (1827–97), manufacturer of farm implements, real estate developer, mayor of Brooklyn, and founder in 1887 of Jones School & Home for Friendless Children, later Jones Home for Children. Several prominent businessmen, including James Coffinbury, Isaac Lamson, and

Samuel Sessions, and Governor (later President) Rutherford B. Hayes served on the home's original corporate board.

Nearby but not on this walk, the three-story brick Jones building (1902) at 3518 West 25th St. was designed by the well-known architect Sidney R. Badgley and is on the Register of Cleveland Landmarks.

To the east of Carlos Jones on a flat ground marker is James Milton Curtiss (1840–1916), a nurseryman and real estate developer who was the first superintendent of Riverside Cemetery. He conceived and promoted the idea for downtown Cleveland's Old Arcade (1890) between Euclid and Superior Aves. and for the Central Viaduct bridge (demolished in 1941 and replaced by the Innerbelt Bridge).

9. A small burial area on the right, identified with a central stone for Emma Tamm, is used by members of Cleveland's Estonian community.

10. Opposite on the left is the grave of Titus N. Brainard (1825–1910) and his son-in-law Harry M. Farnsworth (1881–1955). Note their intertwined initials at the top. Titus Brainard's grandfather traveled from Connecticut by ox-team wagon in 1814 and purchased about 140 acres of land for farming here. In 1876 Titus sold 102.5 acres of his land to Riverside Cemetery Association for development of a new burial ground.

Harry Farnsworth was the Secretary-Treasurer of Brooklyn Savings & Loan. He was instrumental in the formation of Cleveland Metroparks and served on its first Board of Park Commissioners. It was Farnsworth who first proposed the joining of parks to form what is now called the "Emerald Necklace."

11. At the Meyer family plot with the small obelisk are buried more members of a single family than in any other section of Riverside. The plot was chosen to overlook their farmland, now occupied by LTV Steel.

Standing alone on the edge of the embankment overlooking the Cuyahoga River valley and with its back to the road is a headstone with Chinese inscriptions. This memorial for a Chinese woman, Kwan Wai Wah, is situated to face the rising sun.

12. Next on the left is a small ground marker for Diodate Clark (1798–1876), the first male schoolteacher in Brooklyn and later a large landowner and county commissioner, who came to Cleveland nearly penniless at the age of 19.

13. The tall beautiful Lamson-Sessions monument designed by an unknown artist is the most noteworthy memorial in Riverside. Costing $10,000 when it was built in 1877, it was the most expensive monument in Cleveland at the time and quickly became a tourist attraction. The inscription reads: "The trumpet shall sound and the dead shall be raised incorruptible, and we shall be charged."

Samuel W. Sessions (1824–1902), Isaac P. Lamson (1832–1912), and Thomas H. Lamson (1827–1882) all came to Cleveland from Connecticut with a group of skilled workers to establish the Cleveland Nut Company in 1872. Over the next 100 years their success enabled the business at West 14th St. and Jennings Rd., later known as Lamson and Sessions Company, to become one of the country's leading fastener manufacturers with eight plants nationwide in 1930. Lamson and Sessions helped found the Visiting Nurse Association of Cleveland, Tremont's Pilgrim Congregational Church, and the Jones Home.

John Gould Jennings (1856–1937), who is also buried here, was Isaac Lamson's son-in-law, and a director at Lamson and Sessions.

Another artistic carving adorns the monument of Frederick Pelton (1827–1902) to the west of the Lamson-Sessions. Created by an unknown artist, this was on display at the Chicago World's Fair (1894) before being transported here. Pelton, a founding trustee of Riverside Cemetery, was City Council President (1866–69) and Mayor of Cleveland (1871–73).

14. Toward the rear of Section 20, identified by a monument with a seated woman, are Daniel P. Rhodes (1814–75) and his son James Ford Rhodes (1848–1927), members of a prominent West Side Cleveland family who built the c.1874 Robert Russell Rhodes family home at 2905 Franklin Circle, now the Cuyahoga County Archives. Daniel, a Vermonter, became wealthy as a coal mining entrepreneur and founder of Rhodes & Company. He also founded People's Savings and Loan and contributed greatly to the development of the Cuyahoga River's west bank.

James joined the family business in 1870, and embarked on a study of the iron industry in Europe and the U.S. With his older brother, Robert, his brother-in-law, Marcus A. Hanna, and other partners, he reorganized the family's very successful iron, iron-ore, and coal business in 1885 as M. A. Hanna Mining Co. James later became a prolific writer, winning many honorary degrees and awards, among them a Pulitzer Prize for his *History of the Civil War, 1861–1865*. A west side Cleveland high school is named for James Ford Rhodes.

Note another beautiful carving adorning the Schuele burial site near the road. Christian Schuele was co-owner of Fries & Schuele Department Store.

15. Down the road on the right is a polished granite memorial for George A. Tinnerman (1845–1925) and his son, Albert H. Tinnerman (1879–1961). George founded a stove manufacturing business in 1875 that became a diversified multimillion-dollar company. Albert originated the first all-porcelain enameled gas range with concealed fastenings in 1923. He also patented a spring tension speed nut fastener that revolutionized assembly lines.

16. Continue walking west to the next small road and turn right at the three cedar trees. On the left is Charles W. Hopkinson (1865–1950), the noted architect who was twice president of the American Institute of Architects, and whose well-known designs include Riverside's Administration Building, modifications to the Garfield Monument in Lake View Cemetery, Franklin Circle Masonic Temple, the Rockefeller Building at Case Western Reserve University, and Hough Avenue United Church of Christ.

17. On the right is Claud H. Foster (1872–1965), automotive inventor of "Snubber" shock absorbers and the multitone Gabriel auto horn powered by exhaust gases. He was one of the first industrialists to develop an employee profit-sharing incentive program and was also a philanthropist who made large gifts to hospitals and other agencies. Foster donated pipe organs to several churches and built the Brooklyn Branch of the Young Men's Christian Association (located just south of the cemetery) in memory of his mother. In 1952 he divided his fortune of almost four million dollars among 16 Cleveland educational and charitable institutions.

18. Turn right at the next corner. Some members of Cleveland's Ukrainian community, strongly represented in the city's history since the early 1900s, are buried in the Ukrainian section on the right. At the circle just ahead there was once a fountain and pool, and here is where the 1876 cemetery dedication was held.

19. On the left, in the center of this section, is a small obelisk marking the location of Stephen Buhrer (1825–1907), city councilman and mayor of Cleveland from 1867 to 1871. A cooper by trade, he was responsible for building the Cleveland House of Correction & Workhouse during his term as mayor.

On the left near the circle is the memorial monument for Josiah Barber Sr. (1771–1842), whose 1809 Western Reserve allotment encompassed land along the west side of the Cuyahoga River to West 117th St. and north to the lake. He became a land developer and store owner who, with his partners, in 1840 dedicated a large portion of acreage for an open-air market, later to become the West Side Market. Barber was also a circuit judge, the first mayor of Ohio City, and an incorporator of Trinity Parish in downtown Cleveland and St. John's Parish at West 28th and Church Sts. In 1834, Barber incorporated The Cuyahoga Steam Furnace Co. one of Cleveland's first manufacturing companies.

20. The tall obelisk to the left of the circle marks the grave of John B. Cowle (1826–1914). Cowle was the owner of Globe Iron Works, which later became part of Cleveland Shipbuilding, treasurer of Cleveland Drydock Co., and an associate of Universal Machine & Boiler Co. Two Lake Erie ore freighters were named for him.

James M. Coffinberry's adjacent, artistic monument of a woman raising her left arm to heaven contains exquisite carving—particularly in the folds of the woman's dress. Coffinberry, an attorney, journal editor, and Judge of Common Pleas Court, was a Union supporter in the Civil War and, later, legal counsel for the founding of Riverside Cemetery.

21. Past the circle on the left is a large black granite block marking the final resting place of Julius Spang (1852–1950), co-founder with his wife Fredericka of the J. Spang Baking Co. Spang, a German immigrant, managed the baking operations and his wife supervised the financial affairs of the company, which remained at the same site, 2911 Barber Ave., for 70 years and employed 433 persons in three plants before it closed in 1958. Spang served as president of the company until his death at age 98.

Opposite is another artistic monument carving depicting a woman with raised arm gracing the grave of John B. Koelges (1833–99).

22. Turn right at the next corner. Shaded by the large evergreen shrubs on the right are playwright Avery Hopwood (1883-1928) and his mother, Jule Hopwood. Mr. Hopwood was a well-known early-20th-century playwright who wrote such Broadway plays as "Streets of New York" and "The French Doll." He died in a drowning accident in Nice, France. His mother had the monument erected and died herself just eight months later.

Turn right again and continue west on this road past Section 20 and past the road going downhill, to near the end of Section 11.

23. On the left is the 1879 J.J.Cartright mausoleum built to resemble a small chapel.

Next is the Ruetenik family plot. Rev. Herman J. Ruetenik (1826–1914), an educator, author, and editor, came from Germany in 1848 as a political refugee, became a minister and missionary in Cleveland, and established the First through Ninth German Reformed Churches and Calvin College on West 25th St. for German-speaking men. Ruetenik's Fourth Reformed Church founded what is now Fairview General Hospital. Herman's son Martin (1868–1947) founded Ruetenik Greenhouses and Gardens on Schaaf Rd. in Brooklyn in 1885, Cleveland's first greenhouse. Using scientific methods, the three-and-a-half-acre greenhouse became a national leader in the production of hothouse vegetables.

24. To the right (north) is the 1876 Stone Chapel, closed since 1953 because of deterioration. Future plans call for complete restoration of this beautiful little structure.

25. Back on the road beyond the Ruetenik plot and on the left in the small mausoleum is Leonard Schlather (1835–1918). A German immigrant, Schlather founded and operated the L. Schlather Brewing Co. from 1857 to 1902 at Carroll and York (West 28th) Aves., then one of the three largest breweries in Cleveland. Later Schlather became active in financial affairs and banking and built this small family mausoleum in 1882.

26. Continue walking to the Administration Building, turn left (east) at the end of Section 5 and follow this road downhill. In former times a large lake was situated in this depression with several north-south bridges spanning the water. On the left is a small, above-ground columbarium, and next on the left is "Babyland," poignantly decorated with toys, flowers, mementos, and touching inscriptions. This is a very special burial plot for infants and young children. On the right surrounded by evergreen shrubs is a new area planned for more of these youngsters.

27. Continue to the next intersection and turn left. About half-way uphill on the left is the second (1966) Case Western Reserve University Medical School memorial headstone containing the cremated remains of persons who have chosen to donate their bodies upon death for the advancement of science. The first lot, begun in 1947, is southeast of this one and has an identical monument. This stone donated by a monument company in 1967 reads: "In Memoriam . . . they gave in Death for Those In Life . . ." Since 1947 a yearly burial service has been held by the medical school to which families are invited.

Follow this road uphill, staying left at the top and left at the next intersection, and follow the road back to the car parked at the Administration Building.

This chapter was prepared with the generous assistance of William R. Halley, General Manager, Riverside Cemetery and Secretary-Treasurer, Riverside Cemetery Foundation.

8 UNIVERSITY CIRCLE

University Circle, five miles east of downtown Cleveland, is home to more than 70 cultural, educational, health care, social, religious, and other institutions. Information about activities here can be obtained from University Circle, Inc., 10831 Magnolia Dr., Cleveland, Ohio 44106 (791-3900). A University Circle walk is not complete without visiting at least one of the many cultural institutions, such as the Cleveland Museum of Art, Cleveland Museum of Natural History, Western Reserve Historical Society, and Cleveland Botanical Garden. Although many charge an admission fee, some have free admission at certain times.

Distance: 5 miles

Walking time: 3 hours

Description: This easy walk is flat but has many busy street crossings.

Directions: From downtown Cleveland, take Euclid Ave. east to East Blvd., and Wade Oval west to the Cleveland Museum of Art. From I-90, take Martin Luther King Dr. south to East Blvd. From the eastern suburbs, take Mayfield Rd. (S.R. 322) west to Euclid Ave.

Parking & restrooms: At the Cleveland Museum of Art, 1150 East Blvd., for which an hourly parking fee is charged (except Thursdays for senior citizens, when parking is free).

1. Start the walk at the Cleveland Museum of Art and stroll through the galleries to the South Entrance. (If closed during winter months, exit at the North Entrance and take the sidewalk around to the south side of the museum and its Fine Arts Garden.) The museum is open Tuesday, Thursday, and Friday from 10 a.m.–5:45 p.m., Wednesday from 10 a.m.–9:45 p.m., and Sunday from 1–5:45 p.m. It contains one of the world's great collections of art and provides extensive educational programs, films, concerts, and lectures.

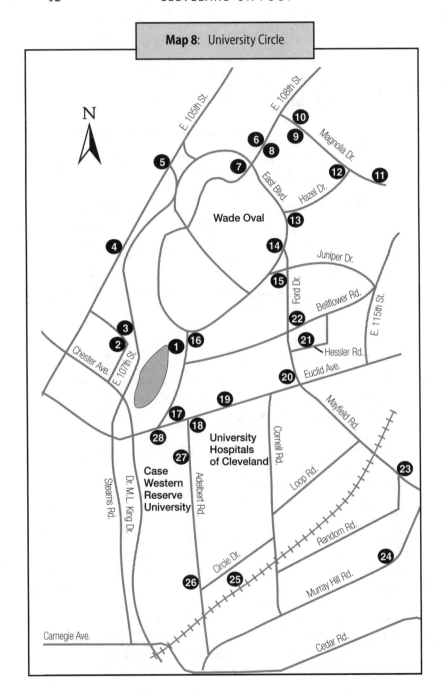

Map 8: University Circle

From the Fine Arts Garden on the south side of the museum, walk around the Wade Park Lagoon, which has beautiful flowering trees in the spring. Take the stone steps at the south end of the lagoon up to the sidewalk along Martin Luther King Dr. (MLK Dr.). Cross MLK Dr. at the traffic light at Chester Ave.; on this corner note the striking Epworth Euclid United Methodist Church. This Gothic Revival church was built in 1928 and contains magnificent stained-glass windows.

2. Opposite the church, at 1890 East 107th St., is Judson Manor. Built in 1923 as Wade Park Manor, an elegant residential hotel, it was renovated to become part of Judson Retirement Community.

3. Continue north along MLK Dr., reaching the Chinese Cultural Garden on the west side of the drive.

4. On East 105th St. is The Temple-Tifereth Israel (Reform) in Silver Park. The Temple Museum of Religious Art is here; it can be viewed by appointment (791-7755), as can the very large temple itself. The museum is dedicated to Judaic cultural, religious, and ceremonial art objects, and artifacts of ancient Israel.

5. Next to The Temple, at E. 105 St. and Mt. Sinai Dr., is the Mount Sinai Medical Center, a 450-bed hospital.

6. Carefully cross MLK Dr. where several streets converge at traffic islands and walk northeast. Go uphill on East Blvd., passing the Veterans Administration Hospital on the left (north) side.

7. The Cleveland Museum of Natural History, on the south side of East Blvd. is open Monday–Saturday from 10 a.m.–5 p.m. and Sunday from 1–5:30 p.m. (231-4600).

8. Turn north onto East 108th St. The Western Reserve Historical Society buildings dominate the northeast corner and consist of the Crawford Auto-Aviation Museum, the Hay Mansion (1910), and the Hanna Mansion (1918), joined together into one building. It is open Tuesday through Saturday from 10 a.m.–5 p.m. and Sunday from noon–5 p.m. Here you can see the oldest enclosed automobile and Cleveland's first airplane and horseless carriages, and a replica 1890s Street of Shops. In the mansions are fine collections of American furniture, period musical instruments, art, and apparel.

9. Turn right at Magnolia Dr. Along this street are once-elegant homes that today house a variety of institutions. The ornate window at the brick Historical Society Library was once the entrance to downtown's Cuyahoga Building (demolished to make room for the BP America Building).

10. At 10831 Magnolia are the offices of University Circle, Inc. (791-3900), where detailed information about the circle can be picked up .

11. At the north corner of Magnolia and Hazel drives is the newly renovated Cleveland Music School Settlement, which offers music lessons, classes, and programs for all persons.

12. The Gestalt Institute, to the south, holds a wide variety of personal growth workshops and courses year-round.

13. Go west on Hazel to the Cleveland Institute of Music on East Blvd. This prestigious conservatory offers many free student and faculty concerts.

14. Cross East Blvd. to the Cleveland Botanical Garden and walk through this building and its lovely gardens. The building is open Monday–Friday from 9 a.m.–5 p.m., Saturday from noon–5 p.m., and Sunday from 1–5 p.m. The gardens are open year-round from dawn to dusk. Educational programs on gardening and horticulture, lectures, workshops, and outstanding seasonal exhibits are featured here.

15. The Gund School of Law at Case Western Reserve University (CWRU) is opposite the Garden Center.

16. On East Blvd. you will pass the Cleveland Institute of Art and CWRU's Freiberger Library.

17. Severance Hall, the beautiful home of the world-renowned Cleveland Orchestra, is at the corner of East Blvd. and Euclid Ave. A tour can be arranged by appointment and is well worth the time to see this lovely 1930 Art Deco building (231-7300).

18. Walking east up Euclid Ave. you will see buildings of CWRU and University Hospitals. On the right is the Allen Memorial Library (1926) with its medical collection and the Dittrick Museum of Medical History, which is open Monday through Friday 10 a.m.–5 p.m. and Saturday from noon–5 p.m. (368-3648).

19. On the left is Thwing Hall (1913), housing CWRU's Student Center and Bookstore.

20. The Mary C. Painter Memorial Arch (1904) and the Neo-Gothic Church of the Covenant (1909) are at 11205 Euclid. The church has an elegant interior with rich wood carvings.

Continue along Euclid one block to Ford Dr. and turn left (north).

21. Hessler Rd. and Hessler Ct., off Ford Dr., comprise Cleveland's first Historic District. The individual 1900-era homes here were saved from demolition, as was the street itself—the only remaining street in the city paved with wooden bricks.

22. Continue out Hessler to Bellflower Rd. and go left (west) past the airy new Mandel School of Applied Social Sciences (CWRU).

23. Turn left (south) on Ford Dr. across Mayfield Rd.. Follow Mayfield to Cleveland's Little Italy Historic District. This Italian neighborhood was developed in the late 19th and early 20h centuries by immigrants who worked nearby in the stone-cutting business and made monuments for use in Lake View Cemetery. Along Mayfield Rd. are Holy Rosary Church, Italian shops and restaurants, and Alta House, a community center named after the daughter of John D. Rockefeller, who helped finance the original structure.

24. Walk back through Little Italy and turn west on Murray Hill Rd. Many artists and craftspeople have located their shops and galleries along this street. At the old Murray Hill School, several artisans have established their businesses in this renovated space and they welcome visitors.

25. From Murray Hill Rd. turn north onto Cornell Rd. and west on Circle Dr. Walking behind the CWRU Medical School, Health Sciences Library, and Power Plant, you will reach Adelbert Rd. Walk north on Adelbert a short distance to the One-To-One Fitness Center. If you have time to see this compact facility, it is worth a visit, if a tour guide is available.

26. Walk past the south side of the Fitness Center to enter the Case Quadrangle on the right with its classroom buildings on either side of this quiet enclave.

27. Adelbert Hall, at the end of the Quad, built in 1881, is the location of the university's administrative offices and office of the president. A devastating fire in 1991 gutted this landmark building, but it has been handsomely rebuilt.

28. Amasa Stone Chapel (1911) is a lovely, small Gothic Revival church with a 121-foot tower topped by three angels and a gargoyle.

Cross Euclid Ave. to East Blvd. and walk along the east side of the Wade Lagoon back to the Cleveland Museum of Art.

9 LAKE VIEW CEMETERY

Lake View Cemetery, founded in 1869, contains the final resting places of some of Cleveland's most illustrious and industrious citizens in a most beautiful horticultural park of 285 acres. The President James A. Garfield Monument and the Jeptha Wade Memorial Chapel are two of the cemetery's most famous and significant buildings. Both are in the National Register of Historic Places. The cemetery lies in three cities: Cleveland, Cleveland Heights, and East Cleveland. Please call the cemetery at 421-2665 to reserve a time for this walk. Walking on the grassy areas of the cemetery is permitted.

Distance: 4 miles

Walking time: 2 to 3 hours

Description: The cemetery is on a hill, the last remnant of the Appalachian Plateau before it descends to Lake Erie. The hills in Lake View are steep but short.

Directions: From downtown Cleveland take Chester Ave. (S.R. 322) east to Euclid Ave., then east again on Mayfield Rd. (also S.R. 322) to the entrance to the cemetery at Kenilworth Rd. From the eastern suburbs follow Mayfield Rd. west to Kenilworth. Enter the cemetery through the Mayfield Rd. gate.

Parking & restrooms: At the Garfield Monument on Garfield Rd., by following the signs toward the left just inside the gate

1. Start your walk at the gate. To your right is the new (1990) award-winning Memorial Chapel Mausoleum. It is open during the day and can be visited now or later in the tour. Near the gate are two very old Japanese pagoda trees, not usually found in this climate, and which bloom gorgeously in August. Note that many trees in the park have been identified by small attached plaques.

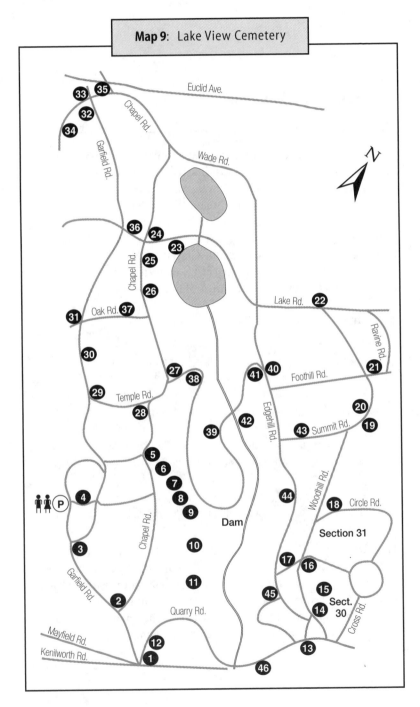

Map 9: Lake View Cemetery

2. Walk left, following signs to the Garfield Monument. Directly ahead is the Upson Memorial with its distinguished Ionic columns. Behind it are several graceful paper birch trees.

3. Pass beautiful old Japanese maples on the right and a hackberry tree on the left. The Coulby monument is next on your right with its symmetrical columns.

4. Ahead is the imposing President James A. Garfield Monument. A large ginkgo tree with its fan-shaped leaves is on the left sidewalk near the entrance. Built in 1890 and restored in 1984–5, the Garfield Monument commands a sweeping view of the city and Lake Erie from its upper porch. It is open daily from April 1–November 15 with an attendant who will guide you through the magnificent interior and show videotapes describing Garfield's life and the cemetery's outstanding horticultural collection. Note the five-part frieze carved by Casper Buberl, a talented sculptor, to depict scenes from Garfield's life (1831–81). Note also the gargoyles projecting outward from just below the conical tower and the rose window directly over the door.

5. From the Garfield Monument walk north and up the steps to the John D. Rockefeller (1839–1937) memorial. This white obelisk, the tallest in Lake View, memorializes one of Cleveland's most notable and distinguished citizens. Founder of the Standard Oil Company of Ohio, Rockefeller lived on a large estate in Forest Hills (East Cleveland/Cleveland Heights). The monument's upper acanthus leaves were carved by Joseph Carabelli. Carabelli was one of the early settlers of Little Italy and founder of a company specializing in cemetery memorials that still bears his name. Many Carabelli carvings can be seen in Lake View.

6. Beyond to the east is the Dr. Harvey Cushing (1869–1939) memorial to the pioneer brain surgeon and organizer of the historical medical library at Yale University.

7. Next is the monument to John Milton Hay (1838–1905), a poet, journalist, historian, and statesman who was secretary to Abraham Lincoln. The angel that guards his grave was sculpted by James E. Fraser.

8. Continue eastward on the grass among the old monuments. A large European beech tree with its purple leaves is near the Amasa Stone grave. Beyond the Corning obelisk on the left and behind the fence can be seen an immense dam spanning the ravine below. Constructed in 1977 to hold back potential flood waters of tiny Dugway Brook, it has left exposed layers of very ancient rock on both sides.

9. Next are the graves of members of the Severance family, major Cleveland philanthropists.

10. Carabelli designed the imposing pair of 35-foot-tall Corinthian columns with a cap to represent the portal to an early Greek temple. This monument to Charles F. Brush (1849–1929) commemorates the inventor of the arc lamp (1879), the first lamp to light any city electrically. Brush, a productive inventor, also perfected a device to power the first electric street railway. The monument reads: "Death is but a portal to eternal life."

11. Beyond is the architecturally significant Stevenson Burke family mausoleum. Herman N. Matzen (1861–1938), a noted Danish sculptor and teacher, was engaged by Burke's widow to design and construct this small building with its four carved allegorical figures representing Law, Art, Commerce, and Benevolence. The bronze door handles are finely sculpted heads wreathed with poppies.

12. Continue southeast to Quarry Rd. to the Memorial Chapel Mausoleum. Take a moment to enter this quiet building of granite and glass, if you did not do so at the start of this walk. Return east down Quarry Rd. and you will see on the right layers of exposed Euclid bluestone, a buff-colored sandstone that is about 360 million years old. This stone was quarried here until the 1930s and, among other purposes, was used for some construction in the cemetery. The massive stone wall along Mayfield Rd. going downhill to Little Italy was constructed of these stones. Across Dugway Brook on the left side of Quarry Rd. are unusually fragrant lacy white flowers of white fringe trees that bloom in May.

13. On the right are the Garden Crypts. From here on, note the cemetery sections marked with small signs.

14. Directly ahead in the center of Section 30 are the graves of Mantis J. (1881–1935) and Orris P. Van Sweringen (1879–1936), bachelor brothers who were railroad magnates and real estate developers of downtown's Terminal Tower, the suburban rapid transit system, and the community of Shaker Heights.

15. The magnificent bald cypress tree near the Lucas mausoleum in Section 30 is a rare specimen that loses its foliage in winter. Scattered throughout the cemetery are very old and extremely slow-growing Japanese threadleaf maples, also called laceleaf maples. Several of these graceful reddish trees can be seen in Section 31 near the Mitchell monument and across the way in Section 35 near the Stone mausoleum.

16. Just around the corner on the left (Section 30) and surrounded by ivy is the flat gravestone of Dr. George Crile (1864-1943), one of the founders of the world-renowned Cleveland Clinic.

17. In Section 8 toward the west (left) is one of four Moses Cleaveland trees still growing in Lake View. They were so named because it is thought that they were growing here at the time of the arrival of the surveyor and city founder in 1796. This one is a magnificent white oak, about 75 feet tall with a spread of 90 feet.

18. Walk past the Holden Mausoleum at Woodhill and Circle roads. This 1917 building is another of Herman Matzen's masterpieces. Its open-work bronze door contrasts with the solid granite building atop the wide steps. Note again the lovely Japanese threadleaf maples.

19. Walk down Daffodil Hill on Woodhill Rd. In April more than 100,000 yellow daffodils are in bloom, a gorgeous spring sight.

20. On the left in Section 3 is one of the nation's largest Sargent's weeping hemlock trees. With a small fence around it, its umbrella-like shape is striking.

21. Near the corner of Foothill and Woodhill roads stands a huge and beautiful fernleaf European beech. Also at this corner is a small building with public restrooms. Turn left at Ravine Rd. in Section 42 and left again at Lake Rd.

22. All along Lake Rd. in section 4 are flowering crabapples that are magnificent in the spring. The row of small houses behind the wall on the right are homes on Forest Hill Ave. in East Cleveland.

23. Lake Rd. bears right and goes between two lakes usually populated with a variety of water birds. Bordering the south side of the lake on the left is a row of very tall bald cypress trees with unusual feathery green foliage that disappears in the winter. Turn next to the small granite building on the right resembling a Greek temple, Wade Chapel.

24. The Jeptha Wade Memorial Chapel (1900) is one of the gems of Lake View Cemetery and is on the National Register of Historic Places. It was built in memory of the founder of the Western Union Telegraph Company who also donated land for Wade Park in University Circle. The entire chapel interior was designed by Louis Comfort Tiffany. A priceless Tiffany stained-glass window depicting the Resurrection is one of the artist's most important works. The gold leaf and glass mosaic walls of Old and New Testament figures, marble ceiling, floor, pews, chancel rail, and lighting stands were all Tiffany-designed. The exterior stonework is by Joseph Carabelli.

25. After exiting the chapel, turn left on Chapel Rd. In Section 6 there is a memorial to Samuel L. Mather (1817–90), a mining and shipping industrialist who contributed greatly to Cleveland's growth. The sculpted Mather cross is typical of the fine stone masonry of the Italian craftsmen who lived in nearby Little Italy. Throughout this older section of the cemetery are examples of their finest work on those elaborate monuments considered necessary for important and wealthy Clevelanders of the 19th century.

26. Nearby is the memorial to Leonard Case, Jr. (1820–80), a benefactor of Case School of Applied Science (later Case Institute of Technology), of the Cleveland Public Library, and of the Western Reserve Historical Society.

27. At the end of Section 6 is an 80-foot-tall dawn redwood tree with its short symmetrical branches. This tree and others like it were cultivated from trees growing in China and thought to have been living at the time of the dinosaurs.

28. At this intersection and to the right in Section 12 is the unusual Lemen Monument with its Doric columns preserved from the demolished Lemen family home, formerly located on Public Square. Directly in front of it is a stately Kentucky coffee tree.

29. Turn right at Temple Rd. and right again at Garfield Rd. At this intersection take note of the beautiful purple leaf European beech standing alone in its own triangle.

30. As you walk down Garfield Rd. heading west, again note the opulence of these remarkable 19th-century monuments to Cleveland's oldest and wealthiest families; Lake View contains one of the country's most significant collections of Victorian monuments.

31. Follow the signs pointing toward the Business Office and Euclid Gate. In Section 23 on the left enclosing the Kunz headstone are Lake View's finest specimens of the incredibly beautiful Japanese threadleaf maples. Some of these delicate-looking trees are more than 80 years old, yet are still quite small. Their gracefully curving trunks show evidence of careful pruning. Their vivid bright red, orange-red, or variegated foliage is especially spectacular in the fall.

32. Follow Garfield Rd. toward the office. You will pass an enormous double-trunked black oak tree on the left.

33. Soon reach the Business Office of Lake View where you may pick up a free brochure describing the monuments of members of the Early Settlers Association Hall of Fame. Opposite the office are two large and rare American elms.

34. Just beyond the office to the south is another Herman Matzen–designed monument commemorating a disastrous 1908 school fire in Collinwood in which 162 students and 2 teachers lost their lives. Nearby are two large, beautiful star magnolias, among the first of the hundreds of flowering trees to bloom in Lake View in the spring. A beautiful Scotch pine stands across Office Rd.

35. Walk north now on Chapel Rd. to the flagpole. The Shaw High School Memorial is just behind it. Busy Euclid Ave. is on your left, as is a lovely Siberian elm tree. Continue along past the Wade Garden on the right. Two more Moses Cleaveland trees are on the right—a beech and a tulip tree.

36. Next is a row of small ornate family crypts. At the end of Chapel Rd. on the right is the Beach Mausoleum; take a peek inside to see the beautiful Tiffany stained-glass window installed by this family.

37. Go past the Wade Chapel again and continue on Chapel Rd. At Oak Rd. in Section 22 is a Herman Matzen–designed monument to the inventor of the White sewing machine, Thomas White and his wife. Courage and Love are on the woman's side, and Diligence and Judgment on the man's.

38. When you reach the dawn redwood tree again (see note 27), turn left this time, going downhill past the vehicle barrier on a small lane to an open, grassy area below the dam. The old wall on the right was constructed of native Euclid bluestone from the cemetery's quarry. Along the right are more small family crypts.

39. Cross the small bridge spanning Dugway Brook and continue uphill to Edgehill Rd. and turn right.

40. On the left is the Herman Matzen–designed John S. Newberry Memorial for Ohio's most prominent geologist (1822–92).

41. A little farther uphill on the right is another Herman Matzen–designed monument—for Frances Haserot. The 6-foot-high seated winged figure, cast in bronze and weighing 1,500 pounds, required over two months of foundry labor to produce.

42. At the top of Edgehill is the Marcus A. Hanna (1837–1904) mausoleum, complete with its own sidewalk doormat. On the hill below it is another Sargent's weeping hemlock with its straight trunk under weeping evergreen branches.

43. The Jeptha H. Wade (1811–90) monument is in Section 3 on the left. The tall angel-crowned Corinthian column overlooking Lake View is a fitting memorial to the cemetery's organizer and first president.

44. Continue up Edgehill, noting another ginkgo tree on the left and the dam below on the right. This structure is 114 feet tall and 520 feet wide, and exposes 400-million-year-old Chagrin and Cleveland shales topped by the younger Euclid bluestone.

45. The magnificent miniature classic Greek temple for members of the Andrews family lies to the right in Section 9. Samuel Andrews became a multimillionaire through his early partnership with John D. Rockefeller in 1865. This imposing structure, reflecting the grace and elegance of another age, contains 36 handcrafted fluted columns and exquisitely carved molding on the entablature.

46. Return to the starting point by retracing your steps on Quarry Rd. to the gate.

Bill Baughman

10 HISTORIC CLEVELAND HEIGHTS

Cleveland Heights, officially established in 1921, was begun as a pioneer settlement of the Connecticut Western Reserve in the early 1800s. It is a well preserved city with many old, gracious homes still very adequately cared for. Its proximity to the city of Cleveland and University Circle's cultural institutions, its thorough building and housing inspection program, strong schools and libraries, and cultural and recreational programs, make it a sought-after place to live.

Distance: 5 miles

Walking time: 2 ½ to 3 hours

Description: This walk will introduce you to some landmarks in the city of Cleveland Heights, from the very old (Superior Schoolhouse) to the relatively new (Cleveland Heights City Hall).

Directions: From east or west take Mayfield Rd. (S.R. 322) to the Jewish Community Center near Taylor Rd. in Cleveland Heights.

Parking & restrooms: Jewish Community Center, 3505 Mayfield Rd.

1. Start your walk at the Jewish Community Center (JCC) at 3505 Mayfield Rd. This JCC (1960) and the Mandel JCC (1987) at 26001 South Woodland Rd. in Beachwood, serve the 65,000+ Jewish population in Cleveland and other area residents with a wide variety of cultural, social, educational, recreational, and physical and health activities for all ages.

2. Across Mayfield Rd. is the Cleveland Heights City Hall (1986) at 40 Severance Circle.

3. Walk west on Mayfield Rd. past another relatively new building, the Cleveland Heights Fire Station (1982) at 3445 Mayfield.

4. Continuing west, at 3352 Mayfield Rd. reach the Sts. Constantine and Helen Greek Orthodox Cathedral (1957). A popular sum-

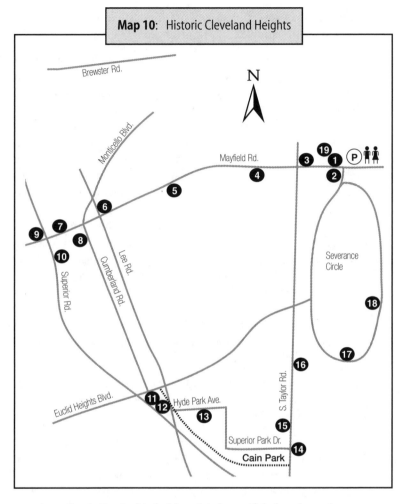

Map 10: Historic Cleveland Heights

mertime Greek Festival is held at this beautiful church, and a tour can be arranged by calling 932-3300.

5. Park Synagogue occupies 33 acres of land with a large complex of buildings at 3300 Mayfield Rd. Built in 1950 by architect Eric Mendelsohn, this synagogue is widely recognized as one of Cleveland's most significant landmarks. Landscaping the site was challenging because a deep ravine bisects the property. The main building, with its 65-foot-high dome, was constructed on three different levels over rock formations that were difficult to excavate but provide a solid foundation to support this massive dome. An opportunity to see the complex may be arranged by calling 371–2244.

6. The Rockefeller Building (1930), at 3099 Mayfield Rd., was built by John D. Rockefeller as offices for his Standard Oil Company of Ohio; it now houses Society Bank in its main second floor space. The facade of the Heights Building is Romanesque, its central portion four stories high under a peaked slate roof with dormers. Its entrance facade features stone quoins and an exposed beam design. Various shops are at ground level, and apartments and offices are upstairs. The bank conducts its business in elegant surroundings. Take a look inside to see the beautiful fireplace and hand-painted ceiling.

The Rockefeller Building was to serve as the gateway for a planned 600-home village; 81 of these French Norman brick homes were built before World War II ended the project. These homes can be seen by driving north on a side trip along Lee Blvd. to Brewster Rd. and adjacent streets. The peaked slate-roofed brick homes once housed Rockefeller's employees. Of interest on these homes are the steel casement windows and decorative trim around the doorways. These houses and the Heights Rockefeller Building are all on the National Register of Historic Buildings.

7. Continue west on Mayfield Rd. to the Cleveland Heights Recreation Pavilion, used for ice skating in the winter and for many community events year-round.

8. On the south side of the road is Cumberland Park with its War Memorial honoring Cleveland Heights residents who served in World War II. Farther south in Cumberland Park is the city's Cumberland Pool, with its architecturally interesting bathhouse built in 1927.

9. Continue walking on Mayfield Rd. to Superior. At the corner, Motorcars Honda occupies the site of the former City Hall. The original entry was incorporated into Honda's new building. In the early days when the surrounding area was only farmland, Phare's Store was on this site. In the 1870s a blacksmith, a cider mill, and a wagon-maker were all clustered around this corner. Later a post office came to Phare's, and this "town" was called Fairmount, Ohio.

10. Walk south on Superior to 14299 Superior, the location of the Preyer House. John Peter Preyer was a wealthy German who established extensive vineyards in the Superior-Mayfield area. He imported workers from Italy who settled in what is now Little Italy, located farther down Mayfield Rd. These Italian workers walked up the hill to the fields to help make the wine. Later they would dig the sewers and water lines needed for expanding Cleveland Heights.

The Preyer House is considered the oldest identifiable residence in Cleveland Heights. Built in 1825 with stone quarried from the property, its walls measure 20 inches thick. Preyer purchased the property in 1864; it originally was on 70 acres with a barn, stables, pond, and gardens. A brook still runs in the deep ravine behind the house. Notice the unusual dormers on the second story resembling Oriental helmets. These were added in the late 18th century to introduce much-needed light into the upper rooms.

11. At 14391 Superior Rd. is the 1882 Superior Schoolhouse containing two rooms that once served six grades. Town meetings were also held here. There has been a school building on this site since 1853. It is virtually unchanged from the way it appeared in the 19th century and was last used as an educational building in 1964.

12. Turning east on Euclid Heights Blvd., go a few steps to enter a green park on the right and walk diagonally through this grassy area to Lee Rd. and the main entrance to Cain Park.

13. The idea for a park, community theater, and recreation area in the ravine along Superior Rd. came from Cleveland Heights Mayor Frank Cain in the 1930s. Cain Park is a 20-acre, steeply graded ravine used for music, art, theater, dance, tennis, and other recreational activities. It was built by veterans, the Works Progress Administration (WPA), and philanthropists in 1934-38; John D. Rockefeller donated hundreds of trees to beautify this area. The refurbished Alma Theater and the Evans Amphitheater were completed for the park's 50th anniversary in 1988. Owned by the City of Cleveland Heights, the brick office and administrative buildings, the arcade above the amphitheater with its Tuscan style columns, and the two brick light towers were designed to fit into the surroundings and to create a village-like atmosphere.

14. Emerging from Cain Park onto Taylor Rd., turn left (north) on Taylor.

15. The Hebrew Academy of Cleveland at 1860 South Taylor Rd. is Cleveland's oldest Jewish day school (1943). With an Orthodox orientation, it serves 700 students from preschool through high school.

16. Along Taylor Rd. are kosher butcher stores, bakeries, grocery stores, and restaurants. At Taylor and Euclid Hts. Blvd. is Mosdos Ohr Hatorah (1994), an orthodox Jewish day school.

17. When you reach Severance Town Center you will be on the former site of the John L. Severance estate. Anchored by Dillard's department store, this shopping complex, remodeled several times, was one of the first suburban malls constructed in Cleveland. Opposite 7 Severance Circle in the south parking lot is an alabaster statuary fountain, the only reminder of the grandiose formal gardens surrounding Longwood, the Severance estate, which was razed in 1961.

18. To the east are the original stables on part of the property now belonging to the Austin Company.

19. Continue around Severance Circle and emerge onto Mayfield Rd. once again at the Jewish Community Center. On the JCC site was once a large estate called Glenallen, the home of John L. Severance's sister, Elizabeth. Her estate and gardens were considered as elegant as Longwood, but they were demolished in 1945.

On the northwest corner of Mayfield and Taylor roads stood another baronial mansion called Ben-Brae, the home of Julia Severance Millikin, a Severance cousin. It was demolished in 1951. Today there is hardly a trace of the opulence that existed in this area where three elegant mansions once stood.

11 CLEVELAND HEIGHTS ARCHITECTURE

The city of Cleveland Heights was established in 1921, but its history goes back to pioneer days in the early 1800s when it was part of the Connecticut Western Reserve. It is a fine, enduring city with many old, gracious homes of varying architectural styles that are still very well cared for. Cleveland Heights is an aesthetic delight to walk (or drive) through because of its wonderful collection of lovely old homes.

This walk begins at the Coventry Library at the corner of Coventry Rd. and Euclid Heights Blvd.

Distance: 5 miles

Walking time: 2 ½ hours

Description: This generally flat walk is mostly on sidewalks. Many of the city's early residences and a variety of architectural styles can be enjoyed. Please respect the rights and privacy of the owners by not trespassing onto lawns of houses. Please call the individual churches on this walk to arrange tours, if desired.

Directions: From the east or west take Mayfield Rd. (U.S. 322) to Coventry Rd. and turn south to the new parking garage on the east side of the 1800 block of Coventry.

Parking & restrooms: Park in the metered Coventry Parking Garage, 1800 block of Coventry Rd. Restrooms are available at Coventry Library (noon–8:30 p.m. Mon, Tue, Thu; 9 a.m.–5:30 p.m. Wed, Fri, Sat; 1–5 p.m. Sun) or at public restaurants.

1. Walk south on Coventry Rd. to Euclid Hts. Blvd. On the southeast corner is Coventry Village Library. It was built in 1926 by the John H. Graham Company in Tudor Revival style of red brick with stone trim, resembling buildings of the English medieval period. Inside are friendly librarians and a wealth of information. Large western windows provide perfect light for reading in this comfort-

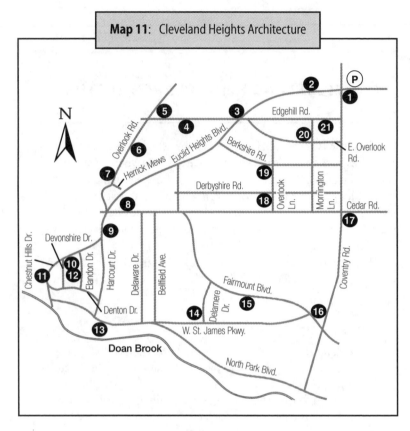

Map 11: Cleveland Heights Architecture

able, heavily used village library. The library's nighttime exterior has been enhanced recently by the addition of floodlights.

2. From the library go west on Euclid Heights Blvd. On the north side of Euclid Heights Blvd. are large, stylish apartment buildings, many now converted to condominiums. Most were constructed in the 1920s and 1930s and remain well-built homes.

3. Turn right (west) at Edgehill Rd. and note the hand-painted Italian tiles on the front of the home at 2555 Edgehill.

On the left is the 1993 St. Alban's Episcopal Church/Temple Ner Tamid, Heights Branch, whose congregations built this interesting house of worship to contain both common areas and separate spaces for worship on different days in the Episcopal and Reform

Jewish traditions. The building, with its many projections, just fits its triangular corner lot.

4. At 2463 Edgehill is an English-style home. Around the turn of the century, this part of Cleveland Heights was laid out by an English landscape engineer who favored homes reminiscent of his native land. He also named the streets after towns in England—Derbyshire, Berkshire, Lancashire, Hampshire, and Coventry.

Opposite at 2460 Edgehill is the Patrick Calhoun house, designed by the architects Alfred Hoyt Granger and Frank B. Meade and built in 1898 on 200 acres of land. This very large wood-frame residence was constructed by the grandson of Vice President John C. Calhoun (under Presidents Adams and Jackson), who wished to be able to view the lush, green landscape of Lake View Cemetery and the newly constructed Garfield Monument. Calhoun was a wealthy attorney and developer who envisioned a noble English village in this setting, featuring mansions and boulevards that would attract wealthy Clevelanders moving out from the city. It was his landscape engineer who gave English names to the streets in this vicinity.

The George Grieble home (1919) at 2432 Edgehill has an interesting multi-level terrace and employs stone decoration over its unusually wide first floor windows.

The Charles Farnsworth house (1916) at 2416 Edgehill was one of the first in the Calhoun development. The arched garage door is balanced by an arched window on the opposite side and an ornate stone arch over the entrance.

5. At the corner of Edgehill and Overlook roads is the three-story sandstone, baronial John Harkness Brown house at 2380 Overlook. Built in 1896, it is one of the earliest homes in Cleveland Heights and was designed by Alfred Hoyt Granger in a Tudor Gothic style. There are handsome window bays in this house, and two main entrances: a walking entrance and a porte cochere on the Overlook side. An inside stairway rises to the third floor. The former carriage house at 2405 Edgehill is now a separate home.

6. Turn left (southwest) onto Overlook Rd. The D.B. Alexander house at 2348 Overlook is now the College Club, a social, philanthropic, and literary organization. It was designed by Abram Garfield (President James A. Garfield's son) in 1904 of handsome hand-crafted materials. Despite additions, it still has a somewhat Victorian look with its tall, narrow front gables, now hidden behind trees.

Farther ahead is Alfred Hoyt Granger's home at 2141 Overlook, now the home of the Cerebral Palsy Association. It is the only surviving building of eight houses on Overlook designed by Granger and Frank B. Meade in the late 1890s.

7. At 2200 Overlook is the striking First Church of Christ Scientist, opened in 1931. Its octagonal, domed interior sanctuary and beautiful woodwork are well worth viewing. Its tall tower, majestically lighted at night, is a landmark in this area. For tour information please call 721-7766. Across the road are the buildings of Overlook House, a Christian Science Sanatorium, at 2187 Overlook.

Just beyond on the left is a cul-de-sac called Herrick Mews containing several charming carriage houses and stables that once belonged to the huge mansions located here. Most of the mansions have been razed and the remaining carriage houses converted to private homes.

8. Near Overlook and Cedar roads is the elegant Buckingham Condominiums at 2330 Euclid Heights Blvd., a handsome structure with stonework on the roof and facade.

Margaret Wagner House of the Benjamin Rose Institute, a 1960 nursing home, is at 2373 Euclid Heights Blvd.

Opposite and farther east on Euclid Heights Blvd. is the tall Braverman Apartments at 2378. This building is well worth noting for its excellent 1930s art deco design. The angular corner balconies are somewhat reminiscent of Frank Lloyd Wright's work. Sigmund Braverman, a noted architect and designer of synagogues, built these apartments in 1937 and lived here until 1960.

9. Return to Cedar Rd. and carefully cross this busy intersection at pedestrian crosswalks to Harcourt Dr. The Georgian style mansion at 2163 Harcourt, formerly the Samuel Halle home, is the residence of the President of Case Western Reserve University. Designed by Abram Garfield, it was occupied for many years by one of Cleveland's most socially prominent families. The Halles were leaders in the city's cultural, civic, business, and musical activities.

On the right is a steep cliff, part of the Portage Escarpment. This slope runs diagonally across Ohio and marks the edge of the 900-foot-high Appalachian Plateau. Uphill roads in this vicinity such as Fairhill, Cedar, Mayfield, and Superior all ascend the escarpment, which continues rising west into the suburbs. Euclid Ave. (Rtes. 20 & 6) delineates its base east of Cleveland. Ancient Lake Maumee, which predated Lake Erie, once reached the edge of this escarpment.

10. Turn right at Chestnut Hills Dr. off Harcourt. Some notable homes are in this quiet enclave of Cleveland Heights. At 2025 Chestnut Hills Dr. is a Frank B. Meade and James M. Hamilton-designed home with unusual window shapes and divisions.

The 1917 Joseph O. Eaton house at Chestnut Hills and Devonshire (2207 Devonshire) forms an angle on the curved street corner. Also designed by Meade and Hamilton, it projects a long horizontal profile with sloping roof, wide eaves, massive chimneys, and bay windows. This house represented the ideal suburban home of the early 20th century.

11. Judson Retirement Community, at 1801 Chestnut Hills Dr., is a multi-building complex with a unique perspective from its perch on a hillside. The entrance to the main building at this level is on the seventh floor; another entrance is several floors below on Ambleside Rd.

Adjacent to the main building is the 1919 Warren Bicknell Mansion, designed and built by Meade and Hamilton and now used by Judson for various purposes. Take a look at the newly landscaped gardens in front with a small waterfall for the residents to enjoy.

As a complete retirement community, Judson maintains independent living apartments, assisted living facilities, and a nursing care center. The newest building, completed in 1992, contains acute care beds, a health center with a pool, and a large parking garage.

12. Continue along Chestnut Hills Dr. as it bends around the edge of the escarpment. In the fall and winter one can see a beautiful view of the city of Cleveland.

On the left is Denton Rd. and two blocks left of it is Elandon. Two Frank Lloyd Wright-style homes are notable on this street. The George Canfield house at 2232 Elandon and another at 2236

Elandon were designed by Bohnard and Parsson and built in 1913 and 1914.

Continue on Denton to Harcourt and turn right (south) to North Park Blvd.

13. At North Park Blvd. turn left (east). Watch for fast traffic when crossing North Park Blvd. to the south side above Doan Brook, or, optionally, remain on the north side of the street.

The cliffs along the sides of Doan Brook gorge are composed of very old, dark Cleveland shale interspersed with man-made stone walls erected to contain the banks from erosion. Here and there above the brook are short woodland trails that can be found winding in and out of the trees. Opposite Delaware Dr. a small trail descends to a rocky ledge on old stone steps. The huge rocky outcrop here is Berea sandstone, a very resistant and hard sedimentary rock that was formed about 345 million years ago out of the sand and silt laid down by an ancient inland sea that covered Ohio.

The ravine below has been carved over the ages by water in the brook running downhill from Shaker Lakes. It flows through a culvert under University Circle, then runs along Martin Luther King Jr. Dr., and empties into Lake Erie at Gordon Park.

14. Continue along North Park Blvd. to Bellfield and West St. James Pkwy. All along North Park Blvd. are beautiful old mansions, many built in the 1920s and designed by Meade and Hamilton.

Near Bellfield bear left (east) on West St. James Pkwy. to Delamere Dr. and follow Delamere past lovely homes to Fairmount Blvd.

15. Turn right (east) at Fairmount. All along beautiful Fairmount Blvd., a National Historic District, are lovely mansions built mostly between 1908 and 1929 as country homes for those who wished to get away from the grand baronial mansions of Cleveland's Euclid Ave. to the rural lands of Cleveland Heights. At one time this wide thoroughfare carried trolley tracks to take citizens to and from some of the finest homes in the Heights. All architectural styles are represented here: New England Colonial, Dutch Colonial, Tudor, Cotswold, and others.

16. At the broad intersection of Coventry and Fairmount are two beautiful old churches: St. Paul's Episcopal at 2747 Fairmount and

Fairmount Presbyterian Church at 2757 Fairmount Blvd. Fairmount Presbyterian is a splendid house of worship containing significant wood chancel carvings. For information about the interior call 321-5800.

St. Paul's Episcopal Church at 2747 Fairmount is a large Medieval Gothic structure built in several stages, the most recent addition being a 1990 south wing containing classrooms, an art gallery, and an enclosed patio garden. An outstanding wood-carved choir screen in the chancel was completed by master woodcarver Edward Fillous and a sculpture, *Hands of the Risen Christ,* was done by Sir Jacob Epstein. Exquisite needlepoint tapestries in both the chancel and chapel were done by members of the parish. For information call 932-5815.

17. Continue north on Coventry. At the intersection of Coventry and Cedar roads is another significant religious building, St. Ann Church. This imposing church complex was dedicated in 1952 but has a long and interesting history predating that.

In 1925 The Reverend John M. Powers took advantage of the fact that historic First National Bank on Public Square in downtown Cleveland was being torn down. From the bank he bought 10 pillars, marble slabs for the sanctuary walls, chandeliers, 2 bronze balcony rails, a clock, 14 tellers' lamps now used to illuminate the 14 Stations of the Cross, and marble drinking fountains now serving as Holy Water fonts. These were all put into storage for what turned out to be more than 25 years.

Powers then found and purchased a Steere-Skinner organ and a set of carillon bells from a Presbyterian church in Massachusetts. Ever resourceful, he acquired oak paneling from the Dan Hanna house for the confessionals and wood paneling for the priest's sacristy. More marble for the private chapel walls came from the razed Ritz Carlton Hotel in New York City, bricks from Cleveland's old Murray Hill School, and the sanctuary rug from Cleveland's Midland Building. Finally, he purchased two bronze sanctuary doors, a wood and bronze communion railing, and marble altar steps from the Central National Bank Building, and lastly, Powers acquired Oriental rugs from the C & O Railroad! Irish goldsmiths crafted the monstrance and the tabernacle on the main altar. Then, amazingly, this eclectic collection was all unified into the present St. Ann

Church in 1952. Information regarding a view of the sanctuary is available by calling 321-0024. The church is open at varying hours.

18. Continue north on Coventry Rd. One block north of Cedar Rd., turn left at Derbyshire Rd. and follow Derbyshire west two blocks to Overlook Lane. On the left is the rear of Cedar Hill Baptist Church. On this site at the turn of the century was the immense mansion of Dr. George Crile, one of the founders of the Cleveland Clinic; the home was demolished in the 1940s.

Turn right (north) onto this charming, brick-paved lane, one of several hidden lanes in Cleveland Heights, and walk one block to Berkshire Rd.

19. The home on the southwest corner (2648 Berkshire) is an 1898 Victorian style home with a magnificent wraparound porch, designed by the architects Frank B. Meade and Alfred Hoyt Granger.

On the right at 2656 Berkshire Rd. is a beautiful 1910 Frank B. Meade and James Hamilton home once called The Henn House after the large family who lived there. It has a long horizontal profile and sloping roof with wide eaves. Note the beautifully designed chimneys and arched windows.

Continue north on Overlook Lane one more block to East Overlook and turn right (east). All along East Overlook are lovely homes of eclectic architecture. Many of these houses were also designed by Meade and Garfield. These remarkable early-20th-century architects always found a way to relate a splendid house to its spacious land and garden.

20. The William H. Warner House at 2689 East Overlook was built in 1908 by Meade and Garfield. A charming architectural design, its east wing has its gabled end toward the street. Note the way the chimney rises through three stories: first as a projecting bay and then as a blank wall. The west wing is turned at a slight angle to rest of the house, and at this angle is a splendid projecting staircase modeled after the famous 16th-century spiral-staircase tower on the Chateau du Blois.

21. Turn left at Mornington Lane. The handsome garden condominiums at Mornington Lane between Overlook and Edgehill roads were built in 1963 on land belonging to the Dr. Charles E. Briggs estate. The original iron gateway, iron fencing, brick walls, stables, and coach house all remain from the original estate. Around the corner on Edgehill Rd. can be seen the tiny children's playhouse still standing behind the blue door in the brick wall. It was designed by Charles Schneider in the 1920s.

Continue up Edgehill Rd. to Coventry, turning left (north) on Coventry past Coventry Library to the Coventry parking garage.

12 SHAKER LAKES AND SHAKER HEIGHTS

Shaker Heights was named for a religious communal sect that lived here from 1822 to 1888. Many artifacts from that period are preserved in the Shaker Historical Museum on South Park Blvd. Shaker Lakes offers an outstanding recreational area for walking, biking, cross-country skiing, and bird-watching within a bustling city.

Distance: 8 ½ miles

Walking time: 3 ½ hours

Description: This tour will introduce you to the Shaker Lakes and to the grand residential architecture of Shaker Heights's most beautiful streets. It is a flat walk on sidewalks.

Directions: Take Shaker Blvd. (Rte. 87) to the Bertram Woods Branch of the Shaker Heights library at the corner of Warrensville Center and Fayette roads.

Parking & restrooms: At the library

1. Starting at the busy intersection of Warrensville Center Rd. and Shaker Blvd. East, cross at the light to the west side of Warrensville above the Rapid Transit Station. Across from the fire station, turn left (west) on South Park Blvd. Many of these large homes were built in the prime of Shaker Heights's development by real estate entrepreneurs Orris P. and Mantis J. Van Sweringen. These brothers were men of vision and taste who conceived the idea of planning an ideal residential community joined to downtown Cleveland by a rapid transit line. They had control over all the buildings erected here through restrictive covenants in each deed that could dictate the location, size, type, cost, and use of every structure. These measures included the proportion of a home's width to depth, its building lines, additions, driveways, and outbuildings. By planning curving roadways, by preserving areas of natural beauty, and by rebuilding

Map 12: Shaker Lakes and Shaker Heights

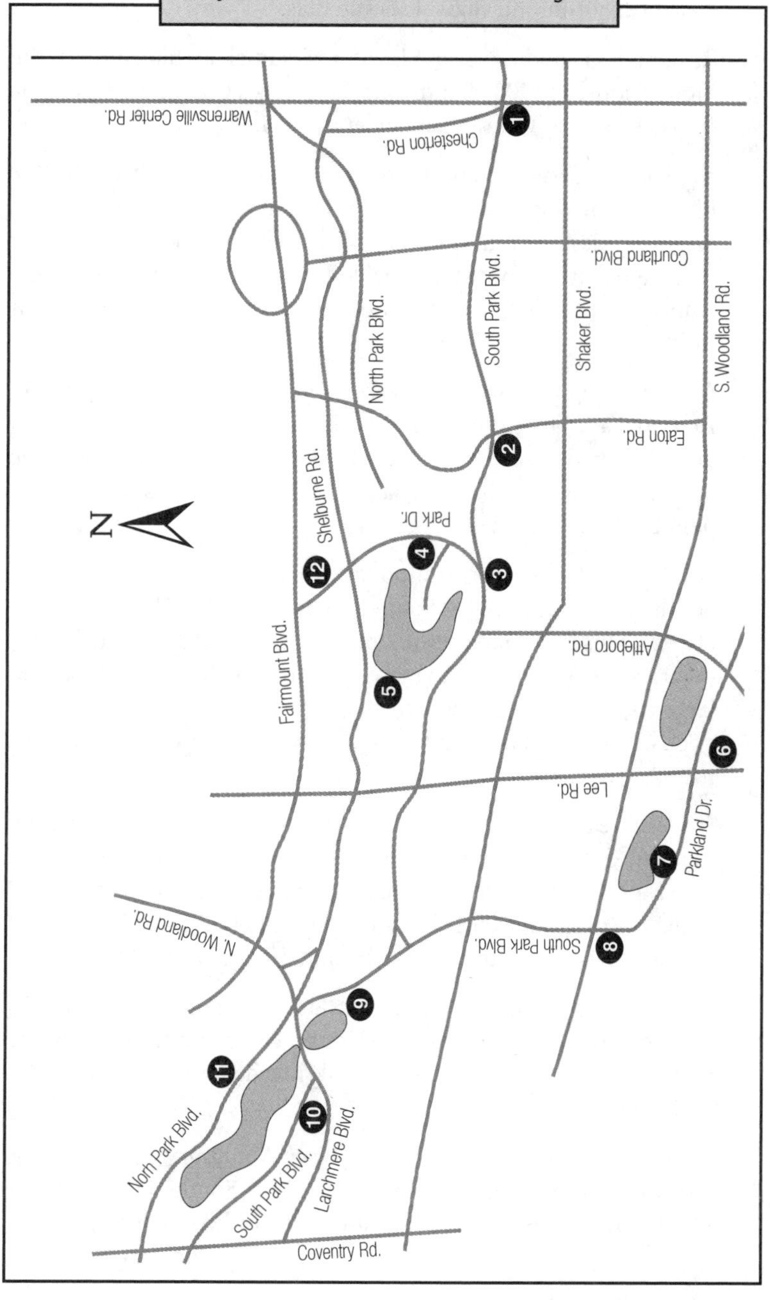

the Shaker Lakes dams and enlarging the lakes, the Van Sweringens created exquisite and valuable home sites.

2. One outstanding example of residential architecture is the Motch House at 19000 South Park Blvd. It is a Classic Revival mansion designed by Charles Schneider in 1924.

3. The Van Sweringen brothers' own home is at 17400 South Park Blvd. overlooking Horseshoe Lake. This magnificent mansion was originally designed in 1912 but extensively remodeled in 1924 by Philip Small into a more fashionable Tudor Revival. It has a steep all-embracing roof, half-timbered dormers, and a three-story tower in front.

4. Turn right (north) at the head of Horseshoe Lake onto Park Dr. At 2701 Park Dr. is the Salmon P. Halle estate, a French provincial villa designed by the firm of Corbusier, Lenski, and Foster in the early 1920s for the brother of Samuel Halle. The Halles were prominent Cleveland merchants.

5. A path will take you around lovely Horseshoe Lake to return to South Park Blvd. At 16740 South Park is the Shaker Historical Society and Museum. Open from 2 p.m.–5 p.m. Tuesday through Sunday, this Van Sweringen-era mansion houses a library, gift shop, and large collection of Shaker artifacts, including furniture, household goods, tools, and farm implements. A tour can be arranged by calling 921-1201.

6. Walk east back along South Park to Attleboro and turn right (south). Cross Shaker Blvd. and South Woodland, and turn right (west) on Parkland Dr. There are many fine homes along here, and two more of the Shaker Lakes—Green Lake (the "Duck Pond") and Marshall Lake, the latter hidden behind homes just past Lee Rd.

7. At 16111 Parkland Dr. is an outstanding example of residential architecture, the Alfred Fritzsche House. This beautiful Tudor house was designed by the architects Frank Meade and James Hamilton and built in 1923.

8. Cross South Woodland Rd. leaving Woodbury School on the left, and continue north on South Park Blvd. Southerly Park will be on the left with its fitness trail just visible inside the park.

9. Cross Shaker Blvd. and follow South Park Blvd. to the Shaker Lakes Regional Nature Center at 2600 South Park Blvd. It is open Monday through Saturday from 9 a.m.–5 p.m. and on Sunday from 1–5 p.m. A variety of trails surround the center, including some boardwalks; they are open from 6 a.m.–9 p.m. A map for exploring this area can be obtained inside the center or by calling 321-5935.

10. Leaving the nature center driveway, turn left, then left again on North Woodland Rd. Cross over the end of Lower Lake to South Park Blvd. Turn right (west) on South Park to Coventry Rd.

11. At Coventry turn north to North Park Blvd. and follow it east to Shelburne. Enjoy the many pleasant homes and tranquil views of the lakes on North Park Blvd. The plaques at the foot of the large old maple trees along North Park honor servicemen who died in World War I.

12. North Park enters Shelburne Rd. Follow Shelburne Rd. east to Chesterton. Turn right (south) onto Chesterton to South Park Blvd. and follow South Park to the start of the walk at Warrensville Center Rd.

13 CHAGRIN FALLS

The picturesque Victorian village of Chagrin Falls has often been featured in magazine and newspaper articles as the quintessential American small town. Located at the far eastern edge of Cuyahoga County only 18 miles east of Cleveland, lovely Chagrin Falls is an old settlement with an interesting history. Noah Graves traveled here from New England in 1833 and was the first visitor to grasp the potential of this territory for settlement. Virgin forests supplied tall trees that could be used for buildings, and a clear, flowing river provided waterfalls that could be harnessed to power mills. Soon a few families from New England settled here, and by 1844 Chagrin Falls became incorporated as a town.

Distance: 2 miles

Walking time: 1 ½ to 2 hours

Description: This walk is almost entirely on sidewalks and includes a 58-step stairway to view the falls under the North Main St. bridge.

Directions: From I-271 take exit 29; follow Chagrin Blvd. east to Chagrin Falls.

Parking & restrooms: Park at the free municipal lot on the north side of West Washington St. at South Franklin St. Public restrooms are not available here.

During the 19th century, the village grew into a bustling metropolis with dozens of mills, factories, foundries, stores, shops, and homes. Today many beautiful Victorian homes built by prosperous mill owners and businessmen still survive and have been lovingly restored to lend this quiet community its charm. Of the many mills here, only the Ivex Paper Mill on Cleveland St. remains and, until recently, was still in operation. The Popcorn Shop on North Main St., the original office building adjacent to the Gates Grist Mill site, dates from 1868. The oldest business buildings remaining in the

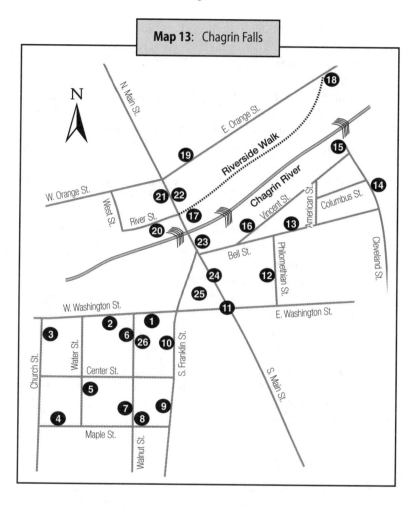

Map 13: Chagrin Falls

shopping district are Millside (1846), at 98 N. Main St. (now The Ohio Bank), and Chagrin Hardware at 82 N. Main St., built in 1857. Many of the old buildings in downtown Chagrin Falls have undergone various changes in their use, but throughout these changes the town has managed to maintain the look of a Victorian village.

Far from being any kind of disappointment, successful Chagrin Falls truly belies its name, whose origin has raised much speculation. According to an 1874 historian, C.T. Blakeslee, Chagrin might have been a corruption of the Indian word, Shaguin, meaning clear river. Another historian, Elizabeth G. Rogers, in 1976 claimed that

Chagrin derived from an Anglicized and corrupted version of the name of a French trader, Francois Seguin, who operated a trading post on the Cuyahoga River in 1742. Subsequently his name was attached to the river that flows through this town.

Though the source of its name may be unknown, the source of the river is known. It arises north of here in Geauga County, gathers several smaller streams along the way, then flows over hard shale and sandstone to form successively larger and larger waterfalls as it approaches Chagrin Falls. The largest waterfall is in the center of town and drops 25 feet. It can be viewed by taking the Stairway to the Falls next to the Popcorn Shop at the bridge on North Main St.

1. From the parking lot on West Washington St., note on the opposite side of the street the 1874 Village Hall, originally the home of Washington Gates, one of the early mill owners and son of the founder of the town of Gates Mills. Gates' mill, located next to the present Popcorn Shop, produced flour and ground feed for many of the villagers and farmers in the area. The mill was removed in the 1930s and the spot where it once stood is now the Stairway to the Falls.

2. On the corner of Walnut and West Washington streets is the attractive First Church of Christ, Scientist. The local Christian Science Society first met as a group in 1931, and in 1944 purchased this property. The 1836 saltbox built by Seth Handerson was remodeled as a church in 1945 and, after more remodeling and a 1960 addition, it has achieved its present appearance.

Continue west on West Washington St. to view beautifully restored homes in the Historic District.

Number 44 West Washington St. was originally built in 1845 on a bed of rock and clay that was later excavated to add a basement to the house. In 1850 it was sold for $500 to a family named Hewes. The west wing and garage were added by the owners in 1982; a porch railing that had been stored under the porch for 50 years was then finally returned to its original place.

Number 49 began as a barn behind the house at *Number 44* and was moved to this plot in 1866 to house Mrs. Hewes's elderly mother. In its early years wings were added to both sides of the home's original peaked-roof center section. The restoration has included landscaping and unusual brick lamp posts on the west side of the house.

Number 54 was built in 1850 for the local druggist and storekeeper, William Waldron, who was a relative of the families living at *Numbers 44 and 49*. Attractive landscaping and removal of some of the Victorian gingerbread trim have created a charming home.

Number 55, a Greek Revival Style home, was originally called The Academy because it housed a small school in the 1840s.

Number 64, now a private home, was until recently the Federated Church parsonage. It was once the magnificent home of the John Bullard family, who operated a thriving wooden ware factory at the rear of the property. This important business produced butter molds, kitchen utensils, and rolling pins for the general population. Examples of the Bullards's products can be seen at the Chagrin Falls Historical Society Museum. Mr. Bullard, the first mayor of Chagrin Falls, moved the house that originally stood on this site in the early 1870s to *86 West Washington,* in order to build this much larger and grander home.

This impressive building is said to be a prime example of Chagrin Falls's Victorian architecture. Homes of this style had all sorts of projections, wings, and bays that were designed to accommodate each family's individual needs. Decorative embellishment or gingerbread on these homes included brackets, scrollwork, bargeboards on the gables, cornices, finials, fretwork, and other ornamentation. The Bullard house is noted for its belvedere, the open-roofed gallery that crowns this striking dwelling.

Note the different styles of roof braces that adorn these beautiful Victorian homes.

Number 86, the original home of the Bullard family, was moved to this site from *64 West Washington* and has been remodeled by various owners, who have added a garage and screened porch.

On the ground at the corner of Water and West Washington streets is a large millstone from a local mill, twin to one located at Triangle Park in the center of town.

3. Now turn south on Church St., but first note *Number 4 Church St.,* with its solid sandstone foundation and forty cornice boards on the roofline. These decorations were common in 1874, when this home was constructed. Recent renovation has restored the original lines of the home except for the screened porch, shutters, and front door.

Many beautiful homes line Church St.

4. Continue two blocks down Church St. to Maple St. and here turn left (east).

Number 93 Maple St. is a modest 1880 home whose additions include a 1920-era front porch and a rear two-story projection built in the 1980s.

Number 83 is another of this district's beautifully restored Victorians built in Italianate style. Its two-story rear addition was constructed in the 1960s.

5. Turn left (north) on Water St. to view more charming Victorian homes:

Number 68 Water St. and its reverse twin next door at *Number 56* were both built by a Mr. O'Malley, a Chagrin Falls lumberyard owner, in 1876 and 1875 respectively. *Number 68* originally had iron grilles over each window that were removed to discourage roosting pigeons; its west wing was added in 1920.

Number 56 (1865) retains most of its early construction details in the exterior trim, front door with iron grillwork, and window casings.

Number 51's original section dates from 1835-40 and features solid rock cellar walls that are two feet thick, hand-hewn log floor and roof joists, and mortised and pegged joinings. In the 1870s, Dr. J.E. Phelps, a Chagrin Falls dentist, raised the house on a brick foundation and built an addition containing a dental office, kitchen and pantry, and wood storage area. In the 1960s, a garage and another addition were built. This home's two chapel windows, one of which is in the facade and the other on the north side, are considered to be fine examples of Western Reserve Gothic architecture.

There is an unusually large old maple tree on the opposite treelawn.

Number 44 is one of the first brick homes in Chagrin Falls, built before 1848 by William Hutchings, a master builder and brick maker from England. Several additions have been made to the house over the years.

Number 29 was built in 1864 on West Washington St. and moved here in 1883, when a bay window and one-story rear section were added. Some of the original work includes the cut stone foundation and hand-hewn beams.

Number 23 was owned from the 1850s to the 1950s by the Porter family. At one time they rented a room to future U.S. President James A. Garfield, who was then employed as a construction worker at the Disciple Church, originally located nearby on Walnut St. A small north wing was added early in the home's life and a 1960 two-story rear wing doubled the size of the original home.

6. Turn right (east) on West Washington St. one block to Walnut St. and then turn right (south) on Walnut.

7. Here are several more of Chagrin Falls's National Historic District homes and the home of the Chagrin Falls Historical Society.

Number 24 Walnut St. originally stood on the site of the old post office on West Washington St. (now a medical building) when it was constructed in 1883 by Orin Frazer. At that time a gazebo stood in front of this stylish Victorian home. Although it has lost its large imposing entrance and two-story bay windows, it retains its typical ornamental cutwork and spindles over the doorway, and has lovely landscaping.

Number 32 features small front gardens and a brick walkway that are characteristic of Williamsburg, Virginia. Although the brick portions of this lovely house date from before 1860, frame additions over the years have enlarged it to accommodate two families, though presently it has reverted to a one-family home.

Number 54 is a beautiful stately home built in the 1840s by J.W. Williams and is one of several remaining mill owners' or businessmen's homes in Chagrin Falls. Mr. Williams, a foundry operator, gave this house to his son, A.C. Williams, and had it moved here in 1873 from its original site. Still retaining its original wood trim under the eaves and iron work on the roof, it was lovingly restored to its former condition in 1963 and a downstairs wing added in the 1970s.

Number 65 Walnut St. was J.W. Williams's original brick stable and carriage house constructed in 1872–3 at the rear of his handsome new brick home (at 60 South Franklin St.). Converted to an attractive home in 1971, its front bow window was once the carriage entrance; the kitchen was the former stable area.

8. Walk east (left) on Maple St. one block and left again (north) on S. Franklin St.

9. *60 S. Franklin St.*, the graceful J. W. Williams home, was owned by this illustrious family whose iron foundry was located on the Chagrin River near West Washington St. The foundry was internationally known for its iron products, especially cast iron toys and sadirons, the implements used in many homes to press fancy Victorian clothing.

This gorgeous house stayed in the Williams family until 1918. Remodelings in the 1940s, 1950s, and 1970s have restored the home to much of its former splendor. The brick is original on all but the north wing addition, and the wrought iron trim in the front doors, and 10-foot doors remain from the early building.

10. Continue north on South Franklin St. to the United Methodist Church (1884) on the left, whose congregation first gathered in 1833–4. The church originally was located in a brick and frame building directly across the street from its present site.

11. At West Washington St. turn right (east). On the northeast corner of N. Main and E. Washington streets, where Society Bank now stands, try to imagine a famous Chagrin Falls landmark first built in 1852: Irving House Hotel. In its heyday it was notable for its fifty-cent oyster suppers, ballroom dances, and many private parties and testimonial dinners. In 1875 the Women's Christian Temperance Union picketed the saloon in this hotel and nine other Chagrin Falls saloons in one epic day. An 1892 grand remodeling added Victorian towers, ornate trim, electric lights, and central heating. But, unfortunately, a fire destroyed the famous Irving House on January 13, 1897, when firehoses froze, an event that prompted the town to establish a central water system. Photographs of this well-known establishment are on exhibit at the Historical Society.

The building owned by Brewster and Stroud on the southwest corner of South Main and East Washington streets has an interesting history. This small white building with red shutters opened as The Falls Hotel in 1897 with central heating, electricity, and plumbing; guests were charged the high price of $2.00 a day for these then very modern conveniences.

Continue walking east on East Washington St. to Philomethian St. All along here are many lovely restored homes.

At *87 East Washington* is Reed-Nicols Funeral Home in a building once owned by one of the members of the Ober family. The Obers operated a large sawmill at 210 Bell St., of which the main building (1873) is still standing, and were the inventors of the Ober lathe.

12. At Philomethian St. (this name means both love of learning and love of methodism) turn left (north). Here are smaller homes once owned by workers in the various mills of Chagrin Falls.

The large school building complex on the left houses Chagrin Falls Middle School. The center section of the building is the oldest part—the 1914 High School facing East Washington St. It is surrounded by additions built in 1940 and later. As the town and school populations grew, many of the elementary and high school grades were moved to a campus on East Washington St. on the former East Cuyahoga County Fairgrounds.

13. Continue north to Bell St. and turn right (east). On the left is the Valley Art Center at 155 Bell St., open 10 a.m.–4 p.m. Monday through Friday and 10 a.m.–2 p.m. on Saturday. It was built in 1922 as a service garage.

14. Turn left (north) on American St., where there are no sidewalks, and right onto Columbus St. to Cleveland St. Please use caution along here because Cleveland St. also has no sidewalks. Pedestrians, however, may walk on the left facing traffic and on the grassy area just above street level.

The entrance to Hamlet Retirement Communities at 150 Cleveland St. is opposite on the right. This extensive community was constructed on land originally belonging to Dr. Justus H. Vincent, who in 1837 built the large white frame home directly opposite at 170 Cleveland St. The Hutchings family added on to the home and lived in it in the 1870s, and the Crawford family occupied it in the 1890s.

Established in 1965, Hamlet offers retirees a variety of beautiful rental accommodations and common areas at Hillside Garden Homes, Atrium Apartments, and Hamlet HealthCare. You may wish to stroll through the attractive grounds. For information and a tour of the facilities, please call ahead at 247-4201.

15. Continue north on Cleveland St. past Vincent St., using great care on this busy sidewalk-less road, to a bridge overlooking a beautiful, wide waterfall on the Chagrin River. Here is the last remaining mill building in Chagrin Falls, which has seen service under several different names and purposes since the 1840s, most recently the Ivex Paper Mill. The Chagrin River becomes a beautiful pond behind this magnificent waterfall, called the Upper Dam. As you look east beyond the falls and the dam, you will see the site of the once thriving community of Whitesburg. In the 1840s, Whitesburg supported a woolen mill, an axe factory, and small workshops. Later the town was incorporated into the Village of Chagrin Falls.

16. Retrace your steps to Vincent St. and turn right to follow Vincent west to Bell St., noting the river below on the right. At Bell St. is the landmark Federated Church, whose spire can be seen for miles around. Its congregation first worshiped in 1846 in a frame church on Bell St. as the Bible Christian Church. In 1884, Bible Christian merged with the Congregational Church and, in another merger, the Disciple and Congregational Churches formed the present Federated Church.

17. Continue to North Main St., turn right, cross the bridge, and turn right again into pretty Riverside Park and the brick-paved Riverside Walk. This pleasant walk alongside the Chagrin River affords a magnificent view of another of the town's waterfalls, Upper Falls. Riverside Park was once the site of the mills of Chagrin Falls Paper Company established by Noah Graves in 1841, but the buildings were razed in the 1930s to create this lovely park. Follow the brick walk eastward past the children's play area to its end, and go up the steps to reach the Chagrin Falls Library, a branch of Cuyahoga County Public Library.

18. Among the treasures in the library are microfiche copies of the well-loved *Chagrin Falls Exponent*, published from 1874 to 1964. This acclaimed newspaper contained national as well as local news, vital statistics, industrial information, and advertising. Original copies of *The Exponent* are preserved at the Historical Society Museum.

From the library, walk westward on East Orange St. passing the Valley Lutheran Church on the right. This church first met in the

Town Hall in 1932 and built on this property in 1946, adding a Sunday School and church offices in 1954 and other additions in the 1960s.

More turn-of-the-century homes line East Orange St.

19. At the corner of East Orange and North Main streets is a shopping center called Stepnorth, housing a variety of shops and the old Hunters Hollow Taverne.

On the southeast corner is Millside, the oldest building in Chagrin Falls still in use, now housing The Ohio Bank. It was built in 1846 and has seen various uses in its approximately 150-year existence.

20. Continue across N. Main St. onto West Orange St. and turn left at one-block-long West St. On both sides of this small street is a dense cluster of historic and commercial buildings. To the south of Hearthside Clothing is the newly and beautifully restored Inn of Chagrin Falls at 87 West St., and next to it is old Gamekeeper's Taverne. All three of these yellow buildings once comprised Crane's Canary Cottage, an inn offering dining rooms, reception and card rooms, and living quarters. Owned by the family of poet Hart Crane, who occasionally visited here, the establishment opened in 1928 and closed in 1942 because of the difficulty of obtaining food and supplies during World War II.

The Village Exchange at 79 West St., the former Joseph O'Malley residence, is an interesting consignment shop that is well worth visiting.

Turn left onto River St. Near the west end of River St. is Chagrin Valley Little Theatre, which opened in 1949 and began presenting legitimate plays after the decline of The Opera House. At the end of River St. is the theatre annex, River St. Playhouse.

On the south side of River St. is a new restaurant overlooking the magnificent Lower Falls. Next to it is a small frame structure that was originally a Chagrin Falls shoe store owned by W.H. Caley. In 1910 it was moved to West Orange St. and later to this location. For many years it was a barber shop, but at present this quaint historic building houses a clothing store.

21. Walk back to North Main St. and note Township Hall on the left at mid-block. Its original portion was built in 1848 to house a library. In 1874 the town purchased the building, made improvements to it by adding a stage to the second floor and the building became known as The Opera House. In 1875, Henry Church, Jr. (the sculptor of Squaw Rock in South Chagrin Reservation) designed and made the weather vane that sits atop the cupola.

In its heyday The Opera House provided the town with minstrel and vaudeville shows, drama and musical performances, and an arena for political activities. The Chagrin Valley Little Theatre used this building from 1930 until 1943, when a fire destroyed the upper half of the building. When it was rebuilt in 1944 it became Chagrin Falls Township Hall, and it now consists of a large one-story room that is rented out for public and private gatherings.

22. Across the street is Chagrin Hardware at 82 N. Main St., another old store worth visiting because it remains in virtually the same condition as when it was built in 1857.

23. All along N. Main and S. Franklin streets are commercial buildings with long histories. The two-story brick building at the southwest corner of River and N. Main Sts. was where *The Exponent* was published from the 1880s to 1964.

At the Popcorn Shop, take the 58-step Stairway to the Falls alongside the shop down to the foot of the 25-foot Lower Falls for a glorious view of this turbulent waterfall. Imagine how this river must have looked over 150 years ago when many busy mills lined both sides of the embankment! By looking up under the bridge you can still see some of the original stonework done by William Hutchings, one of the occupants of the home at 170 Cleveland St.

24. Return up the stairs and continue on S. Main through the central shopping district of Chagrin Falls to note some of the interesting commercial buildings.

The 1882 McClentic Building, on the west side of the street, was once considered the finest building in town; it had 54 gas jets to light the lower story dry goods store and a modern basement furnace. It was completed at a cost of $20,000.

The 1891 sandstone building marked "Bank"—above the women's clothing store on South Franklin St.—once housed The Chagrin Falls Banking Company.

The I.O.O.F. (International Order of Odd Fellows) building on

N. Main St. above Dink's Restaurant once housed City Hall and the Fire Department.

25. The 1877 Bandstand in Triangle Park was the site of the Buckeye Carriage Shop until the city decided to create a new park here in 1875. It was and still is the location of the "Concerts in the Park" series of Thursday evening summer band concerts sponsored by the Chamber of Commerce. An Honor Roll dedicated to the memory of those who died serving their country in World War I is here, as is an old millstone and a 1983 Time Capsule to be opened in 2033.

26. Before returning to the starting point at W. Washington St., it is well worth your time to view interesting relics of an earlier time at the Chagrin Falls Historical Society and Museum at 21 Walnut St. Please call ahead (247-4695) or plan to visit on a Thursday afternoon when the Historical Society is open. (You might then want to stay in Chagrin Falls for dinner and a summertime Thursday evening band concert, at 7 p.m. in June and July.) The museum has many photographs on display and in its collections that show how Chagrin Falls looked in earlier times during its industrial era, before it became a quaint Victorian village. Also on display are many fine examples of items made in Chagrin Falls during this time.

This walk was prepared with the generous assistance of Pat Zalba, volunteer curator of the Chagrin Falls Historical Society, and Scrap Zalba, president of the Chagrin Falls Historical Society, with additional valuable contributions by Annie Gumprecht. The Historical Society is located in the 1965 Shute Memorial Building at 21 Walnut St. Its interesting museum is open on Thursdays from 2–4 p.m. and by appointment, by calling 247-4695.

Section IV
Easy Trail Hikes

14 HACH-OTIS SANCTUARY STATE NATURE PRESERVE

This small 81-acre park offers spectacular views of the Chagrin River Valley 150 feet below. Tall cliffs stand above the river, which is still cutting this valley through glacial drift left from the last Ice Age, about 12,000 years ago. Bird-watching is excellent here, as migrants often rest and feed in the tall trees before or after a flight across Lake Erie. Colorful spring wildflowers and brilliant fall leaf colors are beautiful in this sanctuary.

Distance: 2 miles

Hiking time: 1 ½ hours

Description: The walk is flat, on trails and boardwalks.

Directions: From I-271, exit at Wilson Mills Rd. Follow Wilson Mills east to Chagrin River Rd. Turn left (north) on Chagrin River Rd. (Rte. 174). Cross Chardon Rd. (Rte. 6), pass Garfield School, then turn right (east) on Skyline Dr. and follow it to its end.

Parking: In a small lot at the end of the drive. (No restrooms here.)

1. The boardwalks near the entrance were built to ease walking over wet spots on this flat plateau. At the entrance sign, take the boardwalk immediately ahead and then turn quickly left (north) at the next boardwalk which soon ends onto a trail.

2. This is a short loop trail, which, if you stay to the right at an intersection, ends at the edge of the cliff with a magnificent view of the Chagrin River below.

CAUTION: Use much care in viewing the river from this and several other vantage points in the sanctuary because the cliffs are con-

Map 14: Hach-Otis Sanctuary Nature Preserve

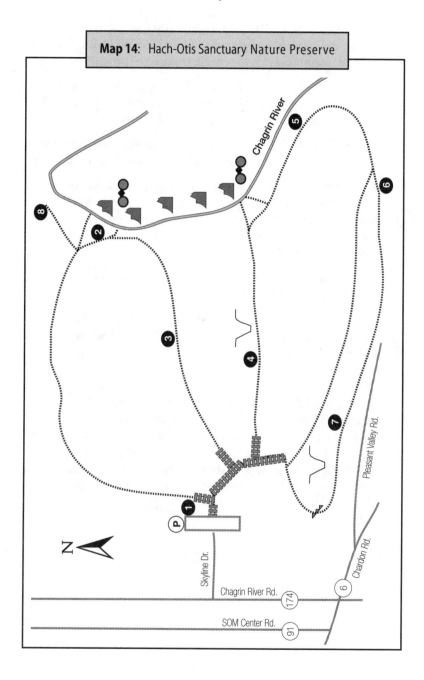

tinually eroding and remain highly unstable. Especially in wet, snowy, and icy weather use great caution. STAY WELL BACK FROM THE RIM, and take care to restrain children or pets.

3. Continue on this trail (white tree blazes) going south to the boardwalk again. Rather than returning to the parking lot, turn left, then left again, still on the boardwalk, which soon ends onto a trail.

4. Cross a small bridge, reach another sweeping view of the valley and houses below. In the distance is Little Mountain, five miles away.

5. Continue east on this trail (red blazes) as it loops through a mature forest of beech, maple, and oak trees. As the trail parallels the river below, note the vast commercial nursery located beside the river on Pleasant Valley Rd. The cars you hear are on Chardon Rd. (Rte. 6) to the south.

6. The trail loops around to the southwest and passes a connecting trail on the right. Bear left.

7. The path dips down to a ravine, over which a set of stairs takes you north again to the main boardwalk. Follow it back to the parking area.

Optional
8. To see a little more of the sanctuary in an undeveloped section, take the white-blazed trail again until it reaches the first viewpoint. Continue northwest on a narrow cliff-top trail along and just below the top of the cliff. Use extreme CAUTION on this portion of the trail. It will soon veer away to the west. It gradually descends the nose of the ridge to the bottom of a deep ravine. Beyond this point you are on private property, so the trail cannot be pursued to its end. Return to the car by retracing your steps.

15 CANAL TOWPATH TRAIL
Cuyahoga Valley National Recreation Area

The Cuyahoga Valley National Recreation Area was created by Congress in 1974 to preserve a valuable scenic park corridor of 22 miles between the cities of Akron and Cleveland. The Cuyahoga River runs through this beautiful valley, as do the Cuyahoga Scenic Railroad and the partially preserved Ohio and Erie Canal with its Towpath Trail alongside. A historic 1853 house at Lock 38 now contains the National Park Service's Canal Visitor Center. The Ohio & Erie Canal Towpath Trail has recently been completed for 19.5 miles between Rockside Rd. in the north and Indian Mound Trailhead, just south of Bath Rd. It is a popular trail for bicyclists; thus, walkers are cautioned to walk on the left facing oncoming bicycle traffic.

Distance: 3 ¼ miles

Hiking time: 1 ½ to 2 hours

Description: This hike will follow a restored section of the old Ohio & Erie Canal towpath going south and will return on the same paved towpath.
As an option, the flat Towpath Trail can be walked northward instead, to Rockside Rd. for pretty views of both the canal and the Cuyahoga River. This walk is 3 ½ miles round trip from the visitor center and will also take about 1 ½ hours.

Directions: From I-77 take the Rockside Rd. exit. Go east on Rockside Rd. to Canal Rd. then south on Canal to Hillside Rd. At this intersection is the Canal Visitor Center.

Parking & restrooms: At Canal Visitor Center

Park rangers and volunteers are in attendance at the visitor center during the day year-round. The center contains exhibits on the Ohio & Erie Canal and 12,000 years of human history, an informative slide show and films, maps, books, and a schedule of park activities and programs. In summer, demonstrations of the restored

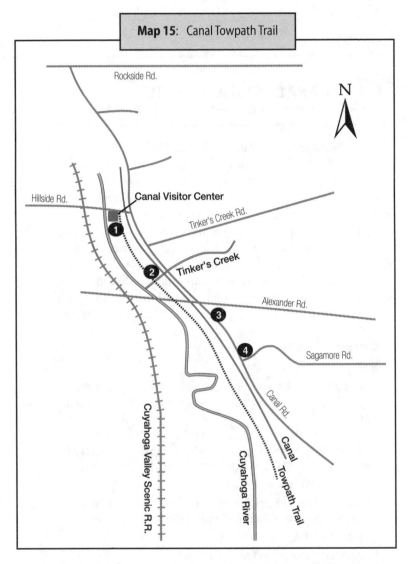

Map 15: Canal Towpath Trail

Twelve-Mile Lock (12 miles from Lake Erie), also called Lock 38, are held in front of the visitor center. It is helpful to view the interesting exhibits and slide show before embarking on the walk.

1. Start the hike going south along the towpath above the restored lock and canal. To the right (west) are the Cuyahoga River from which the canal was watered, and the tracks of the old railroad, now the Cuyahoga Valley Scenic Railroad (CVSR). The railroad is used in the summer to take visitors through the Cuyahoga Valley from Independence, just north of here, to Hale Farm and Village, near the south end of the CVNRA, and on to Akron. A variety of trips are offered by the CVSR. For information call 800-468-4070.

Walking along this flat towpath, used at one time by mules towing the barges, one cannot help but think back to the canal era and the sensation that occurred with the opening of this section of the Ohio & Erie Canal in 1827. Between Cleveland and Akron there were 42 locks, of which this one is among the few that have been restored. The 308-mile canal's 146 locks enabled a complete lift (or descent) of 1,207 feet. When it was opened, the people of Ohio joined in the excitement of vast new opportunities for commerce and travel. This activity extended from southerly Portsmouth on the Ohio River to Columbus and Coshocton in the central part of the state, to Akron and Cleveland in the north. The canal also opened up markets for farmers, by way of the Great Lakes to New York's Erie Canal in the east and by way of the Ohio River to markets in the south. Products such as flour, timber, pork, beef, lard, cheese, stone, straw, and whiskey were shipped out of the Cuyahoga Valley. Into it came manufactured merchandise and furniture. With the completion of feeder canals to Pennsylvania, coal was added to the list of commodities.

2. At about 0.5 mile south of the Visitor Center is the unusual Tinker's Creek Aqueduct. This engineering marvel was constructed to enable canal traffic to continue passage above Tinker's Creek as it plunged down to its confluence with the Cuyahoga River to the west. When the canal boats reached this point they simply floated over the creek within the aqueduct bridge.

3. Just past Alexander Rd. and on the left is the tall, white Alexander (now Wilson) Mill. This 1853 building was the last operating mill on the canal and now is a feed and seed store. Originally it was water-powered by a horizontal, interior turbine engine rather than the traditional waterwheel. Alongside the mill can be seen the Fourteen-Mile Lock, or Lock 37. Just beyond is a wastewater weir, or sluice gate, used to control the canal's water level.

4. Just before Sagamore Rd. on the hill on the left is the Frazee-Hynton House (1827), a red-brick house that once welcomed canal and stagecoach travelers as overnight guests. It is being restored by the National Park Service to become a museum. Although this hike ends here, you may continue farther along the towpath if time allows. Return to the Visitor Center by retracing your steps.

16 BIG CREEK RESERVATION

Big Creek Reservation, one of 13 Cleveland Metroparks reservations, lies on both sides of Big Creek Pkwy. and parallel to Pearl Rd. (U.S. 42) in the towns of Brooklyn, Parma, Parma Heights, Middleburg Heights, and Strongsville. Between Fowles Rd. and Main St. in Middleburg Heights is Lake Isaac, a major waterfowl refuge. This small lake, one of northeast Ohio's few natural basins, is a glacial pothole created by the melting of a large layer of ice left by the retreat of Ohio's last glacier about 12,000 years ago. This three-acre lake is named for an early Berea settler, Isaac Fowles.

Distance: 1 ¼ miles

Hiking time: 1 hour

Description: This is a short hike on a flat, wide trail that begins at the north end of the parking area and makes a loop through land west of the lake, passing a marsh pond, pine woods, and an old orchard.

Directions: Lake Isaac can be reached from I-71, exiting at Bagley Rd. (east) in Middleburg Heights. Turn left on East Bagley Rd. and right (south) at Big Creek Pkwy. Follow the parkway south past Fowles Rd. to Lake Isaac on the right.

Parking & restrooms: Park in the parking area adjacent to Lake Isaac; restrooms are not available here.

Before Cleveland Metroparks acquired this land in 1975, the lake was lower than it is now because of the mining of peat along the west and southwest shores. It has been restored to its natural elevation and has become a major attraction for migrating birds, ducks, and other waterfowl. Because Big Creek Reservation is a wildlife sanctuary, the park also attracts deer, fox, opossum, and many other animals, and surprises the visitor with many lovely aquatic plants and wildflowers. A large sign prohibits feeding any of the wildlife in the park to prevent them from becoming dependent upon humans and

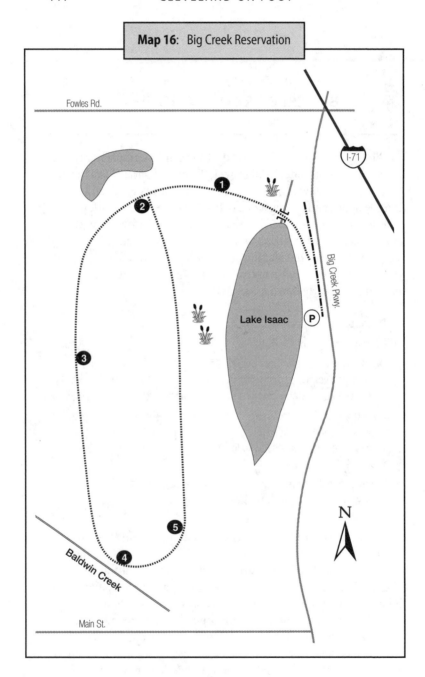

Map 16: Big Creek Reservation

Fowles Rd.

I-71

Big Creek Pkwy.

Lake Isaac

P

Baldwin Creek

Main St.

N

therefore unable to find their own food, escape predators, or migrate.

It is worthwhile to take along a bird identification guide when visiting Lake Isaac, especially when visiting the refuge during the spring or fall migrations, when a variety of birds and ducks stop here on their flights north or south. Especially prevalent are wood, mallard and black ducks, and Canada geese. Less frequently you may see ducks such as the canvasback, hooded merganser, shoveler, pintail, or green- and blue-winged teals; occasionally a tall, long-legged great blue heron finds fine fishing here. In mid-May the courtship dance of the male woodcock has often been spotted in the woods behind the lake.

1. After stepping down onto the trail and crossing a footbridge over the lake outlet, you will pass a sign for the Meadows Area, home to field mice, rabbits, woodchucks, and other small mammals. Go through a red pine woods and under power lines to reach a trail juncture.

2. The trail straight ahead is the beginning of the loop and the trail to the left is where you will end—either may be taken. Continue straight ahead (west) and you will pass a sign indicating the Ponds Area on the right, home for aquatic mammals such as muskrat, painted and snapping turtles, and frogs. Dragonflies and waterstriders may be seen among the water lilies and cattails.

3. The trail passes through an open area, formerly an orchard, and then curves east under power lines and past moisture-loving cottonwood trees.

4. At about the half-way point, enter another short red pine woods to reach a bench overlooking Baldwin Creek. You may hear a train whistle breaking the silence of the woods; railroad tracks form the western boundary of the park.

5. Follow the path to the next trail intersection, where a sign indicates no trail beyond this point: stay to the left. Pass under the power lines again and return to the same trail juncture described in note #2. above. Follow the trail to the right to return to the parking area.

Optional

For further trail walking you will find a well-worn dirt path going both north and south in the center strip of park land adjacent to Big Creek Pkwy. The paved All-Purpose Trail alongside the parkway is also open to hikers as well as bicyclists.

17 BRADLEY WOODS RESERVATION

Bradley Woods Reservation lies on a massive formation of 350-million-year-old Berea sandstone that causes the soil to hold moisture and Bradley Woods to be Cleveland Metroparks' only swamp forest. Old sandstone quarries scattered throughout the park produced fine-grade grindstones and millstones until the 1930s. Because of its generally wet environment, beautiful spring wildflowers and lovely fall foliage enhance Bradley Woods. This relatively undeveloped park, located in Westlake and North Olmsted, has a tendency to be buggy in the summer, so it is preferable to visit it in the cooler months of early spring and late fall. Among the trees thriving here are red maples, sour gums, tupelos, yellow birches, and pin oaks.

Distance: 2 miles

Hiking time: 1 hour

Description: This short walk leads through woods around Bunns Lake to one of the old shallow quarries where a few large blocks of Berea sandstone still lie on the ground. The sandstone ledge beneath this park lies only three to five feet below the soil, causing rain water to accumulate on the surface as many small puddles. Therefore, except for the higher trail around Bunns Lake, the paths in Bradley Woods can be muddy. In summer, mosquitoes breed readily in the stagnant pools.

Directions: Bradley Woods can be reached from Center Ridge Rd. (Rte. 20) in Westlake or Lorain Rd. (Rte. 10) in North Olmsted. From I-480, exit at Lorain Rd. and take it east to Barton Rd., Barton north to Bradley Rd., and Bradley north to the park entrance on the right; follow White Oak Lane to the end.

Parking & restrooms: At Bunns Lake Picnic Area

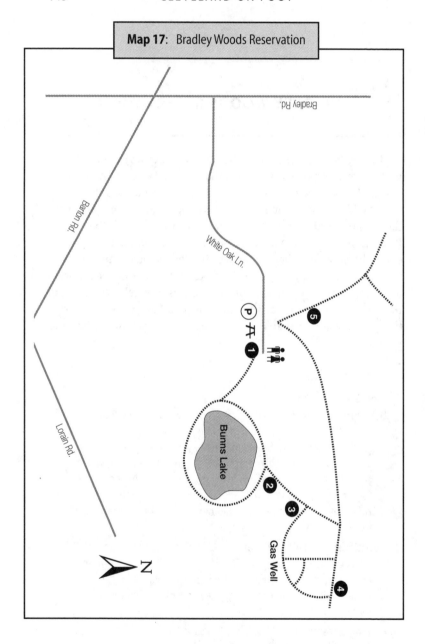

Map 17: Bradley Woods Reservation

Hiking on the short, flat trails, picnicking, and fishing in small Bunns Lake, which was created in 1986, are popular activities for visitors to Bradley Woods. The reservation supports a large population of waterfowl near the lake and white-tailed deer in the undeveloped areas of the park west of Bradley Rd.

1. Start the walk by entering the wide dirt pathway to the left of the picnic shelter. The path is lined with interesting interpretative signs that describe some of the park's history, the habitat for wildlife, and the native trees. Because this area was once farm fields and orchards, you will see here and there some of the old farm roads still intact. The dam created to form Bunns Lake rises up to impound water that originally filled one of the old quarries. The majority of the trees surrounding the small pond are red maples, gorgeous in the fall, and pin oaks, characterized by downward-pointing lower limbs and upward-pointing higher ones.

2. After circling the pond, the trail bears right (north) onto a woods path at a sign for the Meadows.

3. Next it takes a right turn onto a wider dirt path and passes an old natural gas well on the right. At the next intersection stay right and follow the trail through deep woods.

4. A left turn brings you out onto a dirt road, which leads to the left (west) back to the picnic and parking area.

5. At the far west end of the parking area follow the trail to the right of the road (north) as it leads northwest across an open grassy expanse to a trail on the west side of the grassy patch. This trail enters the woods on a dirt path. At an intersection, bear left to reach one of the old Berea sandstone quarries. These huge blocks of sandstone were used to produce fine-grade sandstone for millstones and grindstones up to about 60 years ago.

Follow the path in reverse back to the grassy area and out to the road and picnic and parking area.

18 GARFIELD PARK RESERVATION

Garfield Park Reservation is one of the most recent additions to Cleveland Metroparks. Garfield Park Nature Center (open daily 9:30 a.m.–5 p.m.) was completed in 1987. Smallest of the Metroparks at 177 acres, Garfield Park Reservation nevertheless has a long history. This area of Garfield Heights was first settled in 1786 and became known later as Newburg. Because of its higher elevation, it was considered healthier than Cleveland, and for many years it was a haven for people escaping the swampy conditions and diseases of the Cuyahoga River area.

Distance: 4 miles

Walking time: 2 hours

Description: This hike is on short woods trails and abandoned roads, goes up and down several small hills, and past Wolf Creek. It is a pleasant, non-strenuous hike with varied scenery in all seasons.

Directions: From I-480 exit at Broadway Ave. (Rte. 14) in Garfield Heights. The entrance to Garfield Park Reservation is on the left just past the railroad overpass. After entering on Garfield Park Blvd., take an immediate left onto Mill Creek Lane to reach the nature center on the left.

Parking & restrooms: At the Garfield Park Nature Center

In 1895 the city of Cleveland purchased several properties to form a new country park called Newburg Park, which was later renamed Garfield Park. It became a pleasant place for city dwellers to enjoy nature in a grand setting of tall trees and hills, to go boating on the upper and lower lakes of dammed Wolf Creek, and to take home water from a mineral spring. The Cleveland Railway Company laid tracks to the park in 1917, opening it up to all. In the 1930s recreational facilities were added, including tennis, football, sledding, swimming, and picnicking.

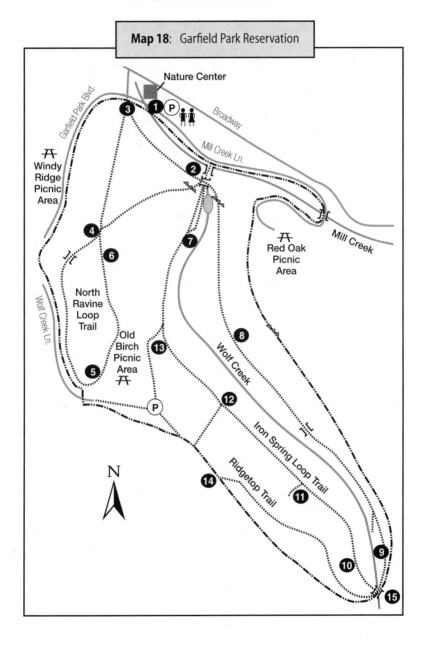

Map 18: Garfield Park Reservation

The southwestern portion of Garfield Park Reservation has been set aside as the Iron Spring Wildlife Preserve for management of upland wildlife species and is especially lovely in spring and fall. Lack of care reduced Garfield Park to a hazardous place in the 1970s until Cleveland Metroparks acquired it in 1986. Now, this lovely small park supports many waterfowl, songbirds, and other wildlife, and numerous varieties of trees, shrubs, and wildflowers. The nature center offers a wide variety of interesting nature programs and events, as well as information and early photographs of the park.

1. Start the walk at Garfield Park Nature Center. Inside the building are many interesting exhibits pertaining to the park's history and to nature study. Park personnel are available to assist the hiker with information, brochures, and maps of Cleveland Metroparks. An active beehive is on exhibit, and a short Garden Walk with interpretive signs is just outside at the rear of the center.

2. Cross Mill Creek Ln. to the asphalt-paved All Purpose Trail and turn left (east) toward the old stonework bridge over Mill Creek. Turn right to cross this bridge, then right again to cross the arched stone bridge over the pond spillway where Wolf Creek enters Mill Creek. These old stone structures are a legacy of the early days of Garfield Park.

Mill Creek is a swiftly flowing stream that eventually enters the Cuyahoga River west of here. Wolf Creek Lake on the left was once a swimming pool and, even earlier—in the 1890s—a boating lake. The sediment that has filled the pond and allowed trees and shrubs to grow up in the mud has come from more than 20 years of highway and home construction in this area. The trail leads up some stone steps on the right to an old blacktop road.

3. Turn right (north) on this road and take it to the sign for North Ravine Loop Trail, on the left. Enter the trail going left (south) and uphill.

4. At the intersection with the North Ravine Loop Trail (identified with blue tree markers), bear right to start this pleasant 0.5 mile loop trail over a bridge and through a lovely woods of maple, tulip, oak, and beech trees. The path circles a ravine through which a small stream runs on its way down to Mill Creek.

5. Follow the trail alongside the paved All Purpose Trail and, at the end of the fence, reenter the woods (north). An open playing field and Old Birch Picnic Area are on the right.

6. Before passing a park bench on the right, take the trail on the right to cross the playing field at its north end, keeping the meadow on the left and the playing field on the right. Reach the sign for Iron Spring Loop Trail. Here, descend some stone steps on the left. At the foot of the steps is a sign identifying these as "Historic Stairs" that were part of an 1890 Master Plan developed by early Clevelanders and Frederick Law Olmsted, a noted landscape architect who designed many parks, including New York City's Central Park.

7. Turn right (south) on Iron Spring Loop Trail, a weedy old blacktop road. Continue 200 yards to a gravel path on the left. Bear left (north) at the Y fork. Below the trail on the right are the remains of the original dam that impounded water to create Wolf Creek Lake for boating. Here also are remnants of old stonework walls that edged the boating lake. Future plans for this park include dredging and refilling the once scenic lake to attract more waterfowl.

Continue north on this trail to return to the arched stone bridge over Wolf Creek.

8. Head east and then south (away from Mill Creek Ln.) on the Iron Spring Loop Trail. Continue past the steep flight of steps on the left leading up to Red Oak Picnic Area. The trail here is marked with black and white hiker signs posted on trees.

Interpretive signs are found at frequent intervals along this trail. The first sign points out tall sycamore trees with white trunks and always-peeling bark that thrive in this watery environment. Next on the right is another view of the broken Wolf Creek dam lying across the creek bed. The stairs on the left also lead up to the Red Oak Picnic Area and playing field.

The next sign notes a giant oak that was only a sapling in 1896 when the park opened. On the right are stone steps that lead down to the creek and circle back up again (an optional detour).

Farther along is a sign on the right noting a beautiful stone wall still remaining on the opposite bank of Wolf Creek. This siding was built in the 1930s by the Works Progress Administration (WPA) without mortar by fitting the stone blocks closely together. Amaz-

ingly, the wall is still in place after 60 years of spring floods! The erosion-resistant sandstones were quarried near Bedford.

On the left is an interesting sign pointing out ancient layers of sandstone rock with interbedding of more layers of stone. These large blocks of Berea sandstone were under an inland sea about 320 million years ago and show evidence of periods of drought and water erosion. Cross a bridge. Farther along on the left is a large witch hazel bush, the last flower to bloom in late October and early November, with yellow blossoms that resemble frizzy witch's hair.

At a trail intersection, bear left and go uphill where the Iron Spring Loop Trail joins the asphalt All Purpose Trail. The next sign identifies a black cherry tree, favored for furniture making because of its beautiful reddish-colored wood.

9. Follow the Iron Spring Loop Trail alongside the All Purpose Trail to the next sign, which describes the early settlements in the area—by Moravians in 1786, ten years before Moses Cleaveland landed in Cleveland, of Newburg in 1814, South Newburg in 1919, and, later, Garfield Heights.

The next sign points out the beautiful sandstone ledges over which cascade tiny waterfalls as the creek makes its way down a 70-foot drop to Mill Creek.

10. At the 2.0-mile point on this hike, cross Wolf Creek over an old stone bridge. Turn right (north) to follow the west side of the Iron Spring Loop Trail, again on the old blacktop road.

At the next sign is a view of the beautiful arched bridge just crossed. It was built of native sandstone hauled from Bedford in the 1890s. Note the small round indentations that the stoneworkers chiseled to fit hooks and tongs into in order to move the huge blocks to this site.

Next on the right is delightful Green Springs Pool. This beautiful emerald pool was created by large volumes of water falling over erosion-resistant sandstone onto much softer rock, which has eroded away leaving a pool eight feet deep.

11. Opposite the pool and on the left is a small path going to the old Garfield Park Quarry. Take this path west past the small natural amphitheater bowl to the small quarry from which stonecutters obtained rock slabs used for the stone steps in Garfield Park. There are still a few stonecutters' marks on rocks and outcrops.

12. Return to the Iron Spring Loop Trail. Farther along on the left is Iron Spring, for which this trail was named. Early visitors to the park believed that the dark rust-colored water gushing from this spring was a curative for various ailments. The spring has slowed to only a trickle now because of changes in the groundwater table. The water is not drinkable but still paints the nearby rocks and soil a very dark rust color. Continue north on the Iron Springs Loop Trail.

13. Reach a trail on the left leading to Old Birch Picnic Area. Turn left (south) at the sign going toward the parking area.

Follow the All Purpose Trail from the parking area south past the picnic tables; note the magnificent white birch tree on the left.

14. Pass the sign for Iron Spring. Along the All-Purpose Trail in this section are Solar Walk signs featuring information about the planets of our solar system. Continue to a bench and the sign on the left indicating the 0.4-mile Ridgetop Trail (blazed with red markers). This is a most rewarding trail to take in spring, when many varieties of beautiful wildflowers can be seen. Avoid taking any side trails.

Follow the Ridgetop Trail eastward to a small wooden bridge on the left, and cross it over a tributary of Wolf Creek. Continue on this trail until you reach the paved All-Purpose Trail.

15. Turn left (north) on the All-Purpose Trail. Follow it downhill past Red Oak Picnic Area and alongside Mill Creek Lane to the nature center.

Optional

As an option, at point #15 where you emerge from the Ridgetop Trail onto the All-Purpose Trail, you can instead turn right (west) and take the All-Purpose Trail northward past Old Birch and Windy Ridge Picnic Areas, then alongside Garfield Park Blvd. Turn right at Mill Creek Lane to reach Garfield Park Nature Center again. You will pass the start of the Solar Walk on this part of the All-Purpose Trail.

19 HUNTINGTON RESERVATION

Huntington Reservation was named for its owner, John Huntington, a prominent Cleveland industrialist and philanthropist. His vineyard and botanical park were located here long before a reservation was created for public use in 1927. Huntington Beach, with its picnic and fishing areas, is a very popular spot in summer. Lake Erie Nature and Science Center is home to Schuele Planetarium and a wildlife rehabilitation program. Baycrafters Shop and Huntington Playhouse are affiliates of Cleveland Metroparks. Baycrafters presents a popular Renaissance Fayre each year on Labor Day weekend.

Distance: 4 miles

Hiking time: 2 hours

Description: This hike contains a variety of terrain and vistas. It winds through lovely woods along Porter Creek, goes along sandy Huntington Beach, and reveals the various features of this park and adjacent Cahoon Park.

Directions: Take I-90 to the Columbia Rd. exit (Rte. 252) and go north to Wolf Rd., then west to the sign on the right for Lake Erie Nature and Science Center and Huntington Reservation, and enter the park on Porter Creek Dr.

Parking & restrooms: Lake Erie Nature and Science Center, 28728 Wolf Rd., Bay Village (871-2900). The center is open from 1–5 p.m. Sun–Fri and 10 a.m.–5 p.m. Sat. Alternative parking and restrooms are at Wolf Picnic Area, east of the center.

1. Start this hike by visiting the nature center, if open, to see interesting exhibits and a variety of wildlife. The trail leads from the rear of the center and is bordered by a wooden railing on both sides. It circles around a ravine and at an opening in the railing descends downhill on a dirt path above the ravine.

Map 19: Huntington Reservation

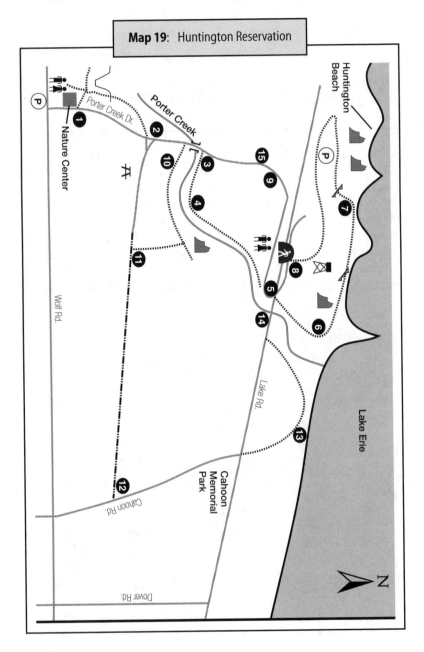

2. The trail exits to Porter Creek Dr. at the Wolf Picnic Area sign. Walk on the road downhill under concrete pillars that once supported the Lake Shore Electric Railway. This interurban line carried commuters between Cleveland and the northwestern suburbs in the early 1900s.

3. At the foot of the hill cross the bridge over Porter Creek and turn right (east) onto a trail on the north side of the creek.

4. The trail winds along the creek. Without crossing the stream, follow this trail through deep cool woods, keeping the creek on your right. Where the creek bends to the south away from the trail, take the path on the left leading uphill away from the water.

5. Enter Porter Creek Dr. on the left as it crosses beneath Lake Rd. and follow it briefly until you emerge onto sandy Huntington Beach straight ahead.

6. Go north and then west along the beach and enjoy fine views of Lake Erie.

7. Ascend the second set of stairs on your left going up the cliff. Walk along the top of the cliff to the far west end of the beach. Return east along the upper walkway to the Huntington Water Tower, an 1890s structure that once pumped water to Mr. Huntington's grape fields. The tower is made of cypress wood, but the outside is covered with siding. The original water pipes, stairway, and water tub enclosure still exist inside the building.

8. At the tower, turn right (south) and walk through the marked pedestrian underpass under Lake Rd. Beyond the restrooms and to the west are Huntington Playhouse, Baycrafters Shop, a restored train caboose, and reservation maintenance buildings.

9. Descend Porter Creek Dr. east of the playhouse to the same bridge crossing the creek. This is about the 2.0-mile mark on this hike.

10. Across the bridge and at the top of the hill, turn left and enter the trail that goes east along the top of the cliff on the south side of Porter Creek. This trail eventually leaves the creek and bears right toward the Wolf Picnic Area and emerges onto a paved All-Purpose Trail.

11. Turn left (east) on the All-Purpose Trail and follow this paved pathway to Cahoon Memorial Park.

12. Continue east through Cahoon Park to Cahoon Rd. and turn left (north) toward Lake Erie. Watching busy traffic, cross Lake Rd. and enter Cahoon Park on a trail on the opposite side of the road.

13. Enjoy another view of Lake Erie and the Cleveland skyline to the east. Caution: do not cross the target-shooting practice area.

14. Return to Huntington Reservation by crossing Lake Rd. again and following it west to the reservation entrance.

15. From the entrance, follow Porter Creek Dr. south back to the nature center parking area.

20 EUCLID CREEK RESERVATION

This long, narrow park is one of the most geologically interesting reservations in Cleveland Metroparks. Euclid Creek flows north through the park before emptying into Lake Erie. As the creek descends, ancient rock levels are exposed. The youngest level is the 345-million-year-old Euclid bluestone at the upper (south) end; and the oldest is 400-million-year-old Chagrin shale at the lower (north) end. Near Anderson and Green roads was once located the small village of Bluestone, from the late 1800s to the early 1930s. The workers who lived here quarried Euclid bluestone from the creek for use in construction, especially for Cleveland's sidewalks.

Distance: 5 miles

Hiking time: 2 hours

Description: This hike begins on the paved All-Purpose Trail and follows it uphill alongside Euclid Creek Pkwy. to Anderson Rd., then returns for a part of the distance on a well-traveled woods trail.

Directions: Take Euclid Ave. to Highland Rd. (called Dille Rd. north of Euclid). Go south on Highland a short distance, turn right on Euclid Creek Pkwy., and enter the Highland Picnic Area.

Parking & restrooms: Highland Picnic Area

1. Start the hike on the paved trail at the Highland Picnic Area heading south and forward in geologic time. The cliff on the left above Euclid Creek is composed of the 400-million-year-old Chagrin shale.

2. Continue on the paved trail as it makes its gradual ascent, going past Welsh Woods Picnic Area at about the 2.0-mile mark. Begin to see the darker Cleveland shale here, its darkness due to its increased content of organic material and fossils of primitive life forms. The trackways of some wormlike fish with feathery tails can be seen fossilized in the rocks alongside the stream just off the trail.

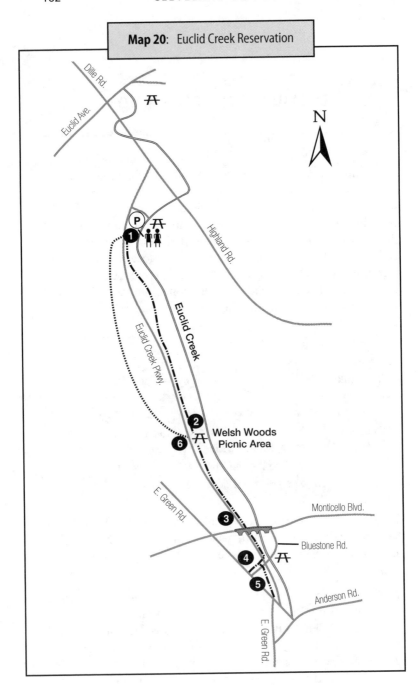

Map 20: Euclid Creek Reservation

3. The trail passes under the Monticello Blvd. bridge to Kelly Picnic Area and a winter sledding hill. The reddish-gray rock of the Bedford Formation appears here with the grayish, flat slabs of Euclid bluestone visible in the creek bed and along the eastern embankment.

4. At Bluestone Rd., descend on the left to the bridge over Euclid Creek at Quarry Picnic Area. Look for interesting prehistoric ripple marks on the surface of Euclid bluestone remaining in the creek. They were formed by wave action of an underwater current when an inland sea covered this part of Ohio. The old Bluestone Quarry is now filled in, but reminiscent of its former activity is an iron hook in the ground above the embankment once used to hoist heavy rock slabs out of the quarry.

5. The stone house at the top of Euclid Creek Pkwy. overlooking the creek and the house at 100 East Green Rd. are constructed entirely of Euclid bluestone. These were built by, and occupied by, quarry workers who once lived here in the village of Bluestone.

6. Retrace your steps and return along the All Purpose Trail to Welsh Woods Picnic Area. Cross the parkway opposite it and enter a woods trail, which continues downward to the parking area at Highland Picnic Area.

21 ROCKY RIVER RESERVATION (NORTH)

Rocky River Reservation is the largest reservation in Cleveland Metroparks. The reservation's size and shape were determined by the flow of the Rocky River in its twisting, turning course from Strongsville in the south to Rocky River and Lake Erie in the north.

Distance: 6 miles

Hiking time: 2 ½ to 3 hours

Description: Rocky River Reservation is a long, narrow park through which the Rocky River courses on its relentless flow north to Lake Erie. The valley created by the Rocky River is characterized by steep shale cliffs rising impressively above the river's floodplain and broad valleys. Many beautiful old trees stand in this lush valley, including cottonwoods, willows, sycamores, and others. This hike begins at Scenic Park Marina and generally follows both Valley Pkwy. and the Rocky River as it twists and turns along its winding course. The All-Purpose Trail crosses and recrosses the river several times. The hike will retrace the same trail coming back and affords different views of the river and valley on the return.

Directions: From I-90 westbound, take Hilliard Blvd. east to Wooster Rd. Turn left (north) on Wooster Rd. Turn right (east) on Detroit and cross the bridge. Turn immediately right onto Valley Pkwy. At the foot of the hill turn right to enter Rocky River Reservation's Scenic Park Picnic Area and the public marina.
From I-90 eastbound, take Wagar exit and follow Detroit Rd. east past Wooster Rd. and across the bridge. Turn immediately right onto Valley Pkwy. At the foot of the hill, turn right to enter Rocky River Reservation's Scenic Park Picnic Area and the public marina.

Parking & restrooms: At Scenic Park Marina and picnic area

The valley of Rocky River was settled early in Cleveland's history (1800s), and its own history is interpreted at the Frostville Museum,

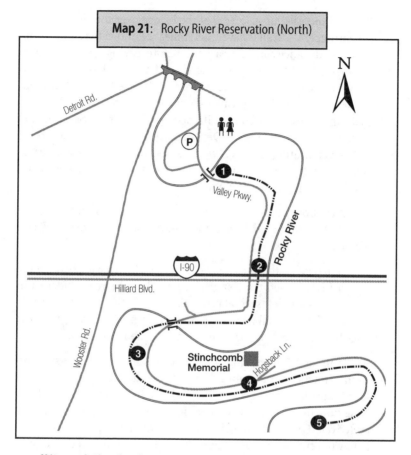

Map 21: Rocky River Reservation (North)

an affiliate of Cleveland Metroparks managed by the Olmsted Historical Society. The museum is located west of Valley Pkwy. off Cedar Point Rd. (777-0059).

A visit to Cleveland Metroparks Rocky River Nature Center will introduce the fascinating geology of this interesting reservation. The nature center is about 10 miles south of Detroit Rd. at 24000 Valley Pkwy., just past Shephard Lane. Nearby streets such as Detroit and Center Ridge roads are slightly higher than neighboring terrain and represent ancient beaches of the once much larger Lake Erie. Many exhibits explain how the valley was formed and much supplementary information is available from naturalists in this wonder-filled nature center, which contains treasures from the past and materials relating to the present.

1. Find the All-Purpose Trail at the bridge over the river near the car entrance. The trail is paved, and mileage is indicated along its full length so distance can be measured. Before leaving the marina note the massive shale cliff above the river. The river has cut through many layers of earth since the last glacier retreated from Ohio about 12,000 years ago. The soft blue-gray shale on this cliff is Chagrin shale, the oldest exposed rock in the park. It was formed about 400 million years ago during the Devonian geologic period. The vertical marks penetrating the rock were caused by erosion. Each visible layer probably represents a major storm event when silting occurred in the warm inland sea that once covered Ohio.

2. After about a mile the trail crosses under the I-90 bridge and the beautiful Hilliard Blvd. bridge and passes a physical fitness trail and picnic tables.

3. Soon pass on the left a ball field located along a wide bend of the Rocky River. When the last glacier retreated, the river widened in some places and left several broad flat areas in the Rocky River Valley, of which this ball field is an example. In its wake the glacier left huge boulders that can be seen in the river, hence its name.

4. At about 2.5 miles, Hogsback Lane off Valley Pkwy. leads east up to the Stinchcomb Memorial, a tribute to the founding father and long-time director of the Cleveland Metropolitan Park District. Note how the river has been held in check with a man-made concrete wall. Originally, the river was located farther to the left just below the cliff. At this point note the slight difference in the color of the shale. The darker, black shale now coming into view is the slightly younger Cleveland shale, also of the Devonian period. Beneath it, of course, lies the older Chagrin shale seen earlier. Cleveland shale is black because it contains large amounts of decayed organic matter. Ancient fish and shark fossils have been found in this layer, as well as brachiopods, some examples of which may be seen at the nature center.

5. At the 3.0-mile mark on the paved trail, turn around and retrace your steps, retreating in time to when this glacier valley was formed 12,000 years ago. Even today the river continues its relentless cutting of the rock layers.

22 HINCKLEY RESERVATION
Worden's Ledges

In 1851 Hiram Worden bought land in Medina County from the estate of Samuel Hinckley that would later become Hinckley Reservation, one of 13 Cleveland Metroparks reservations and the only one located outside Cuyahoga County. The Worden Heritage Homestead at 895 Ledge Rd. was built by Hiram Worden in 1862, the year his daughter Nettie was born, and occupied by his farming family and their descendants until the 1980s. Nettie, who lived in the house all her life until her death in 1945, married her third husband, Noble Stuart, 20 years her junior, in 1944. Noble and his son, George Stuart, continued to stay in the house until George's death in 1984, when Cleveland Metroparks acquired the home and Hinckley Historical Society became its manager.

Distance: 1 mile round trip

Hiking time: 1 hour

Description: The trail is not marked, but it can be followed with this description and map or by referring to the map posted on a garage adjacent to the house. The ledges are located directly under the hill below the homestead, and the carvings are not difficult to find. Worden Heritage Homestead is managed by the Hinckley Historical Society, Susan Batke, curator, and is usually open on Sunday afternoons in the summer (278-2154).

Directions: From Cleveland, take I-271 south to the exit for Rte. 94 (North Royalton). Go right (north) on Rte. 94 (Ridge Rd.). Turn right (east) on Ledge Rd. Pass Kellogg Rd. and Ledge Lake Pool to the Worden Heritage Homestead, about a mile ahead on the left.

Parking & restrooms: Very little parking is available at Worden Heritage Homestead, but cars can be parked along the side of the driveway. A restroom is available inside the museum, when open.

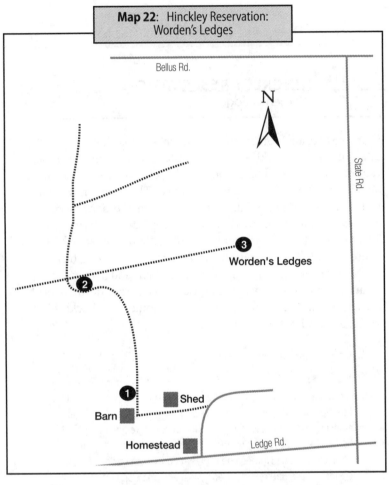

Map 22: Hinckley Reservation: Worden's Ledges

Bellus Rd.

N

State Rd.

③ Worden's Ledges

②

① Shed

Barn

Homestead   Ledge Rd.

Noble Stuart, a bricklayer, home builder, wanderer, and, most significantly, folk artist, began carving wood and wet concrete after his marriage to Nettie. He discovered huge sandstone ledges a half-mile beyond the Worden home and proceeded to carve figures and faces and other objects in the ledges over a period of several years. Although the carvings are gradually deteriorating, they represent aspects of Stuart's life that were important to him: a cross over an open Bible, baseball player Ty Cobb, whom he took hunting and fishing in Detroit, a schooner, representing his father's death in a shipwreck on Lake Superior, a bust of Hiram Worden on a corner of a rock with his named inscribed, "Nettie" carved in script, George

Washington and Marquis de Lafayette (reflecting Stuart's historical interests), and an eight-foot-long sphinx lying atop a large boulder.

Stuart's concrete carving of Christ on the Cross lies on the ground north of a small shed on the property. Although Stuart was a skillful craftsman, authorities do not consider him a significant artist. He died in 1976 at the age of 94. When asked in 1948 why he did the carvings, he said he simply wanted to keep practicing stone carving and leave something that would last.

West of Worden Heritage Homestead on Ledge Rd. is popular Ledge Lake Pool and Recreation Area (234-3026). A small admission charge allows visitors to use the 80-foot by 100-foot pool, changing facilities, and picnic area. Seniors over 65 and children 5 and under are admitted free. It is open 10 a.m.–8:30 p.m. Memorial Day to Labor Day.

Hinckley Reservation contains hiking trails, picnic areas, and an additional swimming area on Hinckley Lake that can be reached from Bellus Rd. Trail information is available from Cleveland Metroparks.

1. From the homestead, reach the trail to the ledges by going west parallel to Ledge Rd. (on your left) and past the sheds (on your right). Turn right (north) just before the barn and follow an old farm lane past an abandoned gas well on the left. Soon the path curves around left and gently descends a small hill. This trail may be muddy, as it is also used by horses.

2. Near the foot of the slope ignore the minor trail going off to the left and turn right (east) immediately. Follow the trail until you see large sandstone ledges on the path directly ahead.

3. At the farthest set of rock outcroppings, you will see on the left a large sphinx carved on top of a rock. This imposing creature seems to guard the entrance to the ledges area. Next is a large rock with "H.M. Worden 1851" carved on its face. On the northwest corner of this rock Stuart carved a bust of his father-in-law, but later added a cement beard when he noticed a photo of him sporting this adornment. "Nettie" is deeply incised in the next rock. A schooner can be seen high up on a ledge to the right, and farther along, also on a ledge to the right, is a cross with a Bible intricately carved into the stone. Ty Cobb's face and name are on a north-facing outcropping nearly obscured by moss.

Worden's Ledges were formed by the same ancient processes that also formed Whipp's Ledges, located in another part of Hinckley Reservation. (These are well worth seeing and can be reached by taking Bellus Rd. east to Parker Rd. and following Parker south to Whipp's Ledges Picnic Area.) Other ledge formations are found in Nelson-Kennedy Ledges State Park, Chapin Forest Reservation in Lake County, and Virginia Kendall Park in the Cuyahoga Valley National Recreation Area.

About 350 million years ago this part of Ohio was under a vast inland sea and, over eons, mud and sand washed into the ocean as wave action eroded the land. The sand at the ocean bottom solidified into rock, and as the waters receded and the land uplifted, the rocks became exposed. This rock is called Sharon Conglomerate sandstone because embedded in it are white quartz "lucky stones" that once were beach pebbles worn smooth by wave action at the edge of the sea. Glacial action of 12,000 years ago continued to shape these sandstone ledges, and today erosion and change continue still.

Return to Worden Heritage Homestead by retracing your steps in the reverse direction.

23 SOUTH CHAGRIN RESERVATION
River Walk

The Chagrin River was designated a State Scenic River in 1979. This beautiful riverside area is well known for its spring wildflowers and fall foliage. There are many tall hemlock, oak, hickory, beech, and maple trees here. Cleveland Metroparks Polo Field, where this walk starts, is used by the Cleveland Polo Club for horse and dog shows and periodically for the Cleveland Hunter/Jumper Classic.

Distance: 8 miles

Hiking time: 3 ½ hours

Description: This hike follows the blue-blazed Buckeye Trail along a scenic section of park land between the Chagrin River and Chagrin River Rd., part of South Chagrin Reservation. An almost flat, wooded trail leads to the main part of the reservation, then follows a paved All-Purpose Trail to Squaw Rock Picnic Area. A set of steep stone steps leads down to the edge of the river, and a short walk along the river leads to Squaw Rock. The walk returns on the same trail.

Directions: From I-271 take Chagrin Rd./Beachwood exit. Go east on Chagrin. Turn left (north) on SOM Center Rd. Turn right (east) on S. Woodland Rd. (Rte. 87). Just past Chagrin River Rd., turn right at the entrance to the Cleveland Metroparks Polo Field parking area.

Parking: Parking and restrooms are at Cleveland Metroparks Polo Field parking area.

1. Look for the rectangular 2-inch by 6-inch blue blazes of the Buckeye Trail (BT) painted on trees and poles along the west side of the polo field. Follow these markers going south.

2. At 0.7 mile, the BT turns left (east) on a bridle trail toward the Chagrin River and follows roughly parallel to the river along a beautiful stretch of woods. There is a variety of birds and flowers in season.

Map 23: South Chagrin Reservation:
River Walk

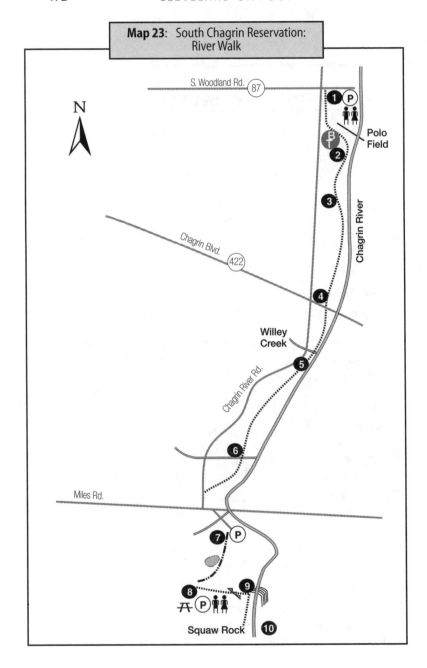

CAUTION: On this heavily used bridle trail the chances are strong that you will meet horses, especially on weekends. When encountering them, stop well to the side of the trail, remaining quiet and still until they have passed, to avoid startling these large and potentially dangerous animals.

3. Continue to follow the BT through open fields and a white pine forest.

4. At 1.7 miles, reach the bridge at Rte. 422 (Chagrin Blvd.). Cross the road and continue to follow the trail along the west bank of the river.

5. At 2.6 miles cross Willey Creek which, if there is high water, can be crossed by going out to Chagrin River Rd., crossing the bridge, then following the creek back to the BT.

6. At about 3 miles the BT crosses another small creek, then goes up a small hill and emerges onto Chagrin River Rd.

7. Cross Miles Rd. and bear left (east) across the River Rd. bridge (not Miles Rd. bridge) to enter the park on the right near Sulphur Springs Dr. An asphalt-paved All-Purpose Trail goes south from the small parking area.

CAUTION: Stay to the left on the paved trail, facing oncoming bicycle traffic.

8. Follow the paved path in a southerly direction, and reach Squaw Rock Picnic Area on the left at about 3.5 miles.

9. At the far east end of the parking area is a pathway leading down stone steps to a beautiful view of the Chagrin River and its scenic waterfall below. Take the steps to the foot and follow the riverside trail to Squaw Rock.

10. This large Berea sandstone rock, carved in 1885 by Chagrin Falls blacksmith and artist Henry Church, depicts a Native American woman surrounded by a quiver of arrows, sea serpent, panther, skeleton, eagle, shield, tomahawk, and papoose. On the river side of this huge glacial boulder are more carvings: a log cabin and the Capitol building in Washington, D.C. The significance of these unfinished carvings is obscure. Some think they could be a spiritual tribute to white man's plundering of the Indians or a depiction of our country's history from the age of Indians and wild beasts to American liberty.

To return to the starting point, follow the trail in reverse. Go back along the river and up the steps to Squaw Rock Picnic Area. Find the paved trail behind the restrooms and follow it back to the bridge and Chagrin River Rd. Here continue following the blue blazes of the Buckeye Trail northward until you reach the polo field and car parking area.

Section V
Moderate Trail Hikes

24 MENTOR MARSH STATE NATURE PRESERVE
Kerven Trail
Wake Robin Trail & Newhous Overlook

Mentor Marsh Nature Preserve is a 750-acre interpretive natural area jointly owned and managed by The Cleveland Museum of Natural History and the Ohio Department of Natural Resources.

The four-mile-long marsh's exceptional features are its diversity of wildlife and plants, and the history of its creation by the Grand River. The Grand River did not always reach Lake Erie at its present outlet at Fairport Harbor. It once flowed through what is now Mentor Marsh and emptied into the Lake several miles west of here. Over the 800 to 1,000 years since the Grand River found its new and present outlet to the lake, the old river channel gradually changed from swamp forest to marsh, and now contains miles of open area enclosing tall plume grass called *Phragmites australis*. Many birds, ducks, reptiles, amphibians, and insects thrive in this rich environment.

Mentor Marsh Nature Center, 5185 Corduroy Rd., Mentor 44060, (257-0777), is open on weekends from noon–5 p.m. from April to October, and, during the rest of the year, on the first Sunday afternoon of each month. Interpretative brochures, reference books, maps, exhibits, a calendar of events, and other data are available from the naturalist-staffed center during open hours. Classes and guided walks are presented at various times throughout the year.

Four marked trails, described below with different access points, are open daily from dawn to dusk. To see all of the nature preserve requires several brief drives. The time needed to complete all the trails will vary depending upon the views of wildlife and plants that attract the hiker's attention. If all are completed, however, allow a full morning or afternoon.

Marsh mosquitoes are part of a wetland ecosystem. It is advisable to take along insect repellent, a hat, a long-sleeved shirt, and long pants when hiking in Mentor Marsh after late May and before the first frost. Open flames and smoking are strictly prohibited, as is the collection of any natural material in the preserve. Pets, motorized vehicles, and bikes are prohibited by state law in the nature preserve.

In 1966 Mentor Marsh became one of the first areas in the United States to be designated a National Natural Landmark, and in 1973 it was designated a State Nature Preserve. It is helpful to take along bird and wildflower identification guidebooks to enhance your visit to these natural areas.

KERVEN TRAIL

Distance: 3/4 mile

Hiking time: Less than an hour

Description: The Kerven Trail begins just north of Marsh House. It is a loop trail on flat forest land with a small enclosed overlook ideal for studying birds of the marsh. Just off the trail is the brief Butterfly Walk, which dead-ends into a field of flowers (in season).

Directions: From I-90, follow Rte. 2 east to Mentor. Take Rte. 44 north, then exit left (west) on Rte. 283 (Lakeshore Blvd.) to Corduroy Rd. Turn right onto Corduroy and follow it to the sign for Marsh House on the right.

Parking and restroom: Park in the Marsh House parking area. A restroom is located inside the small building attached to the residence of the nature preserve caretaker, who is available during open hours.

1. Enter the Kerven Trail just north of Marsh House. This sometimes wet trail is located on abandoned agricultural land, which has been succeeded by a forest containing a variety of trees and plants. Keep on the lookout for owls and deer, which frequent this forest.

2. At the first trail intersection bear right to take the loop in a counterclockwise direction. Following closely by private property, you will soon see a white arrow indicating a left turn toward the edge of the marsh.

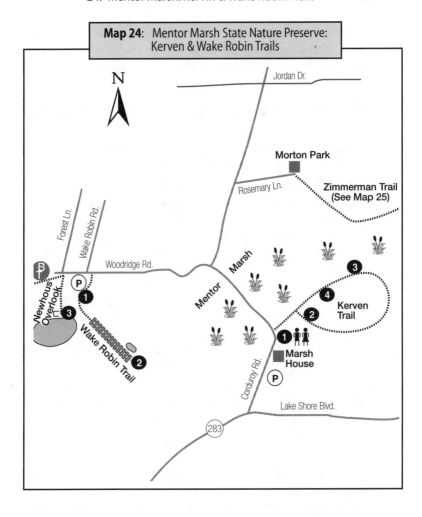

Map 24: Mentor Marsh State Nature Preserve: Kerven & Wake Robin Trails

3. Reach the overlook and tarry a while to enjoy the wonderful view of acres of plume grass dotted with occasional dead tree stumps, reminders of the extensive swamp forest that once covered this marshland. The north shore of the marsh originally contained an oak/hickory forest, and the south shore a beech/maple forest. The riverbed contained willow, alder, buttonbush, and cattails. Some of the birds you may observe here are owls, ducks, herons, shore birds, and migrants during May and September.

4. The trail continues across a footbridge and past an open field on the left, where the dead-end Butterfly Walk is located. Continue ahead past the trail intersection marking the beginning of the loop and follow the path back to the parking area.

WAKE ROBIN TRAIL & NEWHOUS OVERLOOK

Distance: The Wake Robin Trail is a 0.7-mile round trip, and the Newhous Overlook is only a 0.1-mile round trip from the road.

Walking time: Less than an hour

Description: The Wake Robin Trail is a flat boardwalk leading into the marsh that passes several small ponds containing beaver, muskrat, waterfowl, and wading birds. The Newhous Overlook is a two-level wooden structure overlooking a large pond and acres of tall plume grass growing in the marsh.

Directions: For the Newhous Overlook and the Wake Robin Trail boardwalk, drive north on Corduroy Rd. across the marsh to Woodridge Rd. Turn left on Woodridge and follow it to a small parking lot on the left just before Wake Robin Rd. (Corduroy Rd. originally was a bumpy "corduroy" log road, later a paved road, and because of continued sinking, has recently been widened, raised, and resurfaced.)

Parking & restrooms: Park at the small lot identified with a nature preserve sign on the south side of Woodridge Rd. There is no restroom here.

1. The trail from the parking area leads down to a boardwalk that brings the observer directly into the marsh for viewing wildlife. Birdwatchers may see the elusive marsh wren, sora rail, and the American and least bittern. Red-winged blackbirds are almost always prominent. The boardwalk is on a slightly elevated path that once served as a shortcut to a golf course on the other side of the marsh.

Fresh water is supplied by springs throughout the marsh as well as by Black Brook and Marsh Creek, but the water remains slightly brackish due to salt-laden runoff that has seeped in from salt mines located on State Route 44. Water flows slowly through the marsh from east to west and empties into Lake Erie at Mentor Lagoons, about three miles west of here. The lagoons were dredged in the 1920s for a large resort that was never completed. They remain open, but are not yet a part of the preserve.

2. At the end of the boardwalk is a bench to rest on and an open pond where beavers are active. Waterfowl and wading birds nest in the tall plume grass, an invasive salt marsh plant of little nutritive value that tends to crowd out native species. On the edge of the pond, however, there is a small stand of pretty cattails growing. Beaver and other water mammals, such as mink, muskrat, and short-tailed weasel, might be encountered here. Twenty-three species of fish have been identified in marsh waters. The channel alongside the boardwalk was cut to facilitate water circulation to and from a new pond below the Newhous Overlook. Here you may notice midland painted snapping turtles and green frogs, and you may hear peepers in early spring with an almost deafening sound at dusk.

3. Return on the boardwalk to the parking area. Turn left (west) on Woodridge Ln. and continue past five houses to the entrance path for the Newhous Overlook. Here you will enjoy an expansive view of the western end of the marsh and more waterfowl in the beautiful pond below. In summer, hawks and vultures often soar over this part of the marsh, and beaver and muskrats often make an appearance.

Optional

To the west of the overlook is Headlands School Forest, owned by the Mentor Board of Education. As an option, you may follow the blue-blazed Buckeye Trail from the overlook, winding through the site of ancient Indian encampments until the trail exits at Headlands School parking lot. Return to the overlook by retracing your steps. In April and May, beautiful wildflowers, especially trillium, dot the landscape. A map of this trail is available at Marsh House.

The authors wish to recognize the generous consultation and contributions in preparing this chapter by Nancy M. Csider, Cleveland Museum of Natural History naturalist.

25 MENTOR MARSH STATE NATURE PRESERVE
Zimmerman / Buckeye Trail

Distance: 4 miles from Morton Park to Headlands Dr. and back

Hiking time: 1 ½ to 2 hours

Description: The Zimmerman Trail is on a portion of the state-wide, blue-blazed Buckeye Trail. It winds along the western edge of Mentor Marsh and undulates gently up and down through a mature upland and swamp forest with lovely wildflowers in season.

Directions: Drive east on Woodridge Rd. to Corduroy Rd., then north on Corduroy to Rosemary Lane. Turn right on Rosemary and follow it to the end to a large parking lot for Morton Park.

Parking & restrooms: Park near the entrance to the Zimmerman Trail. Public restrooms are in the pool house building, open only in the summer, or at Headlands Beach State Park.

1. The trailhead for the Zimmerman/Buckeye Trail is at the edge of the woods to the south of the Morton Park parking lot. The trail is marked with blue 2-inch by 6-inch Buckeye Trail tree blazes. There are turns in the trail, and side trails off the main trail, so it is important to watch carefully for the tree blazes. Upon entering the trail, bear to the left to go east over gently rolling hills following the edge of the marsh.

2. In autumn and winter there are long views of the marsh on the right. In summer, the trail provides welcome shade from tall beech, oak, and maple trees.

3. After about 1.5 miles you will reach a trail intersection. Bear right. (The left spur, Jayne Trail, goes out to Jordan Dr.—where no parking is available.)

Map 25: Mentor Marsh State Nature Preserve: Zimmerman / Buckeye Trail

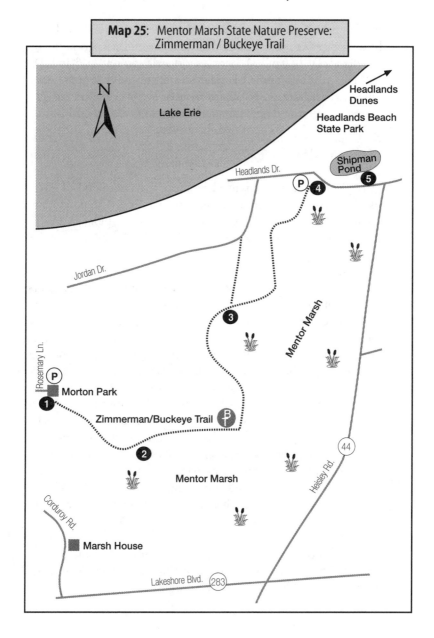

4. Continue following rolling terrain and cross several small foot bridges over wet spots to reach the end of the trail at a parking lot on Headlands Dr. (2.0 miles). Here, a short walk east on Headlands Dr. will take you to Shipman Pond, also part of the nature preserve. Ducks, geese, and other waterfowl may be in evidence; red fox, weasel, raccoon, and opossum may come out to feed at dusk.

5. Shipman Pond, a remnant of the old riverbed of the Grand River, is lined by a buttonbush-willow community. Nearby is where the old Grand River made a sharp turn and gradually eroded through the sand, perhaps in a lake storm or a river flood, to establish its present, more direct course to Lake Erie. The pond commemorates Charles M. Shipman who was a pioneer in the movement to preserve Mentor Marsh in the 1930s.

Optional

Nearby and well worth visiting are Headlands Beach State Park and Headlands Dunes State Nature Preserve. The 125-acre Headlands Beach on Lake Erie offers swimming, picnicking, changing facilities, and a concession stand. To the northeast lies Headlands Dunes State Nature Preserve, a vast accumulation of sand along the Lake Erie shoreline that was created by wind and water along the western side of the mouth of the Grand River. Each year the sandy shoreline builds up and extends farther and farther out into Lake Erie. Access to the preserve is from Headlands Beach State Park. This special place is intended for research, nature study, bird watching, art, and photography. Walking on the dunes is permitted, but visitor are asked not to walk on any growing plants. Monarch butterflies often stop to rest here on their long migration between Canada and Mexico. Plant species found here include dune-making switchgrass and beach grass, and other plants such as sea rocket and beach pea.

The authors wish to recognize the generous consultation and contributions in preparing this chapter by Nancy M. Csider, Cleveland Museum of Natural History naturalist.

26 BEDFORD RESERVATION
Tinker's Creek

Bedford Reservation, located in Bedford, Bedford Heights, Valley View, and Walton Hills, is a link in Cleveland Metroparks' "Emerald Necklace." This lovely park on Cleveland's southeast side is also part of Cuyahoga Valley National Recreation Area. Bedford Reservation contains 2,154 acres of public land, through which beautiful Tinker's Creek cuts a gorge that has been designated a National Natural Landmark. Tinker's Creek drops a dramatic 90 feet during its two-mile course, cutting through many layers of soft bluish shale, and leaving a gorge that ranges from 140 to 190 feet deep.

Distance: 3 miles

Hiking time: 2 hours

Description: This hike follows Tinker's Creek gorge on its northwest side, going steeply uphill with breathtaking views of the gorge at its summit. The trail follows the rim of the gorge to the top and affords nice views of the stream as you ascend. This hike returns on the same path to the picnic and parking area. It is an especially impressive hike to take during fall foliage season, and is also a pretty hike when Tinker's Creek is partially frozen and there is snow on the ground.

Directions: Take I-271, I-480, or I-77 to Rockside Rd. Follow Rockside to Dunham Rd. in Maple Hts. Take Dunham south to Button Rd. Just before the bridge over Tinker's Creek, turn left onto Button and follow it to its end to the Hemlock Creek Picnic Area.

Parking & restrooms: At Hemlock Creek Picnic Area

A wide variety of trees abound here; 29 different species have been identified. Of particular note are tall hemlocks growing in some of the deep cooler areas near streams. Deer may often be seen in some of Bedford's more remote areas.

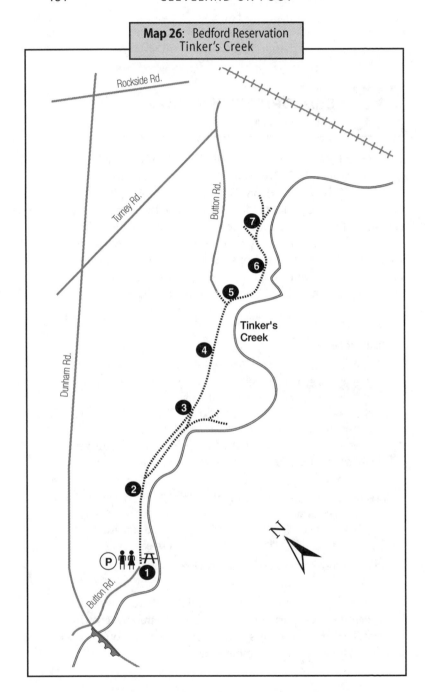

Map 26: Bedford Reservation
Tinker's Creek

1. Start the hike by heading east from the picnic area and ball field. The trail parallels Tinker's Creek on the right. Tinker's Creek flows westward to the Cuyahoga River, at which point it is carried over the Ohio & Erie Canal by an interesting old aqueduct (described in the Canal Towpath Hike).

2. At the first trail intersection, turn right onto the path closer to the creek and view the magnificent cliff across the stream faced with tall hemlock trees clinging to its edge.

These cliffs are composed of very old Chagrin Shale near the water and darker Cleveland Shale above. These shales were formed of mud and silt laid down by an ancient inland sea 400 million years ago and have been exposed by the relentless cutting of Tinker's Creek over the millennia. In winter there are beautiful frozen waterfalls here where small streams flow into the creek. This waterside trail continues for about 0.2 mile.

3. At the intersection, take the trail on the left that ascends the hill to the main trail. (If you stay on the creekside trail or take the trail that goes off to the right, you will see beautiful wildflowers if it is springtime, and enjoy more views of Tinker's Creek, but both trails will eventually come to a dead end at a steep shale cliff.)

4. The upward trail on the left is the old Bridle Trail (now closed) and climbs steeply. In the middle of the trail, about half-way up the hill, is a large boulder covered with ripple marks made by currents on the bottom of the great inland sea that covered Ohio millions of years ago. At the top on the right is a magnificent view of the gorge below.

> CAUTION: Take care not to stray too close to the edge of this cliff. Erosion has occurred here, creating uneven footing and unstable soil.

5. (0.8 mile). As you pass the Bridle Trail sign, turn right toward Tinker's Creek gorge and continue on the trail. The road on the left is the north portion of Button Rd., which no longer connects to the southern part. Button Rd. is of interest because it is one of the oldest roads in northern Ohio. It was laid out in 1801 and enabled early settlers living in the highlands to the east of here to reach the Ohio & Erie Canal lying to the west.

6. Continue on this flat, winding, woodland path high above Tinker's Creek. Several short side trails veer over closer to the cliff edge, but always return to the main trail. (Use CAUTION if you take these side paths for more views of the gorge below.) At about 1.2 miles the trail begins to descend.

7. Reach a trail intersection after another 0.2 mile. Turn right (east) toward the gorge. After 0.1 mile there is another trail intersection, where you will turn left for another beautiful view of the gorge. This is the turnaround point for this hike. You will return to Hemlock Creek Picnic Area by following the trail in reverse.

Optional

If you wish to continue on the trail, it is possible to do so, but the way is confusing because of the many trails that criss-cross this part of the park. Some of these trails lead out to Button Rd., the YMCA camp, or to private property on other roads. If you get onto Button Rd. and take it westward, you will eventually reach the area described in note 5. Then follow the bridle trail downhill to the picnic area and parking.

27 ROCKY RIVER RESERVATION (SOUTH)
Nature Center and Trails

Long, skinny Rocky River Reservation is one of Cleveland Metroparks' 13 "Emerald Necklace" parks surrounding the city. It forms the western part of the "necklace." The reservation encloses Rocky River and its valley on its twisting course from Bagley Rd. in Berea in the south to Detroit Rd. in Rocky River at Lake Erie.

Distance: 4.2 miles

Hiking time: 2 hours

Description: This walk includes a variety of well-marked trails in the vicinity of Rocky River Nature Center. Be sure to stop at the center to pick up brochures and see the many interesting exhibits, which describe the forces of nature at work in the creation of the Rocky River valley and the topography of Ohio. Nearby, the East and West Branches of the Rocky River join together at a point close to the bridge over Cedar Point Rd. The former channel of the West Branch once extended to the west and north of where the center now stands. The old channel still exists in pools and marshes below Fort Hill and west of the Wildlife Management Trail. There are steep hills and sets of stairways to climb on this hike.

Directions: From I-71 south, exit at West 150th St. From the exit ramp turn right onto West 150th, then right again onto Puritas Rd. Follow Puritas west and downhill to Valley Pkwy. Turn left (south) on Valley Pkwy. and follow it to Rocky River Nature Center on the right, just past Shephard Lane.

Parking & restrooms: At Rocky River Nature Center

The largest of Cleveland Metroparks, Rocky River Reservation offers three golf courses, nine picnic areas, a nature center, a museum, a stables, a marina, and other facilities. A 13-mile paved All Purpose Trail extends the full length of the park and parallels Rocky River Pkwy. Outstanding natural features of this park are the mas-

Map 27: Rocky River Reservation (South)

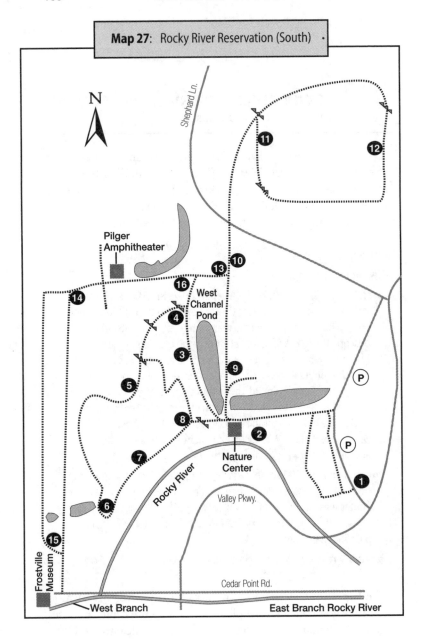

sive Chagrin and Cleveland shale cliffs exposed by the Rocky River in its relentless course to its outlet at the lake. At Tyler Field, the cliff is half Chagrin shale (below), which is the oldest, and half Cleveland shale (above). In the blacker Cleveland shale many fish fossils have been discovered.

Located within eight municipalities, this park contains lovely tall willow, sycamore, and cottonwood trees and beautiful wildflowers, birds, and white-tailed deer. Rocky River Nature Center, at 24000 Valley Pkwy. (just north of Cedar Point Rd. in North Olmsted), contains wonderful exhibits and information about the park. Park naturalists offer programs, guided hikes, and information about the history and geology of the Rocky River Valley. For more information, call the nature center at 734-6660.

Frostville Museum is an affiliate of Cleveland Metroparks and Olmsted Historical Society. Housed in several buildings, it provides the visitor with an interesting history of the people who settled the valley in the early 1800s. The museum is just off Cedar Point Rd., west of Valley Pkwy. It is open Sundays 2–5 p.m. through Labor Day or by appointment. For more information, call 777-0059.

1. Start the walk on the paved Wildflower Garden Trail, just off the main parking lot. By taking the trail entrance nearest Valley Pkwy. you will follow the path alongside Rocky River enjoying a nice view of the water. Then continue around to the Ron Hauser Wildflower Garden, a secluded enclave with benches where each flower and fern species is labeled. April and May are prime times to enjoy this garden.

2. Enter the nature center. There are descriptions of the various kinds of rocks found in the Rocky River Valley, from the 400-million-year-old Chagrin shale near Lake Erie to the 340-million-year-old Berea sandstone near Bagley Rd. Of special interest are fish fossils found in the Cleveland shale layer in the valley. A replica of a fierce armored fish found near here, *Dunkleosteus terelli*, the largest sea creature of that time, is on display.

Huge boulders are scattered throughout Rocky River, thus giving rise to its name. They were deposited by glaciers that slid across all but the southeastern portion of Ohio. The Nebraskan Glacier covered Ohio 1 million to 500,000 years ago, the Illinoran, 150,000 years ago, and the mile-thick ice sheet that extended farthest south was the Wisconsin Glacier of 70,000 years ago. By 10,000 to 12,000 years ago the last glacier had melted, leaving till and debris covering a vastly widened valley—where playing fields and golf courses are now located.

From the center's outside deck there is a beautiful view of the river and Arrowhead Island just across the way. For the next part of this walk you may wish to pick up a Fort Hill map to follow interesting lettered signposts along the way.

3. Take the rear exit from the center to the large trail sign. Turn left to begin the walk on the red-blazed Fort Hill Trail with an arrowhead symbol. Follow the path past a flight of steep steps on the left. On the right is West Channel Pond, part of the former course of the West Branch of the Rocky River. A variety of waterfowl usually are enjoying this pond. Go down the steps and across a short boardwalk.

The post lettered "B" indicates the obviously rusty water that has leached out of the shale. This mixture of mud and iron eventually hardens into a heavy rock called bog iron. It was once harvested by pioneers, who smelted it down and made tools from it.

The shale cliff at signpost "C" was formed by the West Branch of the Rocky River before it changed its course and joined the East Branch after severing a narrow isthmus between Fort Hill and Cedar Point Hill.

4. Bear left up the steps, avoiding the trail that goes off to the right, and remain on the main trail without taking any crossover trails. The path bends left and continues uphill on several sets of steps to make a 90-foot ascent.

5. At the top, turn right at the fork. (The trail to the left is a shortcut back to the nature center). Here at the top, evidence has been found that this site was occupied by Native Americans about 1,000 years ago.

Oaks and maples grace the woods of this beautiful hilltop. Stay on the main trail, avoiding a trail that goes off to the right, downhill. Continue along the trail until you reach a triangular point of land, Fort Hill.

6. Across from Fort Hill is Cedar Point Hill, composed of Cleveland shale, and between these two hills was the isthmus of land that over time was eroded away by both the East Branch and the West Branch of the Rocky River, enabling the latter to join the East Branch's channel and abandon its old riverbed. Below, the Rocky River is formed from the merger of both branches just south of here.

7. Continue on the wide main trail along the fence without taking any of the cross-over trails. Evidence of erosion is visible in many places—such as the exposed tree roots. Below is the Rocky River, flowing northeast toward Lake Erie, and the nature center, with its deck overhanging the river.

8. On the left of the trail are small parallel, finger-like mounds that once were thought to be indicative of Native American Earthworks (1000 to 1640 A.D.), but are now considered to be much older and built, perhaps, for native rituals.

Bear right past the juncture of the shortcut trail on the left to a set of 135 steep downward steps. Turn right at the bottom and follow the same trail back to the large trail sign where this walk began.

9. Turn left at the sign onto the blue-blazed West Channel Pond Trail, with its flying bird symbol. Follow this path across the man-made dam that impounds water from the old riverbed to form a pretty pond for waterfowl. Stay left past a connecting trail on the right that leads back to the parking area.

10. At the next trail intersection, leave the West Channel Pond Trail and stay to the right on the yellow-blazed Mt. Pleasant Trail. This enjoyable path will soon reach busy Shephard Lane.

CAUTION! Cross the road carefully as traffic moves fast on this curving street.

11. Follow the wide gravel path to a point where the trail begins to ascend the hill. Bear right at the steps to make a counter-clockwise loop. Another set of steps eases the climb to the summit where a bench invites a rest overlooking Rocky River valley.

12. Continue on this pleasant hilltop walk on a dirt pathway. The traffic you hear below on the right is on Valley Pkwy. Next descend the slope on wide steps. The freeway in the distance on the right is I–480. At the end of the loop, retrace your steps back across Shephard Lane to the intersection with the blue-blazed West Channel Pond Trail.

13. Turn right at this intersection and follow the path past the pond on the right—another remnant of the old riverbed. A variety of waterfowl can often be observed here. Continue now on the brown-blazed Wildlife Management Trail. By remaining on this wide path without taking any cross-over trails, you will pass small Pilger Amphitheater on the right, used for park programs.

14. Cross a service trail and turn left (south) at the next trail intersection, heading toward Frostville Museum and Cedar Point Rd. Keep to the main path (avoid taking any of the crossover trails) and note the marshes that represent more of the former riverbed of the Rocky River West Branch.

Frostville Museum is open only on Sundays, 2–5 p.m., Memorial Day through Labor Day. Admission is free (but donations are accepted) to view the Prechtel House, Briggs House, a one-room pioneer cabin, a barn, and a general store.

15. Before reaching Cedar Point Rd. and the museum, the Wildlife Management trail turns right. Rows of apple trees along here attest to the former use of this fertile land for farming. The trail bends to the right again and passes more marshland with cattails growing in the water of the old channel. This trail is also used for cross-country skiing and is marked with a blue-blazed ski sign.

16. Reach the same trail juncture passed at point #14 and continue past the service trail and Pilger Amphitheater; turn right at the blue-blazed West Channel Pond Trail. At this right turn there is a bench marked "Generously donated by Fred R. Jones." Follow the path past the pond on the left to return to the nature center.

28 NORTH CHAGRIN RESERVATION
Hemlock Trail

The North Chagrin Reservation of the Cleveland Metroparks is located just east of S.O.M. Center Rd. (Rte. 91) in both Lake and Cuyahoga counties. It is distinguished by deep ravines, a pretty waterfall, a modern nature center, several ponds, and the large Sunset Wildlife Preserve. There are many marked trails in North Chagrin, some steep and hilly, some flat, such as the paved All-Purpose Trail, and others moderately hilly over gently rolling terrain. There are five large picnic areas in North Chagrin with picnic tables and shelters, ball playing fields, and restrooms. Sanctuary Marsh Nature Center is a large building staffed by park naturalists who offer information about facilities in the park, trail maps and brochures, educational programs and activities, and nature exhibits. EarthWords, a bookshop of Cleveland Metroparks, is located in the nature center and offers various nature publications and guidebooks.

Distance: 6 miles

Hiking time: 2 ½ to 3 hours

Description: This hike is on flat terrain for the first and last parts, and in the middle portion goes over a moderately rolling section of the yellow Hemlock Trail.

Directions: From I-271, exit at Wilson Mills Rd. Follow Wilson Mills east to S.O.M. Center Rd. (Rte. 91). Turn left (north) on S.O.M. Center Rd. Turn right (east) at the park entrance on Sunset Ln., then right onto Buttermilk Falls Pkwy. Turn right into the parking lot for Sanctuary Marsh Nature Center.

Parking & restrooms: At Sanctuary Marsh Nature Center

1. Begin this hike at Sanctuary Marsh Nature Center. Circle the building to view Sunset Pond, an excellent habitat for plants and wildlife. Several interpretive signs warn visitors not to feed the ducks and geese. In August, 1993, Cleveland Metroparks joined state, fed-

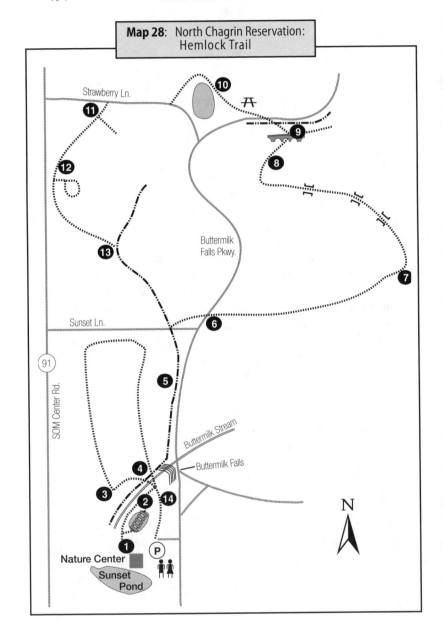

Map 28: North Chagrin Reservation: Hemlock Trail

eral, and international conservations agencies in adopting a non-feeding policy to better protect the wildlife from overpopulation, disease, and non-migration.

2. Leave the nature center and take the wooden Marsh Deck Walk across Sanctuary Marsh. Birds, ducks, and other wildlife can be seen in the marsh, as well as a variety of plants.

At the end of the wooden boardwalk, enter the Wildlife Management Loop Trail on the left, identified by an orange footprint sign. Follow this trail along a wide dirt trail.

Cross a trail, then cross Buttermilk Stream, still following the orange Wildlife Management trail and now joining the Buttermilk Falls Loop trail (blue trail markers). Cross the paved All Purpose Trail and continue on the dirt path.

3. Turn left at the next trail intersection to continue on the orange Wildlife Management Loop Trail (leaving the blue Buttermilk Falls Loop Trail, which continues straight ahead).

Along this mile-long orange loop, you will find pleasant woods and a soft, flat trail through Sunset Wildlife Preserve. The meadows provide homes for rabbits, songbirds, pheasants, deer, and other wildlife.

4. (1.0 mile) At the next intersection (the end of this loop), turn left on the paved All Purpose Trail, which leads to Buttermilk Falls Overlook. This pretty waterfall flows down over many layers of shale exposed by the stream's cutting action over thousands of years. Looking downstream from the overlook and to the right will reveal the ever deepening ravine as the water flows eastward to the Chagrin River far below.

5. Turn back to the paved All Purpose Trail and follow it north to Sunset Ln. (It is wise to stay to the left on the paved trail, because it is heavily used by bicyclists who usually stay to the right).

6. At Sunset Lane, cross Buttermilk Falls Pkwy. and, a little farther along on the right, enter the marked Bridle Trail, which very soon leads to the yellow Hemlock Trail. This lovely path is parallel to, and high above, a very deep ravine carved by Buttermilk Stream.

CAUTION: For safety keep well away from the edge of the gorge, because erosion has created loose soil and gravel underfoot.

7. The Hemlock Trail's gentle ups and downs provide relaxing and enjoyable hiking. At about 2.0 miles the trail begins to bend away from the ravine and crosses several small wooden bridges as it winds north. This is a quiet section of the trail where occasionally wildlife may be observed. The tall beech and hemlock trees are magnificent here. Although there are several turns and intersections on this trail, stay with the yellow tree markers on the main trail and you will not get lost.

8. At about 2.5 miles cross a larger wooden bridge over a stream and go up a small hill. At the top, bear right. (The trail on the left is the Bridle Trail, which leads out to Buttermilk Falls Pkwy. and is a shortcut back to the car if you wish to leave the hike at this point and return via the road).

9. Cross a small bridge with steps and note the infinite layers of shale worn away by the cutting action of the stream. These shale layers were deposited on the floor of the ancient sea that once covered Ohio millions of years ago.

Go uphill on steps cut into the hill and bear left at the top.

10. Cross the All-Purpose Trail and Buttermilk Falls Pkwy. to reach Strawberry Picnic Area. (3.0 miles). At this picnic area are restrooms, a shelter and playing field, and a wildlife pond.

11. Circle Strawberry Pond in a counterclockwise direction. At Strawberry Lane turn right and walk along the road to just beyond the yellow Bridle Trail sign that you will see ahead.

At this sign turn left off the road and enter the Bridle Trail. Almost immediately turn right at an intersection. The trail curves close to S.O.M. Center Rd.

12. At about the 4.0-mile point on this hike you will reach, on the left, a driveway that leads to the Daughters of the American Revolution (D.A.R.) Memorial and Loop Trail. In 1932 a bronze plaque was placed on a large boulder here to commemorate the 200th anniversary of George Washington's birth in 1732. Here the Western Reserve Chapter of the Daughters of the American Revolution planted a large stand of pine trees. The D.A.R. Memorial Loop Trail goes through the 60-year-old and now very tall pine trees. It begins to the right of the wide unpaved open area at the end of the short drive at the sign saying "No Horses Please."

Continue along the narrow 1/4-mile loop trail through quiet and cool pine woods with lovely fragrant needles underfoot, until it ends at the open area again. Return to the Bridle Trail near S.O.M. Center Rd., and turn left to continue on the Bridle Trail as it enters the woods.

13. Turn right at the intersection with the All Purpose Trail (4.7 miles) and continue on this paved trail, past Sunset Lane and Buttermilk Falls Overlook.

14. Continue on the All Purpose Trail to the next intersection (there is no trail sign here) and turn left onto the Buttermilk Falls Loop Trail. (You will leave the All Purpose Trail at this point where it goes out to S.O.M. Center Rd.). The BF Loop Trail leads back to Sanctuary Marsh and the Sanctuary Marsh Nature Center. A trail just east of the pond goes directly to the car parking area.

29 MILL STREAM RUN RESERVATION

Mill Stream Run Reservation is so named because at one time several fast-flowing streams on the property coursed downward about 170 feet to the Rocky River East Branch to power the gristmills and sawmills of the early settlers. Today, because of modern development, the streams have dwindled to just a trickle.

Distance: 6 miles

Hiking time: 3 hours

Description: This trail hike travels over gently rolling terrain, crosses several streams, and reveals a chimney ruin and an abandoned oil well indicating past activity in this area. In the description below, Mill Stream Run refers to the brook flowing from south to north through the reservation.

Directions: From I-71 south, take the Royalton Rd. (Rte. 82) exit. Go east on Route 82 to Valley Pkwy., then south on Valley Pkwy. a short distance to the reservation entrance at Royalview Lane.

Parking & restrooms: At Royalview Picnic Area.

1. Begin the hike at the Royalview Picnic Area and find the trail to the right of and behind the shelter. Follow the path northeast into the woods and to a ravine on the right overlooking Mill Stream Run.

2. The trail leads north high above Mill Stream Run (on the right) and makes a gradual descent to the creek bottom.

3. At about 1.0 mile cross Mill Stream Run and climb a short embankment, where the stream now appears on the left.

4. Walk another 0.1 mile and turn right (south) onto a wide hiking/skiing trail. Without making any turns, continue along it for about a mile as it gradually ascends to high land.

5. Near the south end of this trail there will be a red hiker blaze

Map 29: Mill Stream Run Reservation

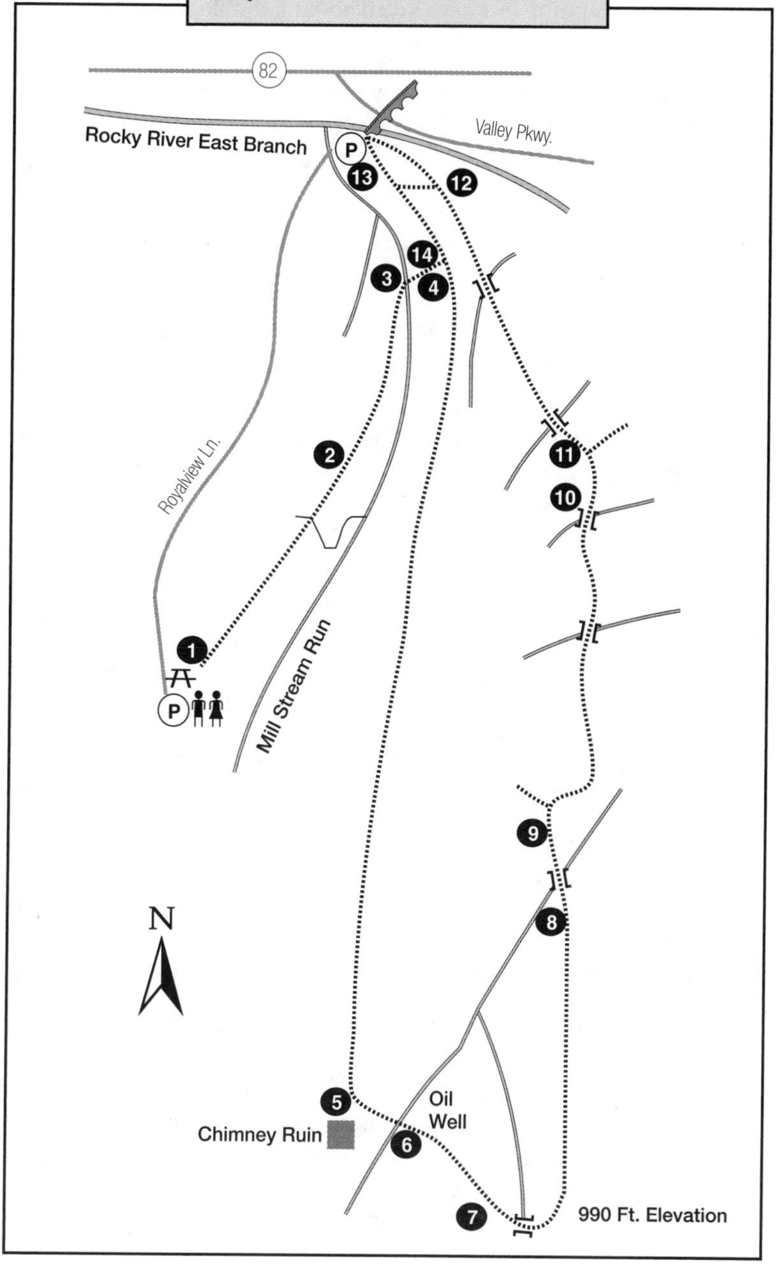

82

Rocky River East Branch

Valley Pkwy.

P
13
12

14
3
4

Royalview Ln.

2

11
10

1

Mill Stream Run

N

9

8

5
Oil
Well
Chimney Ruin
6

7   990 Ft. Elevation

affixed to a tree. Directly ahead in the woods is a tall brick chimney ruin. At this point you have hiked about 2.0 miles. The trail bends sharply left.

6. Heading east, cross Chimney Run Stream and follow red hiker blazes. There will be an abandoned oil well fenced in on the left. Continue straight ahead on the main trail.

7. Cross another stream and continue east until the trail bends left (north). This is the highest point in Mill Stream Run Reservation at 990 feet. White blazes and red arrows now show the way.

8. At about the 3.0-mile point on the left is a huge hollow oak tree. Cross a wooden bridge (constructed primarily for skiers) and follow red hiker blazes.

9. At a trail intersection, bear right to stay on the main trail, keeping the stream on the right. (A side trail goes up to a field on the left.) Still following red arrows, continue as the trail bends to the left. Sometimes deer are seen in this stretch of the park.

10. The trail follows gently rolling hills and crosses two more wooden bridges.

11. Bear left at the next trail intersection and cross another wooden bridge over the stream coming in on the left.

12. Stay on the main trail until the wide Rocky River East Branch appears on the right near the end of the trail. The bridge over Rocky River on Royalview Ln. is ahead on the right. You have hiked about 4.6 miles.

13. At the road turn left and walk to the parking area ahead. Reenter the woods at the trail sign. At the Y-intersection go right and follow red hiker blazes. The trail starts a gradual incline now.

14. Watch for a trail on the right off the main trail about 0.3 mile from the parking lot. (This is the spot described in note #4.) Turn right onto it. The trail descends to Mill Stream Run, crosses it on stream rocks, and then goes up above the ravine hiked previously.

Keeping Mill Stream Run on the left, return to the picnic shelter by hiking on the same trail as before.

Section VI
Moderately Strenuous Trail Hikes

30 NORTH CHAGRIN RESERVATION
Buckeye Trail Loop

There are many kinds of trails in North Chagrin Reservation, which is distinguished by its deep ravines, waterfalls, and large wildlife preserve. Among the facilities here are five large picnic areas, a winter sports area, a scout camp, an education building, Sunset Wildlife Preserve, and Sanctuary Marsh Nature Center. Information and maps can be obtained at the nature center. Trail hikes reveal a good portion of the natural beauty of this area. The following hike is mostly in the southern half of this reservation; the northern half is described in Chapters 28 and 31. Both this and the hike in Chapter 31 have steep hills to challenge hikers.

Distance: 5 ½ miles

Hiking time: 3 hours

Description: This hike is primarily on the Buckeye Trail. It includes two nature trail loops, the Overlook and the Sylvan Trails, and involves a short road walk at the end. The hills are steep.

Directions: From I-271, exit at Wilson Mills Rd. Follow Wilson Mills east to Chagrin River Rd.. Turn left (north) on Chagrin River Rd. Turn right (east) onto Rogers Rd.

Parking & restrooms: Park at Rogers Rd. Field parking lot. Restrooms are along the east side of the field near the river.

1. Rogers Road Field forms part of the east boundary of North Chagrin Reservation. The Buckeye Trail (BT) enters North Chagrin Reservation on Rogers Rd. You will see the blue blazes on telephone poles along Rogers Rd. going west. Follow the blue blazes across Chagrin River Rd. and enter Ox Bow (a paved road).

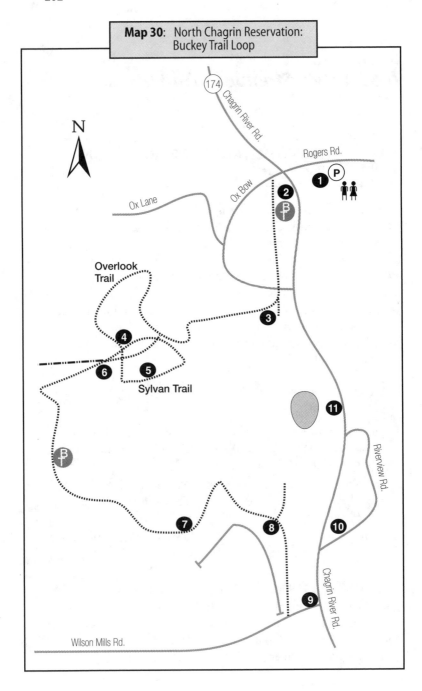

Map 30: North Chagrin Reservation: Buckey Trail Loop

2. BT bends sharply left (south) on the bridle trail at 0.25 mile; at 0.5 mile it crosses the south arm of Ox Bow.

3. Bear right as the BT climbs steeply uphill through a mixed beech-maple-hemlock forest.

4. Reach the Overlook Trail on the right at 1.0 mile. This trail is dedicated to A. B. Williams, Cleveland Metroparks' first naturalist. A plaque is attached to a granite glacial boulder deposited here from northern Canada about 12,000 years ago. This 3/4-mile loop trail with orange-numbered posts offers an interesting nature walk through a mature forest. Interpretive brochures are available at Sanctuary Marsh Nature Center.

5. Reach the main trail (BT). On the opposite side of the trail is a large clearing and the yellow-posted Sylvan Trail. Again, if there is time, this 0.5-mile loop is worth exploring through a beautiful hardwood forest. Reach the main trail (BT) again.

6. Bear left on BT off the paved All-Purpose Trail, which goes right at this point. At 2.5 miles, the BT bends sharply left (south) away from a parking area.

7. The trail winds downhill past an unused roadway and reaches a trail intersection at 3.4 miles.

8. Turn right, still on the BT, and exit the park onto Wilson Mills Rd. (3.5 miles).

9. Turn left onto Wilson Mills Rd. and left again onto Chagrin River Rd., leaving the BT at this point where it continues south.

10. CAUTION: Chagrin River Rd. is an extremely busy, winding, hilly road with very fast traffic. Please use considerable care. Cross it, then walk north and turn right on Riverview Rd. Follow Riverview as it loops close to the Chagrin River.

11. Reaching Chagrin River Rd. again, turn right (north) and continue along the grassy berm back to the Rogers Rd. parking area.

31 NORTH CHAGRIN RESERVATION
Buttermilk Falls Loop

This beautiful forest walk is located in popular North Chagrin Reservation, a park with many enjoyable trails. This loop hike goes through the northern part of the reservation and entails some hill climbing. Be sure to visit Sanctuary Marsh Nature Center, with its library, EarthWords book and gift shop, and many nature exhibits. Naturalists are on duty daily to assist the hiker with information, maps and brochures.

Distance: 4 miles

Hiking time: 2 hours

Description: This loop hike will show the deep ravines for which North Chagrin Reservation is noted, pretty Buttermilk Falls, and Squire's Castle. The terrain is hilly.

Directions: From I-271, exit at Wilson Mills Rd. Follow Wilson Mills east to S.O.M. Center Rd. Turn left (north) on S.O.M. Center Rd. Turn right (east) at the park entrance on Sunset Ln., then right on Buttermilk Falls Pkwy. and follow the signs to Sanctuary Marsh Nature Center.

Parking & restrooms: At Sanctuary Marsh Nature Center

1. From the Sanctuary Marsh Nature Center, cross the marsh on the boardwalk. Follow the blue signs depicting a waterfall for the Buttermilk Falls Loop Trail.

2. This trail will emerge onto Buttermilk Falls Pkwy. Nearby on the left is a wooden platform from which to view Buttermilk Falls.

3. Turn left onto the parkway and cross the bridge over the ravine. Continue on the parkway a short distance to the Hemlock Trail, identified by a yellow hiker sign. Turn right onto this trail. Note the big, old hemlock trees here, an indication of the cool climate of this ravine.

Map 31: North Chagrin Reservation: Buttermilk Falls Loop

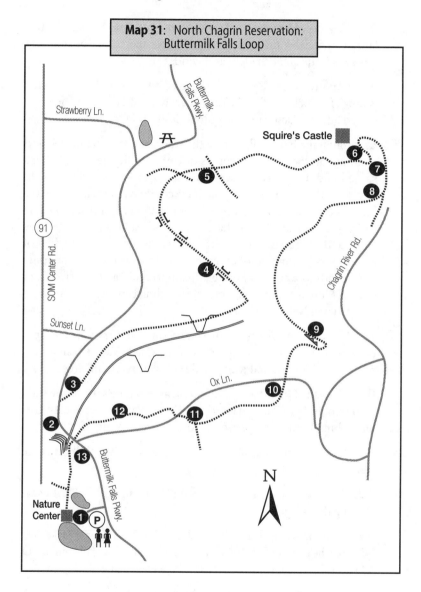

4. The yellow Hemlock trail provides many scenic views of the two largest ravines in the park. It soon leaves the ravine behind and crosses several small bridges as it winds north.

5. Near Strawberry Picnic Area, cross the bridle trail and soon the yellow Hemlock Trail ends. Turn sharply right and enter the blue-blazed Squire's Lane Trail to Squire's Castle.

6. Still on the blue trail, go past the wooden railing on the left and continue on the trail as it curves downhill to Squire's Castle. This stone building was constructed in the 1890s by Englishman F. B. Squire as the gatehouse to a planned country estate that he never built. Squire and his family used it as a summer residence to enjoy the 525 acres of land he purchased. The land was acquired in 1925 by Cleveland Metroparks for North Chagrin Reservation. Stripped of all its doors, fixtures, floors, windows, and furnishings, the building now stands as a shell of Squire's dream to build a grand riverfront estate. (More information about the building can be found at Sanctuary Marsh Nature Center.)

7. Continue east down the driveway to reach a trail on the right crossing over a stone bridge. This is the Castle Valley Trail and is marked with occasional white castle signs affixed to the trees.

8. Follow the Castle Valley Trail south as it parallels the bridle trail, below on the left. The path goes past River Grove Winter Sports Area and cabins, both on the left, and crosses several bridges.

9. The trail turns sharply right and goes steeply uphill on some steps.

10. Cross Ox Lane and continue on the Castle Valley Trail overlooking the ravines.

11. Bear right and leave the Castle Valley Trail near a large tree lying on the ground, just before a bridge. Follow this trail spur about 40 yards then turn right (north) on the wider Bridle Trail.

12. Cross Ox Ln. and follow the bridle trail west on the north side of Ox Lane until it reaches Buttermilk Falls.

13. Return to Sanctuary Marsh Nature Center along the same blue-blazed Buttermilk Falls Loop Trail.

32 SOUTH CHAGRIN RESERVATION
Buckeye Trail Loop

South Chagrin Reservation is located in Bentleyville, Solon, and Moreland Hills. This lovely, heavily-wooded park was enlarged in the 1960s when Cleveland Metroparks purchased property north of Cannon Rd. formerly belonging to a Boy Scout camp. On the east side of South Chagrin Reservation is the Chagrin River, designated a National Scenic River in 1979. Prominent in the sheer cliff walls of the river are layers of shale, deposited as silt and hardened into rock by the great inland sea covering this area 350–400 million years ago. At the river's west edge is Squaw Rock, faced with carvings by Chagrin Falls sculptor Henry Church.

Distance: 5 miles

Walking time: 2 ½ to 3 hours

Description: This strenuous, hilly hike takes a loop within the park, mostly on the blue-blazed Buckeye Trail. It offers a variety of terrain, from paths in deep woods, to a flat rim trail overlooking the Chagrin River, to the wide Bridle Trail that follows the contours of the hills.

Directions: From I-271 take Chagrin Blvd./Beachwood exit. Go east on Chagrin. Turn right (south) on S.O.M. Center Rd. (Rte. 91). Turn left (east) on Miles Rd., go one mile and turn right at the sign for Look About Lodge.

Parking & restrooms: At Look About Lodge parking area

The forest in this reservation contains many beautiful maples, oaks, hemlocks, hickories, and beech trees, and abundant wildflowers. The park is used more frequently by horseback riders than by hikers because of the large number of horse owners in this area. Part of the path is a designated bridle trail.

Look About Lodge, where this hike starts, was once operated by the Cleveland Natural Science Club. The lodge was built in 1938 by the club to resemble Old Faithful Lodge in Yellowstone National

Map 32: South Chagrin Reservation:
Buckeye Trail Loop

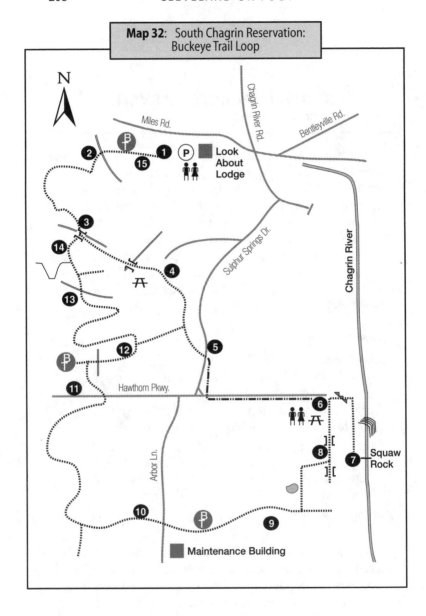

Park. It contains stone fireplaces, chestnut furniture, and cast iron sconces and chandeliers. It is now a unit of Cleveland Metroparks and has been renovated for use as a nature center.

1. Start the hike behind the lodge, following the blue Buckeye Trail tree blazes going west. After entering the woods, soon pass an old chimney and fireplace structure. The trail follows a natural ravine above a quiet tributary of Sulphur Springs stream below on the left.

2. The Buckeye Trail soon gradually descends, crosses a stream, and joins the gravel Bridle Trail, bordered by an old stone wall (0.4 mile). This trail was formerly a vehicular road extending throughout South Chagrin Reservation.

> CAUTION: If you meet horses on any portion of the Bridle Trail, please step to the side and remain still until they have passed, so as not to alarm these somewhat skittish animals.

3. Turn left (east) onto the Bridle Trail and follow it downhill until it reaches an old stone bridge (1.0 mile). At the sign saying "No Horses in This Area," bear left, staying on the Buckeye Trail. (The Bridle Trail continues to the right and will be followed later on during the return portion of this hike.)

4. Cross the bridge to Sulphur Springs Picnic Area, pass restrooms, and enter the picnic shelter. Follow the Buckeye Trail as it continues south of the shelter. Keep to the left at several intersections along this cool, moist trail. At a T-junction, turn left uphill, still following blue blazes.

5. Cross Sulphur Springs Rd. to the paved All-Purpose Trail and turn right (south). Pass a triangular traffic intersection on the right and cross Hawthorn Pkwy. Turn left and follow the paved walkway to Squaw Rock Picnic Area on the right (1.8 miles).

6. Squaw Rock Picnic Area contains picnic tables, a small shelter, a playing area, and restrooms. At the east end of the parking lot is a path leading down stone stairs to scenic Chagrin River.

7. An optional detour is to descend these steps, noting the very pretty waterfall on the left as you go down. Continue along the riverside trail to Squaw Rock, carved in 1885 by Henry Church, a blacksmith and artist from Chagrin Falls.

The significance of the figures carved on the glacial boulder has never been adequately explained. They are a Native American woman surrounded by a quiver of arrows, serpent, panther, skeleton, eagle, shield, and papoose. On the opposite side are an uncompleted log cabin and the Capitol building in Washington, D.C. The Berea Sandstone rock was reinforced with a concrete base to prevent erosion.

Because the stone steps at the south end of this trail have been closed for safety reasons, retrace your steps to ascend the cliff the same way as before.

8. At the top of the steps turn south and enter the cliff-top trail just past the Squaw Rock Trail sign. This wide dirt pathway high above the river still follows the blue tree blazes. Cross a bridge and, just before a second bridge, turn right (west) (2.0 miles).

The trail bends to the left and goes past a pretty woodland pond on the right. Go past the pond, which often attracts playful waterfowl, and at the trail intersection turn right (west).

9. Follow an old gravel road through mixed woods, passing picnic tables on the left. This is the location of the old Boy Scout camp, on land that Cleveland Metroparks added to South Chagrin in the 1960s. Follow the woods road until you reach the service area for the park. There are several maintenance buildings on the left.

10. Cross Arbor Lane and again enter the Bridle Trail, still following the blue Buckeye Trail blazes (2.6 miles). At a trail intersection bear right, staying on the Bridle/Buckeye Trail.

11. At about 3.1 miles you will reach Hawthorn Pkwy. again. Cross it to continue on the Bridle/Buckeye Trail going north. When you reach a wide trail intersection, turn right (east), still following the Bridle Trail, leaving the Buckeye Trail behind as it continues west.

12. Cross a stream on rocks and meet another major trail intersection. Here turn left going uphill (northwest) on the wide gravel trail. This trail winds up and down through deep, quiet woods. Soon pass an old stone wall on the left and follow the trail around a U-turn.

13. At about 3.7 miles you will cross a stream and go uphill. Another old stone wall is on the right, built many years ago when vehicles traveled on this carriage road through the park. Reach another trail intersection and keep to the left. A deep ravine appears on the left.

14. Cross the bridge (4.1 miles). You are now at the same point described in note #3, and will follow the blue Buckeye Trail in reverse. The road goes steeply uphill on yet another ridge. Turn right on the Buckeye Trail when it leaves the road at the foot of a slope and crosses the same stream described in note #2 (4.6 miles).

15. Retrace your steps along the Buckeye Trail until it reaches Look About Lodge and the parking area.

33 BEDFORD RESERVATION
Buckeye Trail from Egbert

Bedford Reservation contains 2,154 acres of land through which Tinker's Creek flows. The creek has cut a deep and spectacular gorge through the park, which has been designated a National Natural Landmark. Numerous trees, flowers, ferns—and often deer—provide enjoyment to hikers in Bedford.

Distance: 5 ½ miles

Hiking time: 2 ½ to 3 hours

Description: This hike on the Buckeye Trail will take you to Tinker's Creek Gorge, a National Natural Landmark. The view from the scenic overlook is particularly impressive during fall foliage season. The terrain undulates up and down small hills.

Directions: From I-271 take Broadway north to Union St.; from I-480 take Broadway south to Union St. Take Union St. to Egbert Rd. and Egbert to the Cleveland Metroparks entrance on Gorge Pkwy.

Parking & restrooms: At Egbert Picnic Area on the north side of Gorge Pkwy. just past the park entrance

NOTE: Watch for sharp turns on the Buckeye Trail. The blue BT blazes are sometimes far apart but generally follow the Bridle Trail.

1. Start the hike from the Egbert Picnic Area. Pick up the Buckeye Trail (BT) behind and to the left of the restrooms. Follow it along the fence and down the ridge overlooking the beautiful gorge of Tinker's Creek.

2. At 0.2 mile, leave the main trail on BT, turn sharply left, and join the graveled Bridle Trail.

3. The BT crosses the paved All-Purpose Trail and Gorge Pkwy. at 0.6 mile and passes Shawnee Hills Golf Course on the left (south).

Map 33: Bedford Reservation:
Buckeye Trail from Egbert

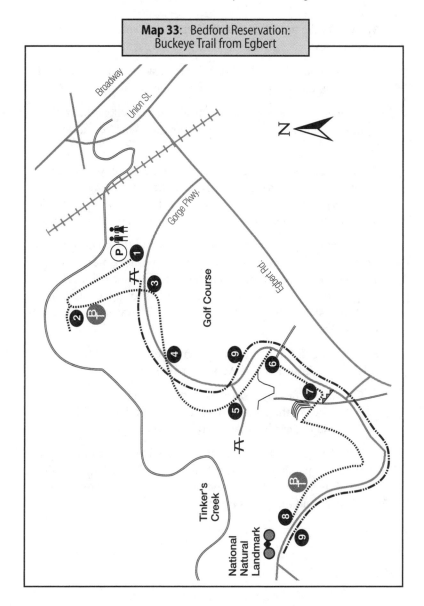

4. At 1.0 mile the BT recrosses Gorge Pkwy. and enters the woods heading west.

5. Cross a paved road leading to Lost Meadows Picnic Area at 1.3 miles. Soon the trail parallels a deep ravine on the right.

6. Reach Gorge Pkwy. again (1.6 miles), and follow the trail as it bears right and reenters the woods above a small stream, Deer Lick Creek.

7. The BT crosses a creek at 2.0 miles on a small wooden arched bridge. On the left is a set of stairs descending from Gorge Pkwy. Follow the sign on the right to the overlook for a scenic view of Bridal Veil Falls. BT leads uphill and continues west on the Bridle Trail.

8. Reach Gorge Pkwy. again at 3.0 miles and the scenic overlook. This National Natural Landmark presents a panoramic view of deep Tinker's Creek Gorge, breathtaking in any season. Tinker's Creek drops 90 feet over its two-mile course, and its gorge has depths ranging from 140 to 190 feet as the creek wends its way to the Cuyahoga River to the west.

9. Leave the BT at this point and cross Gorge Pkwy. to the paved All-Purpose Trail, marked Walk/Bike Trail.

CAUTION: Be careful to walk to the left on the paved trail as it is part of the 20-mile Bedford to Akron Bike and Hike Trail and fast cyclists may be traveling on it to the right.

Turn left (east) on the All-Purpose Trail to return to the Egbert Picnic Area, passing the Bridal Veil Falls parking area, traversing a graceful steel-arched bridge, and passing the road to Lost Meadows Picnic Area and the fitness trail.

34 BEDFORD RESERVATION
Buckeye Trail from Sagamore Grove

This Buckeye Trail hike offers another route to Bedford Reservation's National Natural Landmark scenic overlook onto Tinker's Creek Gorge, and an opportunity to see additional areas of Bedford Reservation and the Cuyahoga Valley National Recreation Area. The trail starts off with a steep climb, then follows a flat plateau above the scenic Sagamore Creek valley, gradually climbing until it reaches Egbert Rd., Overlook Lane, and Tinker's Creek Gorge National Natural Landmark.

Distance: 6 miles

Hiking time: 3 hours

Description: The trail is almost entirely in beautiful, quiet woods on the blue-blazed Buckeye Trail. The terrain is moderately hilly.

Directions: From I-271/480, take Alexander Rd. west; from I-77 take E. Pleasant Valley Rd. east until it becomes Alexander Rd. From Alexander Rd. take Canal Rd. south to Sagamore Rd. Turn left (east) on Sagamore and follow it to the Sagamore Grove Picnic Area. From I-77, take the Rockside Rd. exit. Go east on Rockside to Canal Rd., then south on Canal to Sagamore Rd. Turn left (east) on Sagamore to the Sagamore Grove Picnic Area, only a short distance on the left.

Parking & restrooms: At Sagamore Grove Picnic Area

1. From Sagamore Grove Picnic Area walk east with great care along the left side of Sagamore Rd.

CAUTION: Watch carefully for fast traffic on this short stretch of very narrow, winding road.

Very soon pick up the Buckeye Trail (BT) blue blazes on the left side of the road where it turns sharply into the woods just before the road goes uphill. This tree blaze may be obscured by foliage.

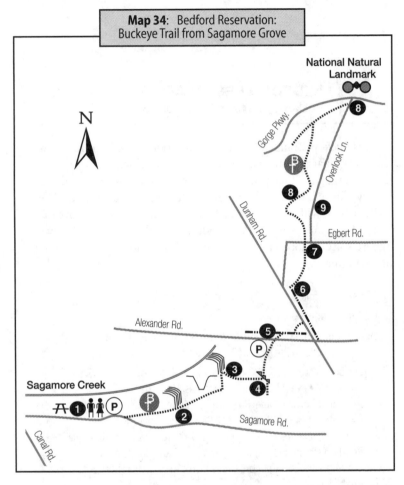

Map 34: Bedford Reservation:
Buckeye Trail from Sagamore Grove

2. Climb steeply to the top of the plateau. At about 0.7 mile on the left is a very pretty waterfall with multiple rock layers exposed. This stream flows down to Sagamore Creek far below. It can be seen only if there is no foliage obscuring the view.

3. At 1.4 miles is another, smaller waterfall and a deep ravine on the left.

4. Reach a set of steep stone steps that lead up to an old railroad bed, which is part of the 20-mile Bedford to Akron Bike and Hike Trail. Turn left (north) at the top of the steps and follow this flat trail to Alexander Rd. and a parking area on the left.

5. At 1.7 miles, cross Alexander Rd. to the paved All-Purpose Trail and turn right (east). After 300 feet, leave the All-Purpose Trail and turn left into woods, now following the BT. Cross Dunham Rd. and bear left (northwest) joining the All-Purpose Trail.

6. At 2.5 miles, just before Egbert Rd., follow the BT as it makes a sharp right turn (east) on a wide trail leading to Egbert Rd. and Overlook Ln.

7. Cross Egbert Rd. Continue north on BT parallel to Overlook Ln.

8. Follow the BT blue blazes past an abandoned quarry to Gorge Pkwy. and the National Natural Landmark, Tinker's Creek Gorge (3 miles).

9. Return south along Overlook Lane to Egbert Rd. and enter the BT at the same place described in note #7. Follow the BT in reverse past Dunham Rd. and Alexander Rd., then take the Bike and Hike trail south to the stone steps. Descend the stairs and retrace the BT along the top of the ravine above Sagamore Creek to Sagamore Rd. and back to Sagamore Grove Picnic Area.

35 HINCKLEY RESERVATION
Whipp's Ledges

Hinckley Reservation surrounds 90-acre Hinckley Lake, into which the east branch of the Rocky River flows. The river was dammed in 1926 to form this beautiful lake. Hinckley is the only reservation of Cleveland Metroparks completely outside Cuyahoga County. In it are Whipp's Ledges and Worden's Ledges formed many millions of years ago.

Distance: 5 miles

Hiking time: 2 ½ hours

Description: This hike, partly on the blue-blazed Buckeye Trail along Hinckley lake, goes to Whipp's Ledges and returns along the east side of the lake to complete a loop. There is one steep hill to climb.

Directions: From I-271 exit at Ridge Rd. (Rte. 94). Go north on Ridge Rd. to Hinckley Hills Rd. (Rte. 606). Turn right (east) on Hinckley Hills Rd. to Bellus Rd., then turn right (east) on Bellus Rd. Turn right (south) on West Dr., entering the Reservation, and follow West Dr. 3/4 mile to a sign indicating Johnson's Picnic Area.

Parking & restrooms: At Johnson's Picnic Area go to the second (farthest) parking area where the road dead-ends.

The Worden Heritage Homestead, managed by the Hinckley Historical Society, is on the north side of Ledge Rd. between State and Kellogg roads. Here you will find interesting information about the history of Hinckley Reservation. In the homestead once lived Noble Stuart, the son-in-law of Hiram Worden, after whom the ledges were named. Stone carvings at Worden's Ledges were made by Stuart sometime in the 1940s. They can be seen by taking a trail from the barn located west of the homestead. A map showing how to get to the carvings, a ten-minute walk, is posted on the homestead's garage. (See Chapter 22.)

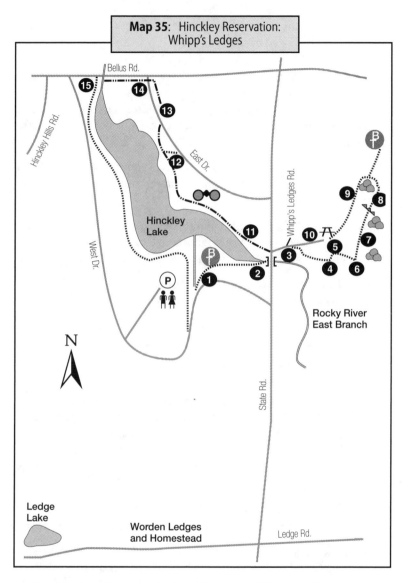

Map 35: Hinckley Reservation: Whipp's Ledges

Bellus Rd.

Hinckley Hills Rd.

East Dr.

Whipp's Ledges Rd.

Hinckley Lake

West Dr.

P

N

Rocky River East Branch

State Rd.

Ledge Lake

Worden Ledges and Homestead

Ledge Rd.

Hinckley is well known for its celebration of the annual return of the buzzards, or turkey vultures, from the southern U.S. around the middle of March. They find the open fields, rocky ledges and cliffs, and abundant food ideal for egg-laying and nesting. In the spring and summer the buzzards can be seen soaring on the rising warm air thermals created by the open fields.

1. Start the hike at Johnson's Picnic Area by finding the blue-blazed Buckeye Trail (BT) heading north on the uphill gravel path just beyond the last parking area. The blue blazes are on the tall trees. The creek will be below on the left. Nice outlooks of Hinckley Lake come into view along this route.

2. Turn left on State Rd. at about 0.7 mile and continue on the road across the Rocky River East Branch on the sturdy pedestrian/bicycle bridge.

3. Cross State Rd. and enter Whipp's Ledges Road leading to a picnic area. Immediately to the right the BT turns east from the road alongside a small creek, a tributary of the Rocky River East Branch.

4. The BT continues through a wet area, past the Rocky River East Branch on the right, then goes into the woods and uphill.

5. At 1.2 miles reach a stone restroom at Whipp's Ledges picnic and parking area. The BT turns right then continues straight ahead uphill.

6. Still following BT blue blazes, start a very steep uphill climb to the foot of the moss-covered ledges, more than 350 million years old. The BT turns left directly under the pock-marked Sharon conglomerate sandstone. These magnificent rock formations rise about 350 feet above the level of Hinckley Lake. The small shiny quartz pebbles that you see embedded in the sandstone once rolled along the shores of a great inland sea that covered Ohio.

7. Hike past small caves and huge boulders, still following BT blazes. At 1.5 miles climb a flight of stone steps between two ledges.

8. Hike along the top of the ledges to a trail intersection. Turn left (leaving the BT at this point) and carefully descend a rocky path on the left between a large split boulder.

9. Reach the trail under the ledges again and turn right onto a path that descends to Whipp's Ledges Picnic Area (2.0 miles).

10. At the picnic area walk down Whipp's Ledges Rd. to State Rd.

Cross the road and, without crossing the bridge again, enter the All Purpose Trail going north alongside Hinckley Lake.

11. Fine views of the lake are enjoyed all along this pleasant, well-maintained walkway.

12. At 3.5 miles, continue straight ahead past an intersection with another trail joining from the right. Follow the path as it soon curves upward to East Dr.

13. Cross East Dr. continuing on the paved All-Purpose Trail, following it left (north) as it leads along the road past Hinckley Lake Bathhouse to Bellus Rd. (3.75 miles).

14. Recross East Dr. to continue on the All-Purpose Trail past the swimming area and spillway on the left.

15. After a short distance, leave the All Purpose Trail to turn left (south) at the top of the spillway and follow a dirt trail downhill adjacent to the lake.

Continue along this lakeside trail to the boat launch area and return to Johnson's Picnic Area.

36 VIRGINIA KENDALL PARK
Ritchie Ledges and Pine Grove Loop

Virginia Kendall Park, one of the first operational units within Cuyahoga Valley National Recreation Area (CVNRA), contains the Happy Days Visitor Center—now operated by the National Park Service. The structure was originally built by the Civilian Conservation Corps (CCC) in the 1930s as a camp for inner-city children. Information and trail maps are available at the center from park rangers. It is open daily from 9 a.m.–5 p.m. (650-4636).

Distance: 4 ½ miles

Hiking time: 2 hours

Description: Ritchie Ledges and Sharon conglomerate rock will be seen on this hike, as well as beautiful hemlock and pine trees. The trail follows the contours of the land going downhill near the beginning, then steeply uphill at the end.

Directions: From I-271 or I-71, exit at Rte. 303 and go east to Peninsula, then right (south) on Akron-Peninsula Rd. to Truxell Rd., where there is a sign for Camp Manatoc. Turn left (east), passing Kendall Lake and Octagon Picnic Area before reaching a sign for Ledges Picnic Area on the left. Turn left (north) onto this road, which leads to a large picnic area with a shelter and playing fields.

Parking & restrooms: At Ledges Shelter

This section of the park features interesting geological formations called Ritchie Ledges that are similar to other ledges composed of Sharon conglomerate in northeast Ohio. About 350 million years ago this area was covered by a large shallow sea. The conglomerate rock took shape when fast-moving streams from the north and east carried sediment to the inland sea. It was compacted into a cement of sand and small quartz pebbles. You can see these small pebbles, which are round and smooth from the action of the ancient sea, as you walk by the ledges. The erosion-resistant ledges were shaped

Map 36: Virginia Kendall Park:
Ritchie Ledges & Pine Grove Loop

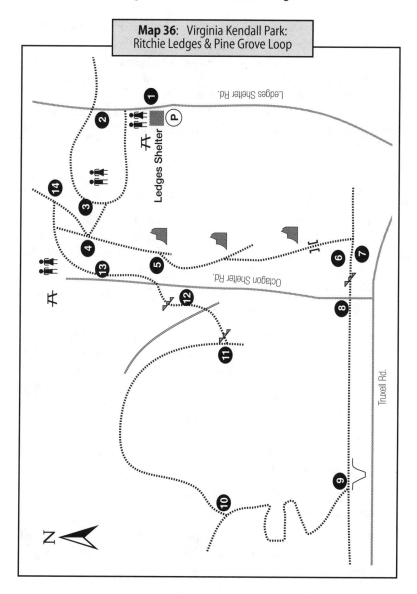

later by the action of an ancient river and still later by the work of the glaciers that covered Ohio.

Now at an elevation of 1,050 feet, the ledges continue to wear away very slowly. Ice Box Cave is the result of a fissure that occurred in the rock many thousands of years ago.

In addition to the hikes described below and in the following chapter, Virginia Kendall Park contains many more trails for hiking enjoyment.

1. Start the hike at the Ledges Shelter and walk north on the trail past the parking area on the left and past the sign marked "To Trails."

2. At the next intersection turn left at the display sign for Ritchie Ledges, and enter the West Ledges Trail, identified by a double-cross symbol. Walk past two brown wooden restroom buildings on the left and picnic tables on both sides of the trail.

3. Shortly this trail jogs to the left and to the right to descend on a steep rocky path, still on the West Ledges Trail, to the ledges area.

4. At the bottom bear left (south) between two enormous boulders to stay on the West Ledges Trail as it follows along under the Ritchie Ledges. Here note the above-mentioned 350-million-year-old Sharon conglomerate with its smooth, quartz "lucky stones" embedded in the rock. The powdery, sandy soil underfoot is a result of many years of erosion of this conglomerate rock that once was beach sand of the inland sea.

To the right and below are Octagon Shelter parking area and Octagon Shelter Rd.

5. At the next two intersections stay to the right, still hiking under spectacular Ritchie Ledges and still on the West Ledges Trail.

6. Cross a wooden bridge just before reaching Truxell Rd. The trail bears right and goes up a short incline at a sign pointing west to Kendall Lake.

7. At this sign turn right (west) and descend a set of wooden bar steps, now on the Pine Grove Trail.

8. At about 1.0 mile cross Octagon Shelter Rd. and enter the pine grove for which this trail is named. This cool, serene, red pine forest is a pleasure to enjoy in any season.

9. At an intersection, stay on Pine Grove Trail on the right. The trail bends away from the ravine on the left and makes several "S" turns as it winds through the forest following the contours of the land.

10. At the next trail intersection go toward the sign indicating Octagon Shelter (not Camp Manatoc) until a wooden stairway is reached (3.3 miles).

11. Turn left to descend the stairs and cross and recross the stream, Ritchie Run, three times on wooden bridges.

12. Ascend a long flight of stairs and reach Octagon Shelter Rd. Cross the road, still on the Pine Grove Trail.

13. At the large, roofed Octagon Shelter sign turn right (east), hiking uphill toward Ritchie Ledges again, completing the loop that was started here earlier.

14. Bear right to reach the top of the ledges and return along the trail straight ahead. On the right is the ball-playing field and the Ledges Shelter and parking area.

37 VIRGINIA KENDALL PARK
Ice Box Cave and Boston Run Trail

Virginia Kendall Park is a beautiful park with rolling hills, ledges, a lake, cross-country and hiking trails, and Happy Days Visitor Center. The center, located on Rte. 303 east of the town of Peninsula and west of Rte. 8, is open daily from 9 a.m.–5 p.m.

Distance: 5 miles

Hiking time: 3 hours

Description: This hike on wooded trails entails climbing several hills and passes Happy Days Visitor Center.

Directions: From I-271 or I-71, exit at Rte. 303 and go east to Peninsula, then right (south) on Akron-Peninsula Rd. to Truxell Rd., where there is a sign for Camp Manatoc. Turn left (east), passing Kendall Lake and Octagon Picnic Area before reaching a sign for Ledges Picnic Area on the left. Turn left (north) onto this road, which leads to a large picnic area with a shelter and playing fields.

Parking & restrooms: Available at the shelter

1. From Ledges Picnic Area walk north on the old roadbed past woodland picnic tables on the right. Turn right (east) at the first trail intersection.

2. Turn right at the sign for Ice Box Cave. The trail curves south along the top of the ledges and descends. At an intersection, turn north along the base of the ancient ledges.

3. Ice Box Cave is on the left. It is so called because it maintains a cool temperature during the hot summer in the depths of the overhanging rock. The trail crosses a wooden bridge and climbs a short flight of steps under the Sharon conglomerate rocks before reaching a Y-intersection.

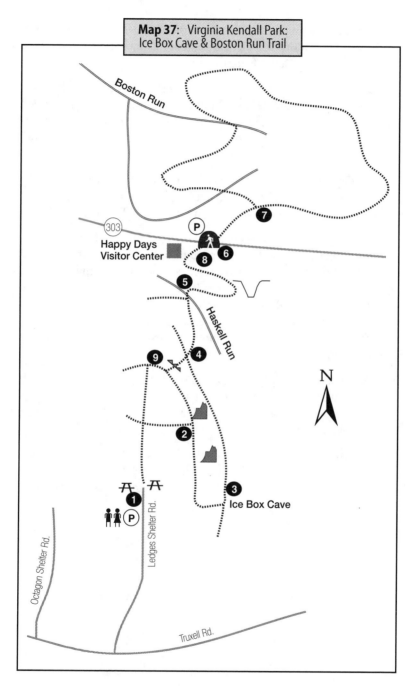

Map 37: Virginia Kendall Park:
Ice Box Cave & Boston Run Trail

Boston Run

303

P

**Happy Days
Visitor Center**

7

6
8

5

Haskell Run

9   **4**

N

2

3   Ice Box Cave

1

P

Ledges Shelter Rd.

Octagon Shelter Rd.

Truxell Rd.

4. After passing a flight of stone steps on the left (built by the Civilian Conservation Corps), bear right at this intersection and follow signs to Happy Days Visitor Center.

5. The trail descends and goes easterly, crossing a bridge over Haskell Run, and ascends the hill to the visitor center on a curved and numbered nature trail. Be sure to stop in at the Happy Days Visitor Center; its exhibits, trail information, and bookstore are well worth a visit.

6. Go east on the visitor center's driveway to a pedestrian underpass under Rte. 303 to a large parking area. There is a sign to the right (east) identifying the Boston Run Trail, a 3.5-mile loop.

7. The entrance to this loop trail is at the far end of the field. Pass the trail exit sign on the left. Continue to the trail entrance sign and enter the wide trail, which traverses small rolling hills and is a favorite for cross-country skiers. It can be muddy in places, because it crosses Boston Run creek several times (though recent trail reconstruction by members of the Sierra Club has improved the path). With one steep climb at the end, this pleasant loop will take about 1 1/4 hours.

8. Back at the Happy Days parking area, retrace your steps through the pedestrian underpass to Happy Days Visitor Center. Follow signs posted here for Ledges Trail and Ledges Shelter, on the same trail, which returns you across Haskell Run back to the ledges.

9. After reaching the ledges, take the flight of stone steps on the right, which were passed earlier (see note #4). Climb these steps to the top of the ledges, turn left, and follow signs to Ledges Shelter.

38 EVERETT COVERED BRIDGE

This hike in the hills and valley of the Cuyahoga River is moderately strenuous but rewarding for its beauty in any season. You will pass four scenic woodland ponds on this hike. The historic Everett Covered Bridge, the last remaining bridge of this kind in the area, was restored by the National Park Service in 1986 after a storm flood in 1975 surged down Furnace Run and washed out the original structure. It is closed to all vehicular traffic; however, hikers, skiers, bicyclists, and horseback riders may cross it. The old buildings on Everett Rd. (formerly the village of Everett) will eventually be restored by the CVNRA for educational use.

Distance: 5.8 miles

Hiking time: 3 hours

Description: This very scenic hike is almost entirely on trails. After a climb on log steps up a very steep trail, the path leads to the Cuyahoga Valley Environmental Education Center (CVEEC). The hike passes several pretty ponds, then descends to the valley floor again and returns to the parking area via the old Ohio & Erie Canal Towpath (Buckeye Trail).

Directions: From I-77, take exit 143, and turn left (east) on Wheatley Rd. (Rte. 176). Continue on Wheatley to the Everett Covered Bridge parking area on the right.

Parking & restrooms: At the Everett Covered Bridge Trailhead

Just south of here, on Bolantz Rd. at Riverview Rd., is Hunt Farm Visitor Information Center where there are exhibits and information.

Hale Farm and Village, operated by the Western Reserve Historical Society, is also south of here at 2686 Oak Hill Rd. in Bath, Ohio. It is open from June to the end of October and also on special dates. Hours are 10 a.m.–5 p.m. Wednesday through Saturday and noon--

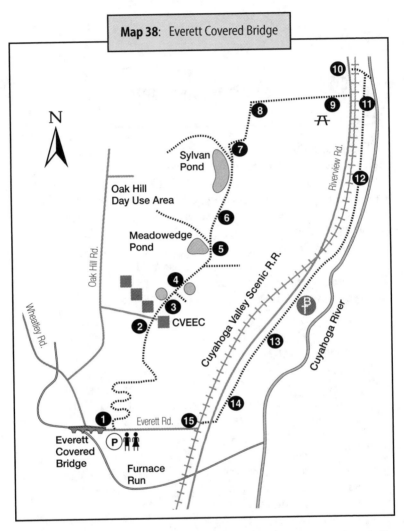

Map 38: Everett Covered Bridge

5 p.m. on Sundays. Call 800-468-4070 or 657-2000 (Akron) for information.

1. Start the hike across Everett Rd. from the parking lot at the trail sign barring horses. Climb steeply to the top on switchbacks and follow the broad path 0.8 mile through open areas and a white pine forest to the entrance road on the campus of CVEEC.

2. This 500-acre center, jointly operated by the Cuyahoga Valley Association and the National Park Service, opened in 1994 and offers a curriculum for school children, who live on campus for a week. Up to 90 students and their teachers participate each week in a multidisciplinary curriculum on ecology and the environment. The Administration Building, the dark brown building in the center of the campus, has information and brochures.

3. Behind the barn south of the Administration Building is a path leading northeast to a small pond on the left. Follow this trail to a fork and bear left, continuing eastward.

4. On the right is another larger pond with a picnic table. Both of these ponds are used for student education. Go to the left around the pond and cross a wooden footbridge at its east end. Stay to the left at the first trail intersection. The main trail proceeds north through pine woods.

5. Reach large Meadowedge Pond on the left. Go around the pond on the earthen dam to the signs that indicate Meadowedge Pond and Sylvan Pond. Take the trail on the right pointing toward Sylvan Pond. (The trail on the left is part of the loop trail returning to the Oak Hill Day Use Area on Oak Hill Rd.)

6. At about 1.6 miles on the Sylvan Pond Trail cross a wooden footbridge.

7. Reach Sylvan Pond at about 2.0 miles. Cross the earthen dam and turn down to the right to find a trail on the left entering the woods. (The trail on the upper left is another part of the loop trail returning to the Oak Hill Day Use Area.)

8. Hike along the lower trail about 0.3 mile to reach a fence on the left. Turn right to take the old woods road eastward downhill.

9. The downhill trail ends at Valley Picnic Area just before Riverview Rd. (2.8 miles).

10. Go north on Riverview Rd. 0.1 mile and cross it to a path that leads across the railroad tracks.

CAUTION! Watch carefully: this is an active railway of the Cuyahoga Valley Scenic Railroad (CVSR). Many trains pass here, especially in the summer months. (For information about the CVSR call 800-468-4070.)

11. Straight ahead is the Canal Towpath/Buckeye Trail. Turn right and hike south on this trail, which parallels the overgrown and partially unwatered historic Ohio & Erie Canal on the right.

12. Soon a beautiful sweeping view of the Cuyahoga River appears on the left where the meandering river comes near the canal.

13. At 4.5 miles note the series of large cornfields planted on the left (east) in the fertile river bottomland. Birds frequently inhabit this part of the valley.

14. At 4.9 miles there are several houses to the right, on Riverview Rd. Here is Johnnycake Lock 27 (27 miles from Cleveland), with its ancient iron fastening for the water gate at the end of the lock. A signboard explains the origin of the name Johnnycake Lock: a blockage of the canal by silt entering from nearby Furnace Run caused barges to be held up for several days until the obstruction could be cleared; neighbors then fed passengers with johnnycakes during the interim.

15. Turn right on the driveway, cross Riverview Rd. and the railroad tracks.

CAUTION! Watch carefully for trains and traffic.

Return along Everett Rd. to the covered bridge parking area, noting on the right several residences, a store, and a barn that the CVNRA will eventually restore.

39 PUNDERSON STATE PARK
Stump Lake

Punderson State Park encompasses 996 acres and contains several glacier-formed lakes and a variety of recreational facilities and accommodations, including a golf course, trails, a small beach, camping area, cabins, tennis courts, a pool, and a lodge with a dining room. The park is open all year and in winter maintains a winter sports chalet for skiing, sledding, tobogganing, skating, and snowmobile riding. This hike will take you on trails to three of the park's lakes that can be enjoyed in any season except winter, when snowmobiles are in use.

Distance: 4.2 miles

Hiking time: 2 hours

Description: This hike is over rolling terrain, primarily on trails with views of three lakes.

Directions: From I-271, take Rte. 87 east past the town of Newbury to Punderson State Park entrance on the right. Follow park road signs to the lodge.

Parking & restrooms: Parking lot is adjacent to the lodge and restrooms are inside the lodge.

1. Start the hike by descending the slope to the left (north) behind the lodge. There is a nice view of Punderson Lake ahead. About 12,000 years ago, as the last glacier retreated from Ohio, the melting of the massive ice sheet left depressions called kettles. This springfed lake and the others in the park are the result of this kettle-forming process. Punderson Lake, at 90 acres, is the largest glacial lake in Ohio. The trail begins at the Nature Trail sign and leads downhill on a wide path.

2. Keeping Punderson Lake on your right (east), continue north along this trail until at 0.3 mile you reach a Nature Trail sign that points to the left. Continue straight past this sign to the sandy beach.

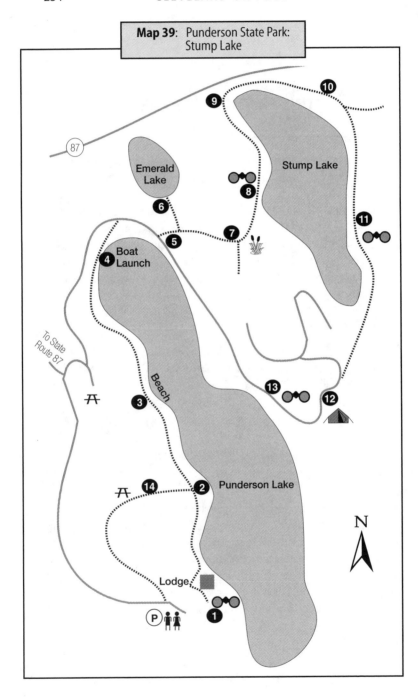

Map 39: Punderson State Park: Stump Lake

3. Walk north across the beach and reenter the trail at the far end, where a sign indicates the concession stand ahead.

4. Reach the boat launch/concession stand at 0.8 mile. Walk through the parking area and turn right onto the paved park road leading to the camping area.

5. After about 0.2 mile more on the left is the entrance to the snow-mobile trail.

6. Turn left to enter the snowmobile trail and very soon reach a fork. Take the left fork downhill a short distance to see the small, deep, glacier-formed Emerald Lake. The cars across the way are on Rte. 87. Retrace your steps on this short side trail and return to the main trail. Turn left (east) and continue along it.

7. At the next trail intersection (1.1 miles) continue straight on the main trail past a sign for a snowmobile area and campground to the right.

8. When the trail reaches a small marsh on the right, bear left onto a wide woods road and soon Stump Lake appears on the right. The reason for its name is evident from the numerous tree stumps peeking above water at its south end.

9. Keeping Stump Lake on the right, continue close to the shoreline toward Rte. 87. The trail squeezes between the highway and lake at its north end and continues around to the east shore of Stump Lake.

10. At 2.0 miles the trail veers away from the lake. At the next trail intersection, stay right, going toward the lake and hugging the shoreline.

11. The trail widens and becomes a more heavily trodden path as it approaches the campground area. Nice views of the lake appear and water birds such as the great blue heron are often seen feeding here.

12. The trail ends at a campground road where a sign identifies the path as the Erie Trail. Cross the road and walk past the check-in station to view Punderson Lake ahead. The lodge and sandy beach can be seen across the water (2.8 miles).

13. Take the park road north to the boat launch/concession area and return along the trail hiked earlier beside the lake past the beach, now on your left.

14. Just past the beach reach the Nature Trail intersection at 3.8 miles. Instead of returning along Punderson Lake as before, turn right on the gravel Nature Trail. Follow this loop trail uphill past picnic tables and a parking area on the right. Continue on this trail (Nature/Iroquois Trail) as it returns to the lodge parking area.

40 PUNDERSON STATE PARK
Pine Lake

Punderson State Park, described at the beginning of Chapter 38, offers a variety of outdoor recreational activities. The park is open all year and offers many opportunities for hiking and cross-country skiing. The trails, following gentle hills up and down, are well maintained and generally clearly marked.

Distance: 5 miles

Hiking time: 2 ½ hours

Description: This hike crosses rolling terrain on trails used primarily in winter for cross-country skiing but also immensely enjoyable in any season. The trail tends to be very muddy in the spring. The route skirts the golf course and affords a view of pretty Pine Lake in the westernmost part of the park. This loop hike starts and ends at the Lodge parking area.

Directions: From I-271 drive east on Rte. 87 past the town of Newbury to Punderson State Park entrance on the right. Follow park signs to the Lodge.

Parking & restrooms: Parking is adjacent to the Lodge and restrooms are inside the Lodge.

1. Begin the walk at the far west end of the lodge parking lot. There is a sign here indicating the Mohawk Cross-Country Ski Trail. The trail is wide and is marked with round orange tree blazes. After sloping gently down to cross a stream on a platform bridge, the trail then goes uphill to the right. (A left trail turn here, also with an orange tree blaze, goes out to the golf course). Shortly there is another trail intersection where you will stay to the right.

2. The trail goes gently up and down before it reaches a paved road leading into the golf course (0.5 mile). Cross this road to a trail marked with a sign showing a variety of cross-country ski trails.

Map 40: Punderson State Park:
Pine Lake

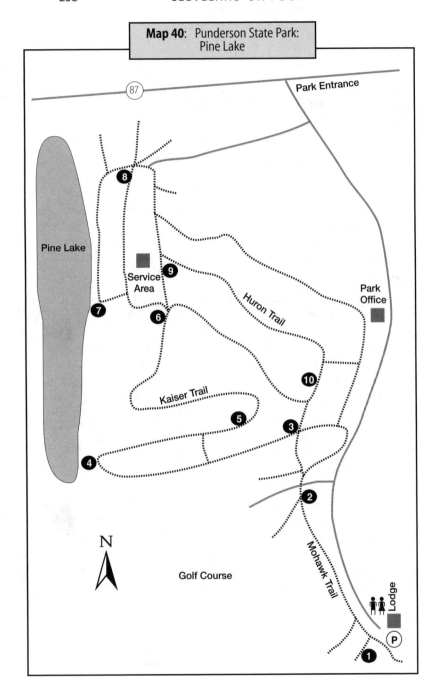

Take the trail on the left. Then, continue straight ahead on the main trail, avoiding side trails going off to the right or left.

3. Turn left at a sign for the Kaiser Permanente Cross-Country Ski Trail, marked with yellow tree blazes. The Kaiser Trail is a serpentine trail that nearly makes a loop, as you will discover on your return. Follow the path westward for pleasant hiking over gently rolling terrain, keeping the golf course to the left (south). These beautiful tall trees are beeches, oaks, maples, tulips, and shagbark hickories.

4. Just beyond the end of the golf course the trail reaches Pine Lake, which always attracts water birds and in summer is filled with water lilies. The trail bends around in a U-turn to head back east (1.5 miles).

5. Continue past a cross-over trail on the right and at about the 2.0-mile point on this hike, the now almost flat trail bends west again. Again, note the magnificent hardwood forest of maples and oaks. After another half-mile of hiking, the trail bends northeast.

6. At a trail junction, leave the Kaiser Trail (which goes off to the right) and take the trail to the left going toward the fence that surrounds the park service area. This area is where dog-sled races are held every winter in Punderson. Just before the fence itself, turn left on a trail that soon enters the woods on the left and goes toward the west. This trail is now marked with red tree blazes. Shortly there is another trail juncture where you will stay to the left on the westward bound path going toward Pine Lake.

7. At 3.0 miles reach Pine Lake and follow the pretty trail along its edge. There may be gulls, ducks, and geese as well as fishermen enjoying this attractive body of water. Midway is a rustic park bench overlooking the lake from which you can pause to rest and admire the view. The cars you hear and may see at the north end of the lake are on Rte. 87.

8. Continue along the lake until the trail bends around away from the water and goes uphill. At a wide juncture of four trails, take the trail farthest to the right (more of the dog-sled racing oval) and go south, keeping the park service building on the left (east).

9. The trail now goes around the park service area, past the Kaiser Trail taken earlier, and past a small snow fence on the right (3.5

miles). Very quickly the trail turns right (east) to enter the Huron Cross-Country Ski Trail, marked with blue tree blazes.

10. Continue on this trail with its gentle ups and downs, eventually past signs for the Kaiser Trail Exit and, shortly thereafter, the Kaiser Trail Entrance, both on the right. From here you will return on the trail taken at the beginning of the hike, but in reverse.

Reach the paved road leading to the golf course, cross it, and enter the Mohawk Ski Trail at the sign, and the trail is again marked with orange blazes. While following this path back to the lodge parking area, take care not to take any of the side trails to the right or left, but follow the main trail that roughly parallels the park road.

Section VII
Strenuous Trail Hikes

41

THREE WATERFALLS
Cuyahoga Valley National Recreation Area

This chapter and Chapters 42–45 describe strenuous hikes in Cuyahoga Valley National Recreation Area (CVNRA). These hikes explore a variety of scenic trails and are designated as strenuous because of the steep terrain found in this lovely green space between Cleveland and Akron. The hikes are also longer than the others in this book and usually require taking a pack with food and water. They are well worth the preparation and effort required to complete, however, and any of these hikes can be shortened by turning around at any point and retracing your steps to the beginning.

Distance: 9 ½ miles

Hiking time: 5 hours

Description: The hike is almost entirely on woods trails with several steep hills to climb. The Stanford Trail is well marked and descends into the valley to the paved Canal Towpath Trail. After crossing Riverview Rd., the blue-blazed Buckeye Trail is followed to Blue Hen Falls, and a side trail reaches Buttermilk Falls. On this last portion of the hike there are many varieties of wildflowers in the spring; bring a wildflower guide!

Directions: From I-271, exit at Rte. 8 and travel south to W. Highland Rd. Go west on W. Highland and at Old Route Eight turn right, go under the bridge, and immediately turn left, still on W. Highland Rd. Follow W. Highland west to Brandywine Rd. and turn left (south). Just past the Inn at Brandywine Falls on the right, cross over the bridge and turn right (west) onto Stanford Rd. On the left is the parking area for Brandywine Falls.
From I-77, take Rte. 82 east to Brandywine Rd. then turn right on Stanford Rd.

Parking & restrooms: Located in this parking area

Map 41: Three Waterfalls

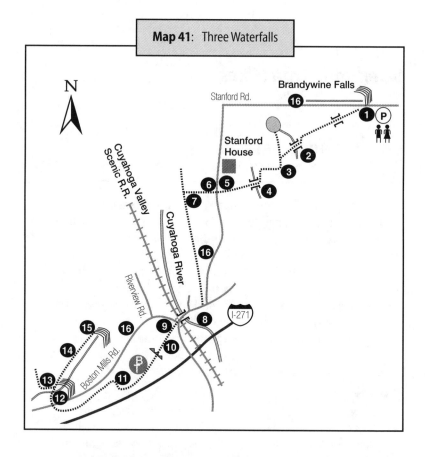

The three waterfalls that you will see on this strenuous hike are Brandywine Falls, Blue Hen Falls, and Buttermilk Falls. Brandywine Falls is a lovely scenic spot with a wooden walkway constructed to enable visitors to step down close to the foot of the falls. The old foundation of the mill once powered by this waterfall is at the far east end of the walkway. Today hardly anything remains of the village of Brandywine except the 1848 Wallace farmhouse, now used as a bed and breakfast, called The Inn at Brandywine Falls.

The second waterfall, Blue Hen Falls, is far across Cuyahoga Valley and, though not as high as Brandywine, is in a quiet woodland spot and easily accessible alternatively by car and a short hike. The third waterfall, Buttermilk Falls, is accessible only by hiking down a streamside trail from Blue Hen Falls.

1. After viewing 65-foot-high Brandywine Falls from the walkway, start the hike by walking along Stanford Rd. to the Stanford Trail entrance, identified by a small brown sign about 0.2 mile on the left.

2. The trail crosses a stream and a wooden bridge before climbing up a set of steps cut into the pathway.

3. At about 3/4 mile turn left at the intersection where a sign points toward the Stanford Hostel. (You may optionally take the short trail to the right to view a small, pretty woodland pond and return the same way to this point.)

4. Soon the trail bears right, winds up and down ridges, and crosses several bridges (1.2 miles).

5. Continue without making any turns, cross one final bridge, then note the large barn in the distance. The path follows a wide swath cut through a meadow to the Stanford House American Youth Hostel, open year-round from 5 p.m.–9 a.m. the following day. This 1843 building has been restored by volunteers and the National Park Service to become northeast Ohio's first youth hostel. The hostel contains 30 beds in two dormitories, common rooms, a large kitchen and dining room, and meeting rooms.

During much of the 19th century, members of the Stanford family included prosperous farmers, dairymen, lumberers, and influential citizens of the nearby town of Boston.

6. Go west across the hostel property to Stanford Rd. Just opposite the hostel's driveway, enter a trail heading west across a field.

7. At the end of this path turn left (south) onto the Towpath Trail, a wide gravel All-Purpose Trail (heavily used by bicyclists) that closely parallels the old Ohio & Erie Canal. Most of the canal to the left (east) of the towpath is overgrown with trees but portions of it can be identified. Farther along can be seen one of the remaining locks (Lock 32), once needed to elevate barges on their way to higher Akron, or to lower them on their way to Cleveland. Used until the great flood of 1913, the canal was watered through weir gates entering from the Cuyahoga River to the west. Often deer can be seen along this part of the canal towpath.

8. At about 2.3 miles reach Boston Mills Rd. and buildings of what once was the old mill town of Boston. One of the mill buildings remains adjacent to the unwatered canal on the south side of the road. Pick up the blue blazes of the Buckeye Trail on Boston Mills Rd. going west.

Cross the bridge over the Cuyahoga River and reach the tracks of the Cuyahoga Valley Scenic Railroad.

> CAUTION! A diesel train uses the tracks to carry passengers from a depot in Independence (near Cleveland) to Hale Farm and Village in the Cuyahoga Valley and to Quaker Square in Akron. (For information about train rides call 800-468-4070.)

9. Continue west across Riverview Rd. Near the southwest corner of Riverview and Boston Mills roads enter the Buckeye Trail at the sign. It ascends a steep hill on small trail switchbacks. The noise of cars you hear is from I-271 to the south.

10. At about 3.0 miles descend a flight of 87 wooden steps.

11. After crossing a wet area, ascend the hill to property belonging to the National Guard and occupied by a caretaker. Cross the property walking west and follow the hard-to-find blue blazes a short distance until the trail emerges onto Boston Mills Rd. (3.5 miles).

12. Cross the road and enter the short drive at the sign to the parking for Blue Hen Falls. The paved trail to the falls descends to a serene and cool open area.

13. Cross a footbridge over Spring Creek. Do not continue to follow BT (which continues uphill). Follow the wooden fence around to the view of Blue Hen Falls. Many layers of dark Bedford shale lie below the more erosion-resistant Berea sandstone cap that lies above this pretty waterfall.

To the northeast is a trail that parallels the stream. Follow it in a northeasterly direction keeping the stream on the right as it carves a ravine below.

14. Cross and recross the stream until it reaches a set of old stone and concrete walls that once supported a now-abandoned road over the brook. Indications of the old road can still be seen on the left. Bear right and cross the stream again, heading up a small embankment as you begin to hear the waterfall.

15. The top of Buttermilk Falls is straight ahead (4.5 miles). Go down to the foot of the falls by means of a trail to the right. This lovely, little-known site is one of the prettiest in our area and contains a 20-foot-high waterfall falling over Bedford shale. As in many areas of Ohio, the last glacier of about 12,000 years ago left this high waterfall overlooking the broad valley below.

Return along the same trail. Watch carefully for the route, because it looks different on the way back. Just above Buttermilk Falls, cross the stream and bear left at the intersection where the woods road is located. Keep the ravine and stream on the left and follow the trail back to Blue Hen Falls as before.

Continue on the Buckeye Trail going downhill at the National Guard property and across Boston Mills Rd., then continuing on the Towpath Trail to Stanford Hostel and the Stanford Trail to the Brandywine Falls parking area.

Optional:
16. For an optional route back from Blue Hen Falls, take Boston Mills Rd. east and downhill to Riverview Rd. Cross Riverview and the railroad tracks and bridge. Turn left at Stanford Rd. and follow the road back to Brandywine Falls.

42 JAITE TO BOSTON MILLS
Cuyahoga Valley National Recreation Area

This trail offers an exceptional variety of scenery, mixed forest of maples and oaks, a fine view of portions of Cuyahoga Valley, open fields, a murmuring brook, and a waterfall. On this hike you may wish to carry lunch and sit down on a mossy spot overlooking a brook for a most enjoyable hiking experience.

Distance: 8 miles

Hiking time: 4 hours

Description: This very rewarding hike on the blue-blazed Buckeye Trail includes a steep hill at the beginning, several more moderate hills, and one steep stairway near the end. The last 2 ½ miles are on the flat Canal Towpath Trail.

Directions: From I-271, exit at Rte. 8 and go south to W. Highland Rd. Turn right (west) on W. Highland to Old Route Eight and turn right. Go under the bridge and immediately turn left, again on W. Highland Rd. At the Summit County line (Cuyahoga River), W. Highland Rd. becomes Vaughn Rd. near Jaite. The small yellow buildings on the left, just past the Cuyahoga Valley Scenic Railroad tracks, comprise the National Park Service Headquarters for Cuyahoga Valley National Recreation Area (CVNRA).
From I-77, take Rte. 82 east to Riverview Rd. Turn right (south) on Riverview Rd. Turn left (east) on Vaughn, cross the railroad tracks, and the Jaite Wayside trailhead is on the left.

Parking: Parking is at Jaite Wayside on the north side of Vaughn Rd., east of the railroad tracks. There is no restroom here, although on weekdays accommodations are available at the CVNRA office.

1. Start at Jaite Wayside Trailhead across Vaughn Rd. just east of the small yellow park buildings. These quaint restored 1906 buildings of the old Jaite Mill Company are offices for CVNRA staff, who welcome visitors and can provide trail maps and information.

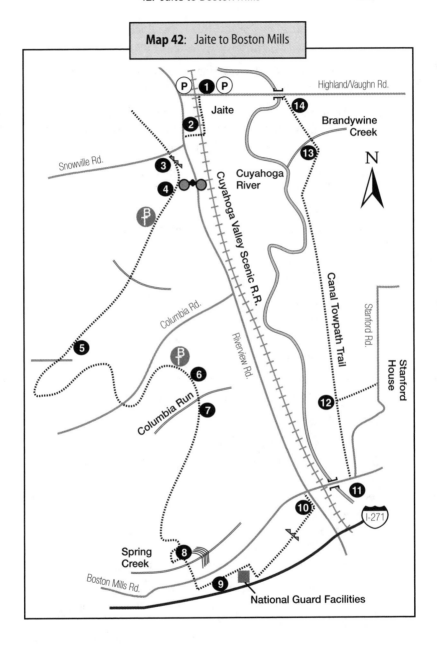

Map 42: Jaite to Boston Mills

2. After crossing Vaughn Rd., follow the Buckeye Trail (BT) signs across a field and across railroad tracks to emerge on Riverview Rd.

CAUTION: Be careful crossing these railroad tracks; they are in active use by the Cuyahoga Valley Scenic Railroad.

Cross Riverview Rd. and stay on the south side of Snowville Rd. Note the sign where the BT comes in from the north and joins the access trail at this point and continues south.

3. Turn left (south) and enter woods on the BT. Climb a set of steep stairs to the top of a ridge through a mixed forest of maples.

4. At 1.0 mile reach an open area with an underground pipeline. Bear left and pause for a lovely view of the Cuyahoga Valley to the east. Proceed south under the power line and along the power line access road lined with lovely oaks and dogwood trees. At 1.6 miles descend to a small creek.

5. At 2.0 miles the trail descends to a larger creek and, farther along, emerges onto Columbia Rd. (2.3 miles). Cross the road to a sign that indicates the distance to Boston Mills as 3.3 miles.

6. At 3.0 miles there is a beautiful mossy stream overlook, an ideal spot to rest under the tall hemlocks and contemplate the quiet sounds of nature—a true wilderness spot.

7. The BT crosses Columbia Run, a broad stream, and at 3.8 miles goes under another power line.

8. At 4.0 miles the trail reaches Spring Creek and Blue Hen Falls. It is worthwhile to go off the BT on the trail parallel to the fence for a short distance to view the falls, with its cap of Berea sandstone overhanging softer Bedford shale. Another option is to take a 1/2-mile trail eastward along the creek to Buttermilk Falls (see Chapter 41).

Cross the bridge over Blue Hen Falls and climb up to the parking area as the trail emerges onto Boston Mills Rd.

9. Cross Boston Mills Rd. at 4.2 miles and cross property owned by the National Guard. Near the caretaker's cabin watch for a sharp turn south. Ahead and on the right is I-271. Pass a creek and ascend the 87-step wooden stairway built to protect the ridge from erosion.

10. The BT descends to the junction of Riverview and Boston Mills roads (5.4 miles).

Ahead is the old town of Boston and the Cuyahoga Valley Scenic Railroad Line tracks.

> CAUTION! Cross carefully: this is an active railroad and trains run frequently between Cleveland and Akron, especially in the spring, summer, and fall.

11. Turn right and proceed east on Boston Mills Rd. across the Cuyahoga River. Walk past the buildings on the right to the abandoned, unwatered canal running alongside the general store on the south side of Boston Mills Rd. (5.6 miles). At this point the BT continues south, but this hike turns north (left) onto the wide graveled Canal Towpath Trail. (The Stanford House Hostel is about a tenth of a mile up Stanford Rd., just north of this point.)

12. Follow the beautiful towpath north. Note the old church and cemetery on the left and, farther along, the interesting old canal lock on the right, Lock 32. The towpath was used by horses and mules that pulled the canal boats during the canal era of the 19th and early 20th centuries. Although somewhat overgrown, the old canal is still visible on the right. At about 6.1 miles the trail from the Stanford House American Youth Hostel enters on the right. Continue straight on the towpath. Deer are frequently seen along this stretch of the Towpath Trail.

13. At 7.0 miles on the left the trail passes the site of the old Jaite Paper Mill (1906) and passes over Brandywine Creek.

14. At 7.4 miles the trail reaches W. Highland/Vaughn Rd. Turn left (west) on W. Highland/Vaughn and follow the road across the Cuyahoga River at the sign indicating the Cuyahoga-Summit County line. At 8.0 miles complete the circuit hike at the Jaite Wayside parking area.

43 BRECKSVILLE RESERVATION
Buckeye Trail to Pinery Narrows

Brecksville Reservation is deeply cut by seven separate valleys and has many different trails throughout its beautiful forested land. Chippewa Creek, in the northern section of the park, cuts through a magnificent gorge formed by the retreat of the last glacier of 12,000 years ago. Within another scenic gorge is Deer Lick Cave, an unusual outcropping of rock formed many years ago. The Brecksville Nature Center on Chippewa Creek Dr. is a good place to stop in for a visit to learn more about the reservation and to obtain a hiking trail map.

Distance: 10 ½ miles

Hiking time: 5 hours

Description: This hike, entirely on the Buckeye Trail, begins at Oak Grove Picnic Area and descends the hill to a beautiful section of the Cuyahoga Valley National Recreation Area (CVNRA). Then the trail follows the flat Ohio and Erie Canal Towpath Trail through one of the most beautiful and scenic areas of northeast Ohio, called Pinery Narrows (although the pines are long since gone). Wildlife abounds here in the valley of the Cuyahoga River. This portion of the trail has recently been improved to accommodate bicycles, strollers, and wheelchairs on the paved pathway. It is best to stay to the left on the Canal Towpath, facing oncoming bicyclists.

Directions: From I-77, take Rte. 82 east to just past Brecksville Rd. (Rte. 21) in Brecksville. Turn right at the park entrance on Chippewa Creek Dr. Follow Chippewa Creek Dr. to Valley Pkwy. and turn right. Take Valley Pkwy. to the entrance for Oak Grove Picnic Area on the left.

Parking & restrooms: At Oak Grove Picnic Area

1. From Oak Grove Picnic Area go out the east exit of the driveway to Valley Pkwy. and find the blue blazes of the Buckeye Trail (BT) on the paved All-Purpose Trail on the south side of the road.

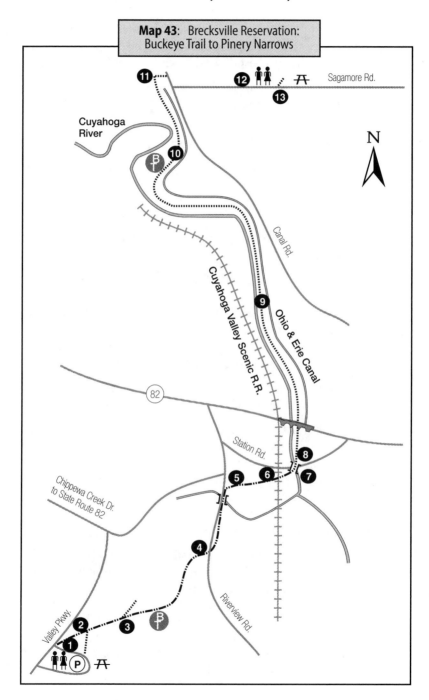

Map 43: Brecksville Reservation:
Buckeye Trail to Pinery Narrows

2. Follow the blazes into the woods. At the double blue tree blaze, turn right (east). The BT is also blazed along here with orange hiker signs. It goes through beautiful tall beech trees, maples, and oaks.

3. At 0.7 mile, the orange-hiker-blazed trail turns left; continue straight and down a steep hill on BT .

4. Turn left (north) on Riverview Rd., going a short distance on the road before crossing it to a blacktop All-Purpose Trail.

5. Follow the All-Purpose Trail east to the Station Rd. parking area.

6. Ahead are the railroad tracks of the Cuyahoga Valley Scenic Railroad.

CAUTION! Cross the tracks carefully: this is an active railroad line.

The recently rebuilt Station Rd. bridge spanning the Cuyahoga River is ahead.

Many years ago there was a railroad depot here and this was an important stop on the line between Cleveland and Akron. The tracks are now used for scenic train rides from Independence to Hale Farm and Village and Quaker Square in Akron.

7. Cross the bridge (closed to vehicles) and note the old wooden bricks used to pave the bridge surface (1.5 miles).

8. Continue east along the All-Purpose Trail and turn left (north) onto the Canal Towpath Trail. Bear left (toward the river) at the next intersection. Near the river are the remains of an old canal gate once used to regulate water levels from the river on the left to the canal feeder on the right. Overhead is the strikingly beautiful Rte. 82 bridge. Pinery Dam, a pretty spillway on the Cuyahoga River, often brings fishermen to try their luck at this spot.

9. The Canal Towpath/Buckeye Trail closely parallels the straight, shallow canal on the right and keeps the wider Cuyahoga River on the left, all through the valley. The river continues gently twisting for several miles through the attractive Pinery Narrows.

Stay to the left on this path to face oncoming bicycle traffic, which is fast-moving along here and usually stays to the right.

There may be deer, waterfowl, and evidence of beaver activity all along this enjoyable stretch of the Narrows.

10. At about 4.3 miles cars can be seen or heard on Canal Rd. to the east. Continue past another of the original waste weir gates and an overflow dam just beyond it.

11. Reach a wooden pedestrian bridge and turn right to cross it to busy Canal Rd. Turn right (south) on Canal Rd. and follow the BT blazes to Sagamore Rd.

12. Turn left (east) at Sagamore Rd. and follow the road to Sagamore Grove Picnic Area on the left, where there are restrooms and picnic tables (5.3 miles).

13. Return along the same trail, retracing your steps through the Narrows, and enjoy new views on the right. Cross the old Station Rd. bridge to the paved path and Riverview Rd.

Watch carefully for the blue blazes of the BT on the right (west) side of Riverview Rd. and ascend the hill to Oak Grove Picnic Area.

44 BRECKSVILLE RESERVATION
Buckeye Trail to Jaite

Brecksville Reservation, one of 13 Cleveland Metroparks reservations, lies within Cuyahoga Valley National Recreation Area. Steep ridges and deep valleys cut by glacier-fed streams characterize Brecksville Reservation, a 3,090-acre park with rugged hiking trails. The Brecksville Trailside Museum (1939) on Chippewa Creek Dr. is open daily and contains interesting nature exhibits. Helpful park naturalists are on duty daily to supply information to visitors.

Distance: 9 miles

Hiking time: 5 ½ to 6 hours

Description: This hike descends from Brecksville Reservation to the Cuyahoga Valley on the Buckeye Trail. It traverses somewhat steep rolling hills and contains some low, wet areas that may become impassable in the spring or after a heavy rain. This pleasant, challenging hike may be best enjoyed in the summer or autumn when the ground is driest. It is a strenuous hike because of the hills and its length, and it is marked in its entirety with blue rectangular six-inch by two-inch Buckeye Trail blazes painted on trees.

Directions: From I-77, take Rte. 82 east to Brecksville Rd. (Rte. 21) in Brecksville. Go south on Brecksville Rd. to Valley Pkwy. Turn left (east) on Valley Pkwy, then right onto Meadows Dr. Turn right at the Cleveland Metroparks Brecksville Stables.

Parking & restrooms: At the stables parking area

1. Begin the hike at the stables and cross Meadows Dr. to find the blue blazes of the Buckeye Trail (BT) a short distance down the road on the left. Enter the trail going east and follow it until it emerges onto the gravel drive to Ottawa Point Reserved Picnic Area.

2. Reach the picnic area via the entrance drive and follow the blue blazes as they continue northeast from the gravel drive on a hogback ridge overlooking deep ravines on either side.

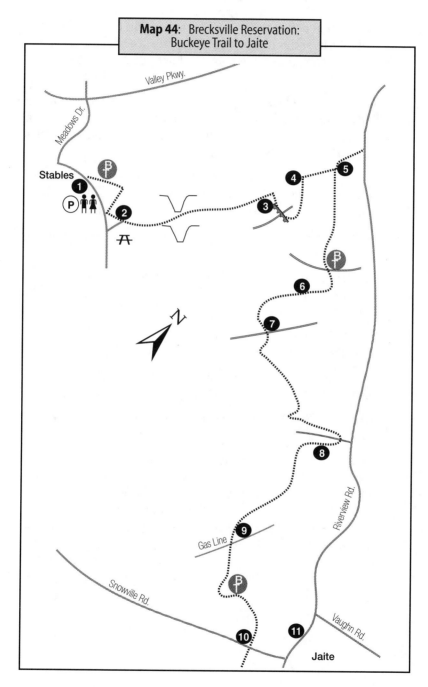

Map 44: Brecksville Reservation:
Buckeye Trail to Jaite

3. The trail descends and makes a sharp right turn off the wider trail. Watch for this turn as it is easy to miss. The double-blue turning blaze is on a post at this point. At about 1.0 mile cross a brook on a log bridge.

4. Follow the trail up along the edge of the hill on the right until it leads out to an old overgrown, blacktop road. This is the old portion of Parkview Rd. that once went through the reservation. Follow this old pavement trail about 0.1 mile.

5. Watch for a double blaze indicating a sharp right turn where the BT enters the woods. This area can be very wet and muddy and contains several small deep water holes on either side of the path.

6. Cross a stream and ascend another hogback ridge at about the 2.0-mile point.

7. The trail descends, crosses a stream, follows the contour of the land going up and down, and finally traverses another hogback ridge.

8. The BT crosses a stream twice and goes up the side of a hill at about the 3.0-mile point.

9. Reaching an open area with a wide woods road, the trail then enters a woods, leaves it at a gas line, and then reenters it (3.5 miles).

10. Follow the BT down a ridge and soon emerge onto Snowville Rd. at 4.0 miles.

11. Leave the BT and turn left (east) on Snowville to Riverview Rd. Turn left (north) on Riverview to the yellow buildings in Jaite at the corner of Riverview and Vaughn roads for an optional stop at CVNRA headquarters (4.5 miles), open only on weekdays.

Return to Brecksville Reservation by taking the trail in reverse and watching carefully for the BT blue blazes at each turn and stream crossing. When hiking in the reverse direction, entirely new vistas open up for continued pleasurable hiking.

45 BRECKSVILLE RESERVATION
Deer Lick Cave Loop

Brecksville Reservation's most outstanding feature is its topography. Seven separate valleys and ridges have been cut through the hills by rivers and streams over many thousands of years. Chippewa Creek has cut a magnificent gorge through the northern section of the park. This gorge was left behind by the retreating glacier of about 12,000 years ago as water flowed east to the Cuyahoga River. Large rocks from northern Canada also remain behind in the gorge and park. The fall foliage is beautiful in all of Brecksville, but especially from the Chippewa Creek Gorge Scenic Overlook.

Distance: 5 miles

Hiking time: 3 hours

Description: This hike starts at the nature center on the yellow and white trails, continues along Chippewa Creek Gorge on the green trail, and then takes the red Deer Lick Cave Trail in a clockwise direction back to the nature center. Traversing all seven of Brecksville's ridges, it is quite a strenuous hike because of the many hills to climb, although not long in mileage.

Directions: From I-77 , take Rte. 82 east to just past Brecksville Rd. (Rte. 21) in Brecksville. Just ahead on the right is the park entrance on Chippewa Creek Dr. Take Chippewa Creek Dr. past Meadows Dr. a short distance to the parking area for Brecksville Nature Center on the right.

Parking & restrooms: Near Brecksville Trailside Museum

Brecksville Trailside Museum, listed on the National Register of Historic Places, is an interesting building to visit to learn more about this Metropark and to obtain a map of the trails in the reservation. Opened in 1939, Brecksville Trailside Museum is the oldest nature center still standing in Cleveland Metroparks. Built by WPA workers with chestnut, walnut, and cherry wood, it reflects the fine craftsmanship of that era.

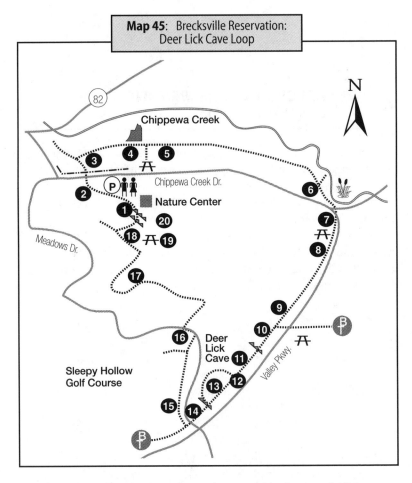

Map 45: Brecksville Reservation:
Deer Lick Cave Loop

1. Follow the sign from the parking area on the paved All Purpose Trail to the museum/nature center. Primitive restrooms are in the woods to the right of the walkway. Before starting the hike, take a moment to view the exhibits in the nature center.

Just before the building is the yellow-blazed Valley Stream Trail on the right. Begin the hike on this trail with its useful tree identification signs. This is the Harriet L. Keeler Memorial Trail, named in honor of a well-known naturalist, botanist, teacher, and author who died in 1921.

Follow the yellow blazes. The trail soon turns to the right to a wooden observation deck for the Prairie Restoration Project. This project was created to encourage the growth of plants that once were common here but no longer are readily found. These plants include big and little blue stem, Indian grass, tall coreopsis, prairie dock, and coneflower.

The yellow trail continues to the west and reaches a large glacial boulder with an attached plaque in memory of Harriet L. Keeler.

2. Here, leave the yellow trail (which goes left) and continue straight ahead beyond the boulder to the white trail. Cross Chippewa Creek Dr. and then the All Purpose Trail, which is identified with both green and white markers. You may begin to hear the rushing waters of Chippewa Creek far below on the right.

3. Almost immediately the trail turns right (east) downhill to a small enclosed shelter. This scenic overlook affords a fine view of the gorge looking north toward the stone bridge at Rte. 82. Berea sandstone blocks have fallen into the gorge and are resistant to erosion even though the creek continues its persistent cutting as it flows eastward to the Cuyahoga River.

4. Follow the green and white trails along the wooden fence; there are nice views of spectacular Chippewa Creek Gorge far below on the left. Proceed straight ahead on the Chippewa Gorge Trail (blazed with green tree markers) where it separates from the white trail (which goes off to the right).

5. Stay on the Chippewa Gorge Trail along the fence, noting that the gorge becomes deeper as you progress, a result of the continued cutting action of the creek. A side trail leads off to the right to the Harriet L. Keeler Picnic Area and the car parking area.

6. The trail gradually winds downhill to a marsh and at its foot meets the Bridle Trail coming in on the left. Very soon the green trail turns right. Stay on the green trail and cross a wooden footbridge over a side stream. The All Purpose Trail is now parallel on the right alongside Chippewa Creek Dr.

Cross a side stream on a wooden suspension bridge constructed by the Ohio National Guard in 1981. Soon after the bridge follow the green trail as it turns right and goes out to Chippewa Creek Dr. (1.8 miles.)

7. Cross the road and opposite you will see a driveway that leads into Chippewa Picnic Area. Here, go south on the red Deer Lick Cave Trail, which will lead in a counterclockwise direction all the way back to the nature center. The red trail begins to the left of the driveway.

8. Follow the red trail on a long, steep uphill trek. Valley Pkwy. is below on the left. Continue following red markers uphill on this ridge, one of the seven finger-like ridges that lie across Brecksville Reservation. Far below on the right is the stream that long ago cut this ravine and today continues slowly to deepen it.

9. At 2.3 miles the red trail is joined by the blue-blazed BT. Signs for the blue ski trail and the orange trail point to the left. Stay on the red trail as it goes downhill in tandem with the Buckeye Trail.

10. Cross a small wooden bridge and ascend a set of wooden steps. To the left and across the parkway is the Oak Grove Picnic Area.

11. Continue on the red Deer Lick and blue-blazed BT. (Note that the Bridle Trail comes in on the left and continues downhill on the right.) Stay on the red trail; the BT loops off the red trail to the right (2.6 miles) but later rejoins it.

12. On the red trail is a bench adjacent to a few picnic tables overlooking the peaceful woods and stream below. Reach a kiosk placed by the Buckeye Trail Association. It identifies this spot as the "Crossroads of the Buckeye Trail." From here the trail extends in three directions: 522 miles south to Cincinnati through eastern Ohio, 441 miles west to Cincinnati through western Ohio, and 65 miles north to Headlands Beach State Park and Lake Erie.

The overlook viewpoint for Deer Lick Cave is on the right, but turn right on the red trail to go downhill to Deer Lick Cave. A small wooden bridge leads to the "cave", which is actually a rock overhang composed of erosion-resistant Berea sandstone. Note how the enormous rock lying on the ground to the left once fit into the overhang. Birds make their nests in and amongst the foliage and crevices on this beautiful rock.

13. After leaving Deer Lick Cave, turn left to cross a wooden bridge, continuing on the red trail, then over another bridge, and finally over a third bridge. Go uphill on a set of stone steps. Note the pretty waterfall on the right. The trail bends to the right at the top of the steps.

14. Cross Meadows Dr. At the next intersection bear right (north) to continue on the red trail—leave the Buckeye Trail behind where it goes straight ahead. Continue following the red trail all the way back to the nature center. This trail is also the Bridle Trail here. If you meet horses, step to the side and remain quiet and still until the horse and rider have passed.

15. At about the 3.2-mile point, the trail goes downhill, crosses a wooden bridge, and then goes uphill. The Sleepy Hollow Golf Course is now on the left. The trail soon goes downhill again, across another bridge, and uphill. You are now crossing some of the beautiful valleys, streams, and ridges that characterize Brecksville Reservation.

16. The ski trail, identified by blue skier signs, comes in on the left to join the red trail. Continue on the red trail. Reach Meadows Dr. again and turn left on the road. Watch for the red trail's reentry into the woods a short distance ahead on the right.

17. At 4.1 miles the trail descends another ridge, crosses a bridge, and goes uphill. Turn left at the top of the hill. Soon there is a view of an open meadows area on the left. The red trail goes downhill again, bends to the right, crosses a small stream on another bridge, curves around another ridge, then crosses the same stream on yet another bridge. Here you are still crossing more of Brecksville's ridges.

18. At about 4.5 miles the red trail again goes up a steep hill along the edge of yet another of Brecksville's ridges. At the top of this hill, turn right to continue on the red trail (the Bridle Trail goes off to the left).

19. Next the red trail turns left just before the playing field, which is on the right. Reach the Meadows Picnic Area and cross through it going past restrooms and picnic tables.

20. The red trail is now joined by the green trail at the top of a set of downhill steps. Turn left to descend the steps, following the sign to the nature center. The red trail meets the yellow trail at the foot of the steps. Cross a small bridge and ascend another set of steps to arrive back at the nature center. The paved walkway to the car parking area is just in front of the building.

BIBLIOGRAPHY

Armstrong, Foster, Richard Klein, and Cara Armstrong. *A Guide to Cleveland's Sacred Landmarks*. Kent, Ohio: The Kent State University Press, 1992.

Blakeslee, C.T. *History of Chagrin Falls and Vicinity*. Chagrin Falls, Ohio: The Exponent Publishing Co., 1903. (Written by Blakeslee in 1874).

Brockman, C. Frank. *Trees of North America*. New York: Golden Press, 1968.

Chagrin Falls Historical Society. *Village Victorian*. Chagrin Falls, Ohio: The Society, 1983.

Cuyahoga Valley Trails Council, Inc. *Trail Guide Handbook, Cuyahoga Valley National Recreation Area*. Akron, Ohio: The Council, 1991.

Ellis, William Donohue. *The Cuyahoga*. Dayton, Ohio: Landfall Press, Inc., 1975.

Field Guide to the Birds of North America. Washington, D.C.: National Geographic Society, 1983.

Fletcher, Colin. *The Complete Walker*. New York: Alfred A. Knopf, 1972.

Folzenlogen, Robert. *Hiking Ohio: Scenic Trails of the Buckeye State*. Glendale, Ohio: Willow Press, 1990.

From Town to Tower. Cleveland, Ohio: Western Reserve Historical Society, 1983.

Gaede, Robert C., and Robert Kalin, eds. *Guide to Cleveland Architecture*. Cleveland, Ohio: Cleveland Chapter of the American Institute of Architects, 1990.

Gieck, Jack. *A Photo Album of Ohio's Canal Era, 1825-1913*. Kent, Ohio: The Kent State University Press, 1988.

Heritage on the Heights. Cleveland Heights, Ohio: Heights Community Congress, 1977.

Johannesen, Eric, *Cleveland Architecture, 1876-1976.* Cleveland, Ohio: Western Reserve Historical Society, 1979.

Lewis, Joanne, and Richard Karberg. *In Our Day.* Cleveland Heights, Ohio: Heights Community Congress, 1978.

Miller, Carol Poh. *Cleveland Metroparks, Past and Present: Celebrating 75 Years of Conservation, Education, and Recreation 1917–1992.* Cleveland:Cleveland Metroparks, 1992.

Newcomb, Lawrence. *Wildflower Guide.* Boston: Little, Brown and Co., 1977.

Ohio's Natural Areas and Preserves: A Directory. Columbus, Ohio: Ohio Department of Natural Resources, Division of Natural Areas and Preserves, 1987.

Ramey, Ralph. *Fifty Hikes in Ohio.* Woodstock, Vermont: The Country-man Press, 1990.

Rose, William Ganson. *Cleveland: The Making of a City.* 1950. Reprint, Kent, Ohio: The Kent State University Press, 1990.

Schmidt, Mark T., and Hannibal, Joseph T. *Guide to the Building Stones of Downtown Cleveland: A Walking Tour.* Guidebook No. 5. Columbus, Ohio: Department of Natural Resources, Division of Geological Survey, 1992.

Van Tassel, David D. (Senior Editor) and Grabowski, John J. (Managing Editor). *The Encyclopedia of Cleveland History.* Bloomington & Indianapolis:Indiana University Press, 1987.

Weber, Art. *Ohio State Parks, A Guide to Ohio's State Parks.* Clarkston, MI: Glovebox Guidebook Publishing Co., 1993.

Williams, A. B. *Geology of the Cleveland Region.* Pocket Natural History No.9, Geological Series No. 1. Cleveland, Ohio: The Cleveland Museum of Natural History, 1940.

More Good Books About
CLEVELAND

If you enjoyed *Cleveland On Foot*, you'll want to know about these other fine Cleveland giftbooks and guidebooks . . .

Cleveland: A Portrait of the City
One hundred brilliant color photographs capture Greater Cleveland in all seasons, showcasing familiar landmarks and uncovering surprising hidden details. Descriptive notes provide historical background. A handsome giftbook.
$35.00 hardcover • 96 pages • 8 ½" x 10 ½"

Best Things in Life
236 Favorite Things About Cleveland
This fun little book collects thought-provoking quotations by Clevelanders— famous and ordinary—about what they like best about living in Cleveland.
$5.95 softcover • 144 pages • 6" x 4 ½"

Cleveland Golfer's Bible
Describes in detail all the golf courses, driving ranges, and practice facilities in Greater Cleveland. Includes descriptions, prices, ratings, maps.
$12.95 softcover • 240 pages • 5 ½" x 8 ½"

Cleveland Discovery Guide
All the best family recreation in Greater Cleveland—in a handy guidebook. Written by parents, for parents; offers detailed descriptions, suggested ages, prices, and more. An idea book for how to share more "quality time" close to home.
$12.95 softcover • 208 pages • 5 ½" x 8 ½"

Color Me Cleveland
The all-Cleveland coloring book. Detailed illustrations showcase a variety of Cleveland landmarks. Fact-filled descriptive captions. Durable, heavy-duty paper.
$4.95 softcover • 32 pages • 8 ½" x 11 ½"

Available at Your Local Bookstore.

These and other Gray & Co. books are regularly stocked at most Cleveland-area bookstores and can be special-ordered through any bookstore in the U.S.

If you don't have a local bookstore, or have difficulty ordering through a bookstore, call Gray & Co. directly for assistance.

Gray & Company, Publishers
11000 Cedar Avenue • Cleveland, Ohio 44106
(216) 721-2665